INNER CITY OUTLIER PAPERBACKS

The Garret Scenario

BOOK SAFE GLACIER

How The Rails Became My Rehab

Circa 2017

Was Written By

In The California House
Circa 1820

"Once stood a barroom and above it a Brothel,
Then lived a scenarist in the garret writing Novels."

- MES not Braze about BrightDawn.

AMAZON - FRENCH MARKET

Inner City Outlier Paperbacks
Presents

BRIGHTDAWN

as BRAZE in
The First Garret Scenario

Without further ado…

Braze Scanlan

I've been a paper boy, artist, manager, dishwasher, honor student, failure, telemarketer, pawnbroker, house painter, junky, art director, dealer, acrobat, smuggler, guilty loving son, sneaky little ass hole, actor, thief, some dude, sometimes student, producer, pusher, delivery person, brother, pretty good friend, really good connect, consumer, tagger, boyfriend, love bomber, addict, jerk off, screenwriter, salesman, pseudo-hobosexual, etc., etc. But most have just called me a hustler over the years. And recently, the term chronic entrepreneur was used to describe me. But really…

"What's the difference?"

BOOK SAFE

I've experimented on the edge, in the streets, various markets, countless rooftops, numerous tunnels, plenty of stages, in the city, up the way, down the tracks, on dance floors and much more. But my experiment *CURE for the CRASH* brought it all together like never before. I can't say making the movie saved me from myself, but it gave me an epic journey in self-discovery through many challenges.

My co-thinkers and I are the curious type who chase bold and mind blowing ideas. Unless there's something outrageous to be had, an underground culture to explore, or wicked chemicals to ingest? We search further chasing dreams in fresh scenes to euphoric highs! We duck the law and exhaust our mania by living large and illegal! We are consumed and governed by risk behavior, driven by dangerous dreams, and passionately broken.

Now, let me try and explain us… the habitual users, the chronic opportunists, and the emotionally bankrupt I'm referring to. And in doing so, I won't pretend to remember everything perfectly, or in order, but with style. As you dig inside the *Book Safe* and explore my art of train hopping, filmmaking, suicide and rebirth, you'll find a shattered life I call my own. And maybe, just ***Maybe***, you're as crushed to smithereens as I am, and picking up the pieces just like me. For those of you who are, this is not a how to, or self-help book. But a guided tour from the emergency rooms that saved me, to the movie I made that taught me how to help myself.

With that in mind, picture the body's most complicated instrument, the piano of emotions. On it, thoughts register as feelings. From it, a psychological soundtrack has been scored on broken chords. The Garret Scenarios begin in four, three, two…

EAST LANSDOWNE

Back in the Day
When kids filled the streets and Played

My success as a trader on the streets began when I earned tips carrying heavy shopping bags for old ladies at my hometown supermarket in East Lansdowne. I hustled so much there that the older guys in town called me ***The Acme Kid***. But I was like any other ambitious young buck from the neighborhood, who like me, raked the neighbors leaves in the fall, or shoveled the snow from sidewalk for a five spot. Later on, I even went legit and got a paper route. To get that gig, I actually had to subcontract a few blocks from an older kid because I was way too young to get a paper route on my own. But I had to work a deal with that kid regardless of my age because she had every goddamn block in the neighborhood under her control! She delivered all the newspapers to every house for eight blocks by three blocks with the help of her dad. He drove her around in his station wagon filled with newspapers while he screamed over Devo *tracks* or she sang along with Madonna songs. Car windows down, music up, they would cruise and toss papers on time and predictable like that.

When I acquired (how is another story) two and a half blocks of the route she had on lock… I pushed a shopping kart filled with newspapers to the beats of Lisa Lisa Cult Jam or the King of Rock on my Sony Walkman every day; rain, sleet, snow and was happy to do so! I felt older than my years to get some work in and money earned before school everyday.

Back then I pursued everything that was slightly out of reach that made me look a little older. I was always drawn to doing things that older kids where doing. And I loved being sceen by my peers hustling at the Acme, shoveling snow into piles taller than me, or pushing my shopping kart filled with newspapers while kids my age where just, just doing chores to get a measly allowance off their parents. It was those kids, who would loose their Halloween candy to me playing poker the first week of November. They were easy to bluff.

Now as chance would have it, my third grade teacher was one of my paper route customers. I loved collecting from her! It made me feel momentarily… superior. But she didn't make it easy. She rarely answered her front door. And I think on purpose! So one day at school I flipped it, I had too, she left me no choice.

"Where's your homework Mr. Scanlan?"
she asked me curiously.

"Where's my $15.20 Miss Shaw?"
I said with a smile.

A bit shocked, but noticing me playing it up, she grinned, looked at me out of the corner of her eyes, and just waited for my homework.

"It's been four weeks,"
I pointed out with a sad, constructed smile.

Then, after I made my point, I casually handed her my homework assignment as if I just found it.

"You have very,
wise penmanship for such a young man."
she remarked.

"It comes natural Miss Shaw.
Better wise writing than a wise…
well, you know."

"I think we're on the same page."
She said to me as if we were on the same level.

The next day, she brought me in the exact amount she owed me in a sealed enveloped and thus, I was Paid In Full long before Rakim! Later that year she casted me in the lead roll of the school play. But I wasn't excited about it, I felt used. She gave me the impression that she was trying to get a little more for her late money, than just the newspapers I delivered on time.

But I actually liked it when people got behind in their bills. Because when I did collect (And I always did.) all that money was mine! So I'd carry dead beats like her and pay their outstanding bills till I collected their entire balance. It was like a having money in the bank to me. Nobody got cut off. They always paid. Well, only once did I have to cut my losses when I found a big pile of papers frozen on the front steps of an old lady's home. But I don't think she beat me, I think she died in there. So I let the family slide when I noticed them cleaning the yard to sell the house. I wasn't a ***Two Headed*** monster yet. I just did what I could to make a buck before I was old enough to get working papers and cash in. And oh boy, did I get encouragement along the way before I was taxable.

"The lil Acme Kid is no joke,"
older kids would say,
"A Big Mac in the making."

They'd cheer me on as I raced my empty shopping kart home to get to school on time. And after school, the streets swarmed with us kids playing tag football, kick the can, skating, breaking. And the older kids always picked me to run with them! We were out in the world loving life long before home computers appeared to rob the joy from generations ahead. We listened to everything from Black Sabbath on Vinyl, to Run DMC from boom boxes. We wore old concert t-shirts and worn out corduroys during the week, and new sweat suits on the weekends. We were kids who enjoyed hanging out together, not logging on at home, alone. We walked to school and never got carpooled. Our messages where tagged not text. And even playing video games got us out of the house and at the corner store with a hand full of quarters. It was an amazing time to be a kid back when, Whodini rapped about Friends.

Yeah so, like I said… I started out carrying bags at the Acme every Saturday & Sunday morning. Why did I work, instead of just riding my Mongoose around with other kids my age? So I could eat lunch wherever I wanted too with the older kids! And buy a Mad, Cracked, or WWF Magazine, and play Pac-Man, Asteroids, or Centipede at the corner store till dinnertime. But mind you, it wasn't just me who hustled; a lot of kids did what they could for a buck in *My Part Of Town* pre

Tuff Crew. And so did my lil brother Richy who, after watching lots of this go down, and was hip to some of my other shenanigans, began hustling even younger than I did!

It started one Christmas morning when Richy maybe… four, when he split his gifts in two piles under the tree as he opened them up. Afterwards, he sat between the two piles and played with his new electronic Epoch-Man game wearing his new Dr.J Jersey over his pajamas. He looked happy to me, but MOM was puzzled by the gifts he separated in two piles.

"What's that pile for Rich?"
she asked.

"Those are the gifts I'm going to keep Mom,"
said lil Richy.

Mom and I gave each other a curious look before I looked over to DAD, who was kind of dozing off on the couch; probably still sleepy from the side jobs he worked so often.

"What's up with the other stack Richy?"
I asked him.

"They're for the front steps,"
he said with a smile,
"I'm a have a sidewalk sale tomorrow!"

It made sense to him, me too. I was really impressed by his business mind. But not Mom! If I tried to pull that one over, she wouldn't have it. I thought she was a little harder on me, and always just… worried about Richy. In fact, I think the only thing Mom let me get away with when I was a lil kid was mispronouncing my name when I was a baby! Brian came out "Braze" when I was just a few months old; it stuck with me as I grew up. Looking back on this, as hard as she was on me at times… that was the beginning of me truly doing no wrong in her eyes. In fact, she never said specifically "don't do" anything. But rather…

"If I catch you doing that!"

And she was serious! So I learned early on that I could do anything, as long as I didn't get caught doing it. As for Dad, he was there too, but seemed to just laugh off more than Mom could. Good times between them were seldom; maybe those two should've never married; I don't know. But their relationship did teach me the importance to never marry someone just because they have the same name as your favorite Beatle.

My dad was hung-over or maybe loaded that Christmas, not sure. I didn't know much about drugs yet to be certain. That is, other than the fact that the mention of drugs in the house would put Mom into a rage! I began to figure out when Dad was on some stuff, when he looked like the bad guys on TV, the dudes who the cops would bust when they found dope on them; who where Kind Of Blue, and tired looking.

Sometimes, I would just stare at my Dad with his eyes cracked and his smile halfcocked as he reached out for my cheek saying…

"Come here Rabbit!"

That's what he called me, but not that Christmas morning. Every so often he would probably take too much and just be out of it. On those days, like that Christmas, I would watch him real close, like a TV. I would imagine what he was thinking, or what he was dreaming about. And sometimes when I was in that mode with him, my mind would drift with his like Siamese Dreams.

That's when I began to see things differently, stuff I wanted to see, or maybe in fact what he was seeing, rather than what was real? I duh-know. Just things far from that of my Dad looking like a bad dude on TV. When he did look a little down, I channel surfed through all the good shows I could find him on in my mind! Doing stuff like… driving a Ferrari in Magnum P.I. or coaching a basketball game on The White Shadow, or wearing a cape in The Greatest American Hero! But that morning, I found him on the Gong Show singing a Beatles tune. Well, kind of…

"Scrambled eggs… Oh my baby how I love your legs, "
he sang out of tune, but with love.

He was playing the inflatable guitar at center stage of my mind as the neck of it slowly deflated in his hand. Off stage, Chuck Barris cringed like he had gas pains as my Dad tried to continue but failed to pronounce another word and just mumbled through the rest of the song under the jeers of the studio audience.

But Dad was in fact not on TV, but on the couch covered in wrapping paper as we come off that drifting moment together, as Mom and Richy sat on either side of him, laughing! When he came to, he abruptly dug himself out of the Christmas paper grave they buried him in while we were lost in the proverbial sauce.

"Look at Dad! Big dumb Dad!"
lil Richy laughed.

We often laughed at him, not with him. And I joined in big time that morning. Laughing and pointing with Richy! So much so, that he yelled at Mom for it. After all, she was slightly amused too. And he didn't like it when we ganged up on him. Who does?

"They shouldn't make fun of their father!
They shouldn't call me dumb!"

"Then don't be such a fool Paul!"
Mom yelled back.

My brother and I would roll on the floor laughing during exchanges like these between Mom and Dad. They really got to each other often. But as far as Dad's go, he was a good one. Both our parents cared for us and worked very hard. Richy and I were just a couple of spoiled kids who fought over what TV shows could be watched on the big TV. Back when you were lucky to have just one 19-inch color TV in the house. That little 12-inch B&W in our room sucked! I could never watch Smurfs in black and white, and Richy liked Transformers at that time.

In fact, I watched so much TV, I learned how to read by picking up the TV guide! Like James Fogel put it, I was one of those a TV babies. When my Grandpa and I weren't watching a double feature of *M.A.S.H* together, he would take me out on Sundays to parks and museums to get me from the television. Mom would tear me away from *Welcome Back Kotter* and take Richy & I to Center City for long cold walks Downtown before warming up in the John Wanamaker Department Store. But I was so mesmerized by the stories I was watching on TV that I didn't just watch the shows, but studied the people on them. I wanted to be some of them so bad, it wasn't long at all before I was strutting like Vinnie Barbarino, anticipate like Radar O'reilly, and soon, wearing as much gold as B.A. on the A-Team! All the while, my brother was watching me, not TV. We were pretty close at that age.

In the beginning I looked out for him when we were outside of the house, but things changed. I don't know what happened to that young protective kid I was on the train platforms when I stood between the tracks and my brother. Back then I always found myself in front of Richy and Mom as subway cars silver surfed under Market Street on the tracks and raced by us with waves of hot air that cut through the old city winters.

"Watch out for the subway train Epoch Man!"
I warned my lil brother.

I instantly pulled Richy farther from the edge of the platform and far from the approaching danger of the racing train. His head was always in his Epoch-Man game back then. Later, my desire to keep my brother out of danger and do the right thing, would eventually, be reduced to me giving him instructions on how not to get caught doing the wrong thing.

When I got a little older, maybe 12, I caught the fever from the photography of Henry Chelphant & Martha Cooper in the book Subway Art. It was being passed around between my friends on the street, so I went out and stole my own from the bookstore. Then, I got ill from the cinematography of Tony Silver's Style Wars doc on PBS! After I watched the graffiti being painted in that documentary, I felt it time to take my name seriously on the streets! The street art of New York City ignited an uncontrollable passion that burned in me for years to come. Subway Art became my bible, and Style Wars, maybe my gateway drug. Once I crossed the line and became criminal minded; my moves had no boundaries. I wrote MES, Mes for Messiah. Creating something out of nothing gave me a god complex long before I could even drive.

At this time I started hopping subway trains; not paying the fare. I did it for the same reason most kids did in my neighborhood, we didn't want to pay the fare when we could buy a slice of 69th Street pizza with that money…

"One cheese slice please!"

East Lansdowne, where I grew up, is at the end of the train line in Upper Darby at 69th & Market. From there at The Terminal, I could venture in any direction both suburban and inner city on buses, trains, and trolleys.

While traveling on mass transit, I studied other writers. Graffiti writers call tagging those transit routes in Philly "walking routes". And to get around and save money for 69th Street pizza, to buy records at Sound of Upper Darby, and pay the admission to the Circus Town night club we all met up at on Friday & Saturday nights, we hopped rides every way we could. Dollar stole, dollar… y'know. It was impossible for SEPTA to make us pay! We began only paying for things we couldn't steal. We had a code name for it called Vic. We'd go out and Vic everything!

"Where are you going Braze?"

"I'm going to the store to meet Vic Mom."

While my friends were stealing cars, stereos, and selling weed, I stole the paint for us; I couldn't drive yet, and didn't smoke. I was always the youngest in my crew, proving myself in my own way was a full time job. So I didn't go out and just steel some paint for us, I'd Vic entire stocks of cans from stores till they eventually put the cans in cages and locked them up! Then, on to the next beat. Which meant I'd have to hop SEPTA once again to get to a virgin store.

BRIGHTDAWN

To get on SEPTA subways, I'd squeeze through top of a turnstile at a platform exit, or sneak jus under the view of a cashier at the booth by the entrance. And often climb around turnstiles high above rush hour traffic, just below the EL platforms, two stories above the cars below! And sometimes… even emerge from a dark subway tunnel like a subterranean alien and climb onto the pedestrian platform to the surprise of bums and bag ladies on benches who kept warm down there in the winter; it's always winter in my memories.

Basically, hopping the EL was my free ticket to the art gallery of Philadelphia, the real birthplace of graffiti! In the 80's, graffiti was a bigger part of growing up in Philly than Little League Baseball or Catholic Youth Organization Basketball. After B-ball practice, a can of paint was to me, what a bag of dope was to Jim Carol. I got high off riding the EL and looking at all the rooftop burners. From there, my first obsession was born. And that was, to stay alive and illegal just as King Suroc coined it. All I wanted was rep, and I went out to get some! And the more rep I went for, the more paint I needed. I made a sport stealing cans. It wasn't a matter of just getting away with it, but how much I could steal at one time! And as soon as the shop owner got hip to my game, he'd put the paint in a cage. And so the story goes… eat, sleep steal, repeat. Hopping trains to hardware stores yet to be screwed! I just fell in love with The Art of Getting Over at a tender age.

THE BOTTOM

Where a Tagger
Became a Pawnbroker

When I was 14, my Dad got me a part time job at a pawnshop on 42nd & Lancaster in West Philly in a part of town call "The Bottom". On Saturdays, I was their "runner". I ran electronics, musical instruments, tools, everything, up and down the stairs and in and out of pawn. But it wasn't long before I went from runner, to writer. I wrote pawn tickets and appraised gold and goods at the age of fifteen. I really dug that scene down there!

Soon, I rolled with a knot in my pocket, Gucci links around my neck, and a Rolex on my wrist that led me to walk with a pimp strut that made pigeons on the street to the rooftops do double takes! Cool-C got his bling for the Glamorous Life from me at Eagle Loans Pawnshop in West Philly. They called me the lil white-delight down there when I turned 16 and rolled up slow and low in a Dookie Suzuki Jeep to work. And around all the local high schools I'd let my gold chains hang off my neck and out of the window before I tucked them in to get out of my ride when I let my presence be known even further in the flesh. When I pimped my Lotto Map sneakers on the pavement and flaunted that tuff strut from my slick ride oozing my pawnbroker wealth in the presence of schoolmates, they knew there was a new player in town when I drove up for the first time. A girl with dollar signs in her eyes asked me…

"Yo, how you be sportin' all that gold?"

"What, you don't know girl?"

I left Public Enemy boom from my kicker box in my fastback of the Dookie Suzuki as I passed by the skaters to my pack of old heads who where all players; hard working dudes. I even heard a dumb jock whisper to a group of cute preppy girls…

"That jerks moving drugs,"

While some, like that dude, initially may have thought I was a criminal, others just thought I was a cheesy rich kid. I mean, I did just transfer from a Private School called Bonner into that Public School to get closer to better friends I had in Upper Darby High who knew what was up in the scene. Most in my grade didn't know what to make of me because I was so young, a sophomore, who looked like me, rolling with seniors as soon as he walked in the front door. It was a little shocking to them! So I left um all guessing for a minute and let them pondered the jocks assumption that I was moving units.

Then I turned back to that dude with the hot preppy girls, switch the compact disk track with my remote, and rocked "Don't Believe The Hype". Then, to get the record straight, I responded …

"I'm no dealer my buddy, I'm a pawnbroker."
I said with smile.

And when that got out in school, they lined up at lunch! I took orders for goods from students of all subcultures, to the faculty in all grades, one after the other. They lined up at my lunch table where I'd be eating with one hand and making notes with the other…

"What chew need man?"
I asked.

"I need a link chain,"
said a Greek Kid,
"It's gotta be dope!"

"Turkish or Figaro, what-chew want?"
I inquired.

"No Turkish malaka!"
he barked.

Next in line…

"How about you hippie?"

"I need a scale,"
said the Dead Head.

"OK, no prob. Triple beam, or digital?"

As that stoner took a moment and thought about his options, I looked to the next guy in line, my Gym teacher, who asked…

"Can you get me a four head VCR Braze?"

"Sure coach. You want a remote?
…That's an extra five."

I was just another Mack at work. While most kids went to high school to read books, or just hang out with their friends, I went there to make money. After making a couple grand a week for a few months, I found I could never get my fill and felt very strong in the middle of it all. I learned in the pawnshop that whenever you touch someone else's money, take some or make some off it. At that time I had money coming in from all directions. I saw opportunity everywhere on the streets at sixteen. Soon enough, I went from running pawn tickets and hustling goods at lunchtime, to having runners of my own on the streets pushin' butter fulltime. My Dad inadvertently introduced me to my first connect, Earl, who was connected with the JBM, Junior Black Mafia. Earl's jewelry and big Mercedes impressed me and we became friends too. Everybody liked me. I took that for granted.

I began running cocaine after a couple druggie friends lured me up to North Philly to get us some blowjobs, but all we came home with were half-gram bags for them. They played me for a ride. But seeing opportunity and liking the taste of the coke myself that night, I bagged my own coke with some weight I copped from Earl. And those two druggie friends of mine, were the first to run butter for me! From there, things got bigger. In a few months I had 6-8 runners pushing coke for me every weekend while I stayed in the shadows, partying hard. I had it all, but all I thought about was more.

Although we started out pushin' dimes, it wasn't long before the customer's appetite grew, so we bumped up the dime bags to half-grams for 25 dollars; bagging that shit was another part time job! Most of my runners ran 16 bag bundles and earned 25 dollars out of every 100 bucks they brought back to me. Each bundle held 16 half grams totaling a street value of

400 dollars. The runners got one yard and I got three. I managed six or more runners a week. By the time I made that money my Pawnbroker cover was solid! And I successfully diversified my interests under the radar at seventeen years old. I got away with it all and looked good doing it because I established myself as a legit Pawnbroker. I was the kid who could get you the goods, on the cheap, from the shop on 42nd & Lancaster. I felt I was ahead of the curve of all my classmates, ducking and weaving like a point guard on an endless break from Long Lane to 69th Street. My Mom knew I was becoming a monster, and hated that Pawnshop and my Dad for introducing it to me. They split up around this time.

I just knew what I wanted and went out there and got it every day since go! And in doing so, all I acquired created a larger than life persona. My little brother Richy was around 12 when I entered this chapter of my life. We were like many others in our neighborhood thinking image was everything and to many, I looked like a pure player. So how could Richy not look up to me? The impression I gave my lil brother was more than inspiring. It was criminal.

One night when I was driving down Long Lane in our neighborhood, I noticed Richy on the corner with a dozen of his boys by the pool hall. When Rich heard my system, he flagged my jeep down, so I pulled over.

"Yo Braze! You got 5 dollars I can borrow?"
Richy asked,
"…I want to chip in on some more beer
with my friends."

I reached into my pocket and pulled out some loot…

"Sure,"
I said with a smile,
"You got change of a fifty?"
"Damn. Naaaw Bee!"

I always followed my sarcasm with an extra sinister smile for an added touch; it was considered charming in the 80's in those parts amongst my kind.

"Will you show me how to make
that money Bee? I know what's up."

I think he was buzzed and feeling extra brave and ambitious, because he never directly asked me about my business. I thought about it for a second, and thought… he's not old enough to run drugs, no way! So, I scratched my head and pointed out the obvious…

"You aren't gonna make a dime chipping in
five dollars on a case a beer,"
I told him.

And then he started to listen to me carefully…

"Take this fifty, and buy a keg.
Then sell all your friends
five-dollar cups. You know the deal."

A month later Richy was throwing weekly parties by the train tracks, and I'd later find out pushing nickel bags of weed, quarters, and a lot more. But, that was his business. Who was I to judge? I found out because the guy who sold him the weed, was one of my runners. They became good friends.

"Does he smoke?"
I asked my guy.

"Nope."

"Is he making money?"

"Bigtime, for a young boy,"
my man said.

"Off weed! How?"

"His people are young, and he knows it."

"So?"

"So when he sells them weight,
he sprays it down
with hairspray to make a lil extra."

I couldn't help but laugh at that one! All in all, I thought it wasn't a bad move, for a pre-teen. Not bad till he got busted at school pushing nickel bags on the school playground. He did a couple days at a juvenile detention center because he didn't want to rat out his connect. When Richy went to juvi, my Moms blood boiled! If she knew I was friends with his connect, I think she may have tried to kill me. To say she despised drugs is an understatement. My Dad's drug use was to blame for their marriage ending.

Our Dad was an on again off again user their whole marriage. Though Mom never used, drugs seemed to always pop up around her. She knew I was up to something when I was a teenager. How could she not? Everyone else bought my pawnshop cover but not her. But when Richy got busted, I think that really caught her by surprise. At that point she had to swallow that everyone in the family was dirty, but her.

CAUGHT NAKED

When a bloody attack on my Neighbor Made the Newspaper

Just before I turned eighteen, I went home dusted and spun out from a Dead Show one night after I ingested two-dozen hits of acid, smoked a bundle of wet, and drank a few beers; great night. And oh what a night it was! When I got home later, Mom had to lock herself in the bathroom with Richy and call 911 as I tore up the house going crazy after the Concert.

That perfect storm of powerful chemicals had me raging and screaming so much it cut through the midnight darkness of the street and woke up most of the residence on the street as sirens approached from blocks away towards my primal howls, breaking glass, and dumfounding good neighbors because… "That couldn't be Braze." Could it?

Outside Mom's, when the paramedics arrived at the house with the cops, they found "the action" at a random house down the street where I was naked and bashing down someone's front door with my bare hands, a bloody mess indeed. In the midst of this overdose of mine, they found me a half block from Mom's crashing my fists through a storm glass window, in winter, naked and bleeding profusely from my right forearm in a rage on some neighbor's home! A neighbor I didn't even know! Let alone have any reason to terrorize. To this day I have no idea what was going through my mind. But there I was, bashing down his front door with my fists as I screamed at the top of my lungs…

"Make it stop! Make it stop MOM!"

I had nothing against that neighbor. I didn't know him or his family when I rushed his home for no reason. That is, other than all the drugs I did that made me crazy. But he knew how to handle such a matter. He wasn't going to let anyone he loved get hurt! From behind his front door, he screamed at me…

"I have a gun! It's loaded! I will shoot you dead!"

He had to do what he had to do. Some naked guy was breaking down his front door! Then, the cops arrived behind me, lights flashing, guns drawn. But that didn't faze me. I just kept raging, screaming…

"Mom! Make it stop! Make it stop MOM! PLEASE!"

My Dad wasn't living with us, but some how he made it there on the scene. When I stopped my assault on the house and turned to face the cops, I'm told I kept screaming and crying covered in blood. Not knowing whose blood was on me, mine or someone else's, the police where ready to shoot. I kind of remember feeling as if I were an infant scared of the world and just wanted to go back in the womb, maybe use the umbilical cord as a noose to kill myself. In reality, the cops were urging me to get on the ground! But I didn't get it. Even with their guns pointed at me, I didn't know what was going on. Surrounded by police, neighbors, and family, I just kept screaming…

"Make it stop Mom! PLEASE?"

Then, the neighbor came out of his house with his gun! When that happened, the cops stopped trying to communicate with me, and zeroed in on him, waving his gun around hysterically!

"This man is insane! My family is inside!
He cut my phone line!"

I was in the middle like a bird in a turkey shoot I suppose. Between them, I stood raging with my naked body covered in blood, as the cops look around me, and at the neighbor pointing his pistol in the officer's direction.

"Put the gun down sir!"
a Cop demanded,
"DROP YOUR WEAPON NOW!"

As I observed the action below, my soulless body continued to scream between the gunplay as my perspective seemed to rise through the clouds and into the darkness devoid of heavenly moonlight; but all too soon came to light in the newspaper the next day with the headline: MAN CAUGHT NAKED. My girl Erica would read about it all too.

MASHED UP

The game of drugs is hard to Play
They can kill you any Day

I finally came to that night in this horror show of mine at a local ER with leaves in my ass, veins hanging out of my arm like spaghetti, and a catheter in my penis.

"We may have to amputate."
said a doctor as I regained consciousness.

Though things were really blurry, I knew I was inside a hospital. But my mind kept playing tricks on me! I felt as though I was outside in a field of chaos, being taken off a helicopter medevac. Did they fly me here I wondered? Then, amongst all this confusion, I heard a sweet unplugged guitar playing while the helicopter blades blew my one eyed doctor's lab coat, and his long dark hair, around the room in hyper exaggerated lengths with the freedom of graffiti wild style arrows.

The doctor had the head of a hawk and was speaking in Chinese, Korean, or something like that, I don't know. And he had one big eye, a birds' eye, huge and real! Three nurses with big oval cartoon eyes who were singing in English with Asian accents assisted him, singing in broken English…

"Through double dip acid I can see…"

They were Japana-Nurses in really tight outfits with outrageously exaggerated figures; who had a lot of talent! Then, I noticed the hawk head doctor examining the spaghetti falling out of my arm, wearing a dancing bear pin on his white jacket? I screamed…

"Suicide ain't painless!
And I have leafs in my anus!"

The very serious, sexy, singing surgical assistants ignored me and kept on with their song, but I was way to paranoid to sing along…

"I see your dancing bear pin
you narc doctor!"
I yelled.

Then it occurred to me…
"Dancing bears?"

That little pin was the first connection I could make to earlier events. And it terrified me! Seeing those bears was a most insane clockwork joke on me; like Alex being forced to watch! The pin induced flashes of memory I wasn't ready to recall at that moment. I began convulsing with recollections of blood, broken glass, guns and primal territorial pissing and prehistoric behavior that was stored in cells turned off in genes millions of years ago; turned back on by the hippie cocktail. I'd much rather have seen a dancing Jesus chorus line pin, or homeboy Smurfs doing a row of head spins pin, but not that dancing bear pin on Hawk Eye at that moment! But then again, there were those cute Japa-Nurses who kept trying to calm me with their song, God bless them…

"The game of drugs is hard to play,
they can kill you any day."

With absolutely no boundaries, my black hole of excess, paranoia and stupidity, ate me up and mind-whammed me psycho that night. Emotionally, I never fully recovered from that overdose, but I survived it. Maybe that's all you can do with certain trauma. You see… it still haunts me frequently with physical twitches when I think of the police pointing their guns at me when I was naked on my block. And the feeling of my bare feet over fences in my neighbor's back yards. And visions of my blood on the front door of that dudes house as paramedics tried to calm me down and restrain me on the sidewalk.

Not being able to regain my business after all this, I began getting high all the time. My runners began running their own drugs, and selling them to me! When I came down from binges, alone and broke, I'd just wish for a UFO to come pick me up with a one-way ticket. I didn't think I was crazy, just a looser with voices screaming in his head, and who woke up in unique places, unaware, of how I got there. And as I spent more time using like this, my binges led me as far down this reckless road that my body and mind could tither. Mom's voice looping in my head…

"Why Braze?
Why? Why Braze?
Why? Why Braze?"

"I don't know why?"
I'd murmur to her as if she were there.

"Why Braze? Why Braze? Why…"
continued in my head.

"…I don't know Mom!"

The cross talk in my mind never ceased after that horrible night. I talked to myself constantly to drown out my Moms voice in my head. I'd chant…

"Guns to head since I was a child,
led taste on tongue is ever so mild.
Guns to head since I was a child,
Led taste on tongue is ever so mild"

I continued with that for days, weeks, years! I don't know where that nonsense came from. Sometimes I'd lay frozen with these demons on cocaine for a couple days chanting that while imaginary snakes coiled around my neck and snuck between my legs, taunting my dick with their tongues. Once my head, could rise from bed, I'd do whatever it took to avoid the flashbacks from consuming me further. I'd jog, drink, or just read out loud, real loud! With manic semi sober energy I'd go bombing my name, on the rooftops by the El train. Drink at dive bars and fuck chicks in the bathroom that liked snorting rails off toilet bowls. And then, when I could, sleep for days to rid the ghosts from my twists. All that business just kept me in shape before another binge that would leave me frozen and chanting somewhere again. I'm told I even spoke in my sleep…

"Stop it. STOP. Why? You put guns to your head?"

But I had regular intervals of sanity through it all. And it probably saved me from being institutionalized. Or maybe, avoided, I should say.

"You're good."
I'd tell myself,
"This too shall pass."

My panic attacks and half-witted comments between my lips and mind regarding life, death and suffering were on regular rotation! Everything was disconnected but still operating on various levels. Random thoughts raced on different wavelengths in my mind, while some fell from my mouth like secret passions of Nasty Nas making love to Deadger Allen Hoe.

Despite the obvious scars left upon my reality and the stitch marks on my arm to remind me how lucky I was to survive that horrible naked night with all my limbs, I still pursued all the drugs and lil bit of drug dealing I could muster. At the lowest points of my paranoid states… I hoped that jail or death would save me from my self-inflicted suffering while I kept using. But I don't think I was ever addicted to anything. I just had consumption problems similar to eating too quickly or, emotional problems. I don't think I ever went through withdraw. Call me a Crack Biggie…

"I'm not an addict I just do a lot."

Then, finally… when my Mom found me crashed in bed after a long binge, she picked the lock, searched through my footlocker, and found a few pounds of mushrooms. She woke my ass up by dumping all the shrooms on my head. We blew up on each other! Later that day, with her encouragement, I moved out. It was just Mom and Richy at that point. I was out on my own with my Giorgio Cologne. While Richy stayed home and kept doing his deals, under her radar of course. At the age of eighteen, when many kids are celebrating a new sense of freedom, I was more concerned about getting busted as an adult, and doing real time!

Though our family fell apart, Mom stayed strong and kept up her business composure at the airlines, but she had to shift gears there because of us. From the time I started hustling, she climbed her way from a temporary position, to regional sales manager in just a few years. But with all the drama at home, she decided to take a front desk job at the airport where her workload was much lighter. Mom deserved a lot more than I gave back to her most of the time.

DEAD END

There was nothing left to Do
But not because of You

I got by on my own the first couple years in South Philly by nickel and diming it below Broad Street. But not long after my 19th birthday, I lost most of the juice that I had when 17th & Mount Vernon & 18th and Wallace got shut down. I had solid connects over there since I was 16. Connects so good that we would bring our girls out together and go bowling on the weekends; as if we were regular co workers not drug dealers. So when that scene, "up the way" fell to a sting & indictments, I had to go back to North Philly to cop weight. But that was OK. I knew how to carry myself, I knew how not to look like a sucker. I made friends up there in places that looked like a third world war zone.

Then, finally, an old friend I knew from the South Street scene began hooking me up. His name was Johnny; real good guy, family was connected. Johnny brought me in on his game and broke me off right from the key, fish scale shine that flaked off crispy. Just like it should when its good white not ghetto butter. Johnny and I became friends because we were dating two sisters who's Dad owned a corner bar on South Street. But my girlfriend Erica, the younger sister, was straight. So juggling my connections with Johnny, my runners, and my own habit often isolated me from my girl, till ultimately… she just moved on. We'd been together since I was thirteen. She noticed me dancing on a TV show back in the day, and had her older sister approached me in a gas station to let me know Erica had a crush on me. I blew them off, but fell for Erica later at a club called Circus Town we all hung out at back in high school. Many years later Erica's sister would date Johnny, the South Philly coke dealer. I was so close to those two sisters it nearly felt incestuous at times! They came from a good family and made me feel apart of it for as long as they could.

At this time, after bouncing all over the city to keep my hustle going, getting kicked out of my house, and loosing my girl, my brother wrote my junky ass off as well to build a small outlaw empire of his own; I was too sloppy for him. Besides having a few runners who connected with me to re-up weekly, I was alone now. I drank and drugged alone. I went for long drives alone. Walked through Longwood Gardens alone. And went to the movies, alone. If it were not for drinks with Johnny sometimes, I'd have had no social life. But Johnny was soon looking at time for a case he couldn't beat, so…

One night, I dragged Richy along with me to The Ritz Cinema on 2nd street where I was a regular. We went to see My Own Private Idaho! As soon as the barn came crashing down in the middle of the highway, I was hypnotized. I think I watched the rest of the movie with my mouth open, head tilted, and eyeballs vibrating.

After that picture, everything became a little clearer to me; though Richy couldn't understand why. He hated the movie! But what I noticed, and he didn't, was the way the characters in the story celebrated their struggle. And that felt fresh to me! Maybe I could create something out of my hard times?

"But what?" …I murmured.

From that point on I dreamed of reinventing myself! Gus Van Sant gave me the impression that living on the edge of society and even in the streets could be exciting. Before the Van Sant Private Idaho picture, despite how low I was, I never thought moving to skid row would be an ambition of mine. But after watching that flic, I wanted to be a part of a story like that! And if it made me homeless, so be it.

I didn't know exactly what I wanted to do, but I knew there was something out there and maybe, just maybe, I could write my way to it. I wanted to feel as good in my own life, as I felt in the movie theater. Drugstore Cowboy and My Own Private Idaho were my favorite pictures. Through them, Gus planted something in one of the potholes in my head that grew to more than I ever imagined for myself growing up. Something birthed inside me that wanted more than that which I was accustomed to. I wanted to get in touch with the emotions that bothered me, and turn them into something other than the pain they brought me.

Inspiring to me was the obvious touch of good taste put into the storyline around riff raff characters, pinched with gritty interviews for street credit, that made me think they were a little more than dramas, but some sort of art time capsule maybe. At that time, I'd often see punk rockers on South Street sitting around with each other having fun. I envied their apparent carefree lust for life. It was then I began to observe subcultures and journal notes. And after reading, writing, and dreaming as much as I was, it occurred to me that… maybe I can create my own story. And the word "maybe" was coming up more than ever. But I continued drugging my way through, night and day. I couldn't talk to anyone about my problems and crimes that troubled me, so a journal became my safe. A book where I could create some poetry and short stories out of the chaos I was living. In between the stories and tea stains, I'd write some rhymes and graffiti between all the journal entries in a stream of wickedness and awareness. And maybe I could do this or that, but to maybe to… stop doing drugs, never came to mind. After all, it was all those stirring emotions that were induced by youth and chemicals that I wanted to feel and write about.

I wrote in journals so much, I thought at the time that the physical act of writing planted my intentions deeper in the universe. But I'm sure it made writing less of a chore. Picking up an ink pen was like visiting an old friend. One who knew me so well I could say whatever I wished. I was honest on the page long before I was honest with myself. And it was the best I could do when I was low, lonely and lost, which was basically all the time. The highpoint of my life at that, if I had any, were in the first second I woke up, wherever. I really loved that blissful, levitating moment I occasionally had in the first second of ongoing bad days. When my eyes began to crack open and my mind had yet to sum it up. At that split second, I was nowhere and completely disconnected from what's to come as I rested off all the chemicals from the night before, or the night before, and the night before. During that first half second, I had no personal debts, no guilt, no lost religion, no broken spirit, no name to reinvent or leave behind, no gut to feed or head to fill with comforting garbage and all the other interests my lower self craved. In that first half second I was weightless on Earth. Then, the back end of that first second approached like an EL train from elsewhere. I'd arrive subway fast from my sleep underneath the sheets; miserable and one cent beyond spent from all the fares and turnstiles that baffled me along my endless tracks to temporary satisfactions.

When I made it from the sheets, I brewed some tea and often wrote in my Journal. I never read what I wrote, I just kept writing as if I could write my way out, but I was buried too deep to actually do so. Depending on my twist, I'd often wake up to find different messages around me that I wrote the night before. I thought of Richy a lot when I was alone, but I had very little to do with him these days, I was lost and always doing myself disservices. But it wasn't his fault, or anyone else's.

Sometimes I'd even wake up on West Philly rooftops with my head on stolen Moleskins under my straight letters with knots of Dirty Frank bar napkins in my pockets scripted with bad poetry in scripts

There's nothing left to do... But not because of you.
Time is lost, a life is gained.
Something should be learned from all this pain.
Style don't care so shave your hair.
And give up this life of mindless despair.
I'm not trying to be the best... Just someday be honest.

I was like any other crazy writer on the street who wrote with no rules. I put together encrypted stories that gushed words of a fading life with a blue coral cap only a veteran graffiti writer could decipher.

KETAMINE DREAMS

Way Gone
Rolling at Dawn

I woke inside a small, intimate aftermath downtown with my head resting on an old paperback titled NORJAK. Music was playing, dozens of people were dancing in front of me, and it was bright. Bright? That was weird. Then I noticed the words Ways & Means scratched into my forearm as house music spun and began to hit me in the heart. It didn't make sense, but neither did my surroundings at first. Then it came back to me… I'm in Brian Norwoods record store in Center City. I got over there some how from the night before after Evolutions, and somewhere else with no name and off the map.

But that was last night, this morning, as I struggled to my feet in the record store, a quarter fell out of my ass and rolled across the floor. Then I noticed it was so bright because I was sleeping in the storefront window of the record shop… in my boxer briefs? Confused, I wondered where my pants were as I watched the coin roll, as they do, in a circle before it fell flat on the ground. Bewildered, I had to admit.

"I put a quarter in my ass
and I played myself."

Standing behind a sign in the widow, I read it aloud mindlessly…

"Help Wanted?"

I pondered that, because I knew I could probably use some. And it was just about then that I began to wake fully and regain my spiritual and schizophrenic self once again. But where were my pants?

Outside, and across the street from a large record store window, I stood there with the HELP WANTED sign covering my head. From over there a Pedestrian screamed…

"Where's, your, head, at!"
with loco charm.

Back to the inside I could care less about my head but my pants had a 40 jug of K in them! A disco ball spun behind me as ravers did the running man with their hands champing overhead! I was at an after party of some sort, I knew that, but where were my pants? Outside, I noticed someone passing by the window behind me with an open umbrella in one hand and a coffee in the other. But she didn't notice me… pale and lifeless as a mannequin in the storefront window. Then, I began to catch the groove inside with the queer crack heads of all genders who danced in the store as music spun like sugar in a cotton candy machine of shared drug dreams.

All I could gather… was that I must have lost my shirt and pants between here and there the night before. I was out of control and going down fulltime and didn't mind. Nor did I, WANT HELP, as the sign said backwards in the window like a Led Zeppelin Stairway to Heaven implication of some kind. But it wasn't time to figure everything out. NO! Instead, I just shook my head to shake the sounds that came to me from the underground. Half naked, I turned and faced music!

"I shake my head to bake the sounds
that come to me from underground!"
I screamed.

Then, Brian noticed I was awake from behind his turntables and threw my pants over at me, hitting me in the face. Instead of quickly putting them on, I looked for the 40-jug. When I found it in them, I immediately gave Brian a fist up in thanks. He shrugged it off like I was crazy. Maybe I was. Maybe I gave him my pants the night before so I didn't loose the jug. It's possible.

Behind me, outside on the street, cars rolled past and people walked to work as I danced my pants back on in the record store window as the HELP WANTED sign fell down. I doubt they were taking applications at this time anyway.

Inside with me as the beat went on, one guy with blonde dreads kept asking me the same question over and over, as if on a loop. I knew the song. I don't know why he was so hung up on it just cause he looked the part. I didn't fully acknowledge him as I was on my own trip, enjoying what was spinning before me. But from the corner of my eye, I knew he was there, asking me over and over again if I were there. Finally, I had to turn to him and scream my answer…

"I'm here MAN!
I'm right fuckin' here!"
I yelled at him.

But to my surprise there wasn't a man beside me saying that, but a Josh Wink video on a TV in the window. Maybe I wasn't really awake yet after all. Ketamine dreams are lucid indeed.

Dazed, I murmured to myself,
"My mind be playing Winks on me."
like a Getto Boy .

Back then, the pills were so primo and water flowed endless like Ponce de Leon, that the nightlife had many of us rolling past the break of dawn and on, way gone, in hyper dramatic chemical "jawns" that only Phunkadelphians of a certain level could ever recall in their fountain of inner city youth.

At that time, I pretty much let the parties take over my dreams of player status. Where once upon a time strutted like a big shot on the streets, I found my spirit on the curb between the hustler I was and the habit I'd acquired. My brother Richy knew me as well as anyone else at this time, and he was very, very disappointed. Even disgusted with me I think. But he didn't say so. He didn't have too. Ignoring me spoke volumes. I was just another guy who grew into his graffiti name… MES.

While I was down, out, and on the duck from all of the players I grew up with, my lil brother Richy became one of the main connections between New York and Philly for certain so called, club drugs. In NYC he made solid connects in Manhattan and Brooklyn. Some mobbed up, others the first on the scene, and at least one, who was BTS. And that one BTS buster, he'd really regret connecting with, later.

During my absence, he worked hard to get big. Once I was his connect, now, he seemed to be everybody's!

But you would never know it if you met him, he was much more humble than I ever was. As it were, my good connects were limited to cocaine. So when I wanted to get into pushing the pills I was rolling on and the ketamine that was seducing me, I had to go to my brother.

"Yo Richy, can you down me with some
records and water?"

Of course he could, and did. He gave me a roll of records and a 12 pack of water. But he was very concerned about my sloppy business that he could catch some heat from.

"But you just come to me,"
he ordered,
"Stay away from the street.
No more buying coke from the mafia."

That was impossible at this point anyway. He was referring to my South Philly connect Johnny; rest in peace. John fell victim to an early morning hit waiting at a red light on Delaware Ave. Someone evidently thought Johnny was going to snitch to do less time. I du-know? But Richy didn't know about all that, so I just moved forward.

"You're my guy."
I assured my little brother,
while looking up at him.

And damn, if I wasn't smaller than him in every way at that chapter of my life. But knowing this, I took his direction to clean myself, flip more drugs, doubled down, and stack paper again. I put the days of pushing cocaine behind me, and placed the records and water (pills & ketamine) on the front burner. Through Richy's fronts, I got up rolling again. And all those coked out spells I weathered came to an end. It seemed as though MDMA and K cured my self-induced cocaine psychosis. These new drugs didn't burn me out… they reinvented me! While I was wrapped up in the dark side of the coke world, lots of my old friends got onto the rave scene. Once I was a leader at lil house parties, now I followed them to mega parties at clubs, convention centers and caves… to outlaws in locations that were hard to believe, such as inside bridges and at the end of airport runways. And soon, Richy and I were having good times and dancing together like never before. I felt like a junky coming out of retirement! The MDMA gave me new life! My prior field experience on the dance floor with freestyle music made it easy for me to adapt to this new thing that was happening in techno. After isolating myself and being out of the loop for so long, I had to learn the scene and get into the music that led it. It was an easy crowd for me to approach; most of the people were just old friends dancing to new music… great music! It was just a bunch of good friends doing choice of drugs, all night in nights that didn't end. It was epic adventures in the making every long weekend! Debbie Deb introduced me to Club Music with Look Out Weekends in Grade School. In High School, The Bank on Spring Garden Street had me starting my weekends on Thursday Night with industrial music. Then there was a party every night from Fluid to Evolutions in the tec-house scene. And in no time at all, between the clubs and the after parties, I had more money and drugs than I could spend or use on any given day. And for the partying I did, that was necessary to stay in business.

With money coming in once again, I found a nice lil loft in Center City and shacked up with a new girlfriend Celene, just a few blocks away from my brother's monster loft. I started to fill a safe full of cash, collected art from New Hope galleries, drove a new BMW off the showroom floor, had shoe racks filled with sneakers, and rolled everywhere I could with my French bulldog; ghetto fabulous indeed.

And through it all, I spent more time with Richy than I ever did before. He had season tickets to the 76ers and we'd often take the subway down South Broad to watch Allen Iverson work a program. We'd scream at Allen from our seats all night! We grew up admiring Julius Erving, but we loved watching A.I. It was good times just… living the high life with my brother.

Most of our close friends were in on it too. I don't think we imagined the party ending, because it basically never did. We got high, shopped, traveled and ate whenever and wherever we wanted, all without college educations or good jobs; any jobs! We hustled easily and successfully for years. Until, Richy lost his connects for Ketamine in New York. His guy up there who brought the water into The City and subsequently into the entire North East of the country, wanted to exit the game; a game that stretched for thousands of miles.

The Ketaset Ketamine, made in Fort Dodge Ohio, was exported to Mexico before it made its way back to New York. This shipment from Mexico was never legal, but was made successfully for years. The guy who ran this in New York, Gaten, was preparing to do time on a big charge; his absence was sure to dry things up. But Richy was real close with this guy Gaten, and Gaten was a real legend in New York. He made millions in his 20's and 30's by diversifying his interests in nightclubs, after creating a home delivery service of drugs known as "The Guest List". But eventually, he got busted manufacturing MDMA; he really couldn't say no to a dollar, ever! That was his downfall. That and keeping too close to his old gang "Born To Steal" around. Dealing with his gang B.T.S. was dangerous. But not Peter Gaten, he retired from robbing long ago.

Now Gaten, out of respect for Richy, and all his business over the years, sold us the last 20 cases of Forte Dodge K to be had in the United States through those channels. When that ketamine was gone, the K game would not be the same. Not to mention that the quality of the pills was getting so shabby, people were counting on the pure K more than ever. And Richy, he was on the shit as much as anyone else.

"When this K is gone,"
Richy uttered
"we have to find an
elephant-tranquillizer connection!"

He was joking, but he would have surely chased it down if it were possible to acquire I think. I drove up to NYC with Richy to get some of those last cases of K. It was a pretty big deal. So big, we had to make a couple trips because it was too much to bring back in one carload, and he insisted on driving his car and having no tails of any sort. On the way back with the second load, he voiced more worries…

"I don't know what I'm gonna do
when this is gone," he admitted, wholeheartedly.

Richy was very disappointed he was going to lose the connection. But that's not what I heard in his voice. Ketamine was his drug of choice, mine too at the time, so we both had dependency issues ahead.

"This water,"
he speculated,
"will be gone in nine months."

"Well, if you sell the bottles for 80 dollars,"
I suggested,
"It may last a year or more."

Rich laughed that one off! Most of our guys in the city paid half that. A little more if you were from somewhere else. Most runners cut the bottles in half and sold 40-dollar jugs. Charging 80 dollars a lick would be no laughing matter to them.

Eventually, on a computer I was learning how to use, I did some research on Ketamine and found some suppliers in Tijuana Mexico. And after making a few phone calls, I flew out to the West Coast to visit an old graffiti pal who moved to The Hollywood Hills. Then from LA I drove to TJ and right to the Veterinary Pharmacia I connected with on the phone. That guy was really surprised to see me! And even more surprised when I bought him out! Inside the store, they opened a trap door to the basement where we went down and did the deal. And once I was back outside and loaded up my car in broad daylight as if I had a permit to do so, I waited in line for an hour at the border. I bought some cheap gum from a desperate looking kid to calm my money nerves. By the time I rolled up to the customs Agent, I was cool and a little cocky when He asked…

"Do you have anything to declare?"

"Just a hang over officer."
…as I handed him my license.

"What's your purpose in Mexico?"

"I'm a writer,"
I continued,
"Doing research on
Pharmaceutical drug smuggling."

Then he handed me back my ID, and gestured me to move on though without giving my comment a second thought; I just knew how to deliver I guess…

"Have a nice day officer,"
I politely responded.

Then I drove the ketamine right by him in the back of a rented Pathfinder and over the border. It was easy, and I enjoyed it! When I got back to LA, I shipped it back East from the Wilcox Post Office in Hollywood.

I made a lot of these runs over the years. I even carried a much longer draft of this story on the passengers seat when I crossed the border in case one of the Agents wanted to take my "research" cover any further. And once, I was asked more about the "story" I was researching! So I offered the agent a draft of it…

"Would you like to give it a read?"

He responded with an enthusiastic,
"Sure thing!"

I autographed the screenplay and told him to keep it. He held the script in his hand with a pleasant smirk, and read the title back to me…

"Bump,"
he laughed.

"My email address is there…
So share your thoughts.
I could use an insiders perspective."

"Will do."
He responded, but never did.

I can hardly believe what I got away with sometimes! What a con I could be with my good teeth, a smile, and bold attitude.

Hours later, when I'd get back to LA, I'd pack the boxes of Ketaset Ketamine and drop the "Inner City Organic Tattoo Supply" packages off at the Hollywood Post Office. Then I'd eat at one of my usual spots, such as Musso & Frank Grill for my turkey in gravy dish, or chicken and waffles at Roscoe's.

Smuggling took a lot of time, energy, and nerve. But mania gave me an abundance of it at the times. But I didn't feel crazy at all, but rather the queer love child of Thompson and Scarface! Which is, all I ever really wanted to be. I made it all look easy, as if I was allowed to do it. And that's how I think I got away with it. I never looked suspicious. In fact, those runs down to Mexico put me back on my feet and gave me some of my balls back! In my head, I wasn't washed up anymore. And I wasn't living off my brother's laurels. I was running my own thing once again. I even got a small apartment of my own in LA for a while where I enjoyed a fantasy of writing movies, part time. I mean, everybody out there was doing one thing but calling him or herself another. Such as my regular waitress at Roscoe's…

"I'm an actress,"
she said; no surprise,
"What do you do?"

"I run an import business,
and write,"
I boasted as Curtis Mayfield flashed
through my pusher man mind.

"Write what? Screenplays?"
she asked, and eagerly waited on my reply.

"Yup. Crime dramas,"
But I'm new…
still haven't landed a lit agent."

"Oh, I see."
She responded, obviously disappointed.

Then, my runs to Mexico went from getting in and out quick, to staying down below the border for days at a time because I was too high to make the drive north. Sometimes I woke up inside my car, parked on the beach by The Bullring before I drove away, swerving slowly around sunbathers by the edge of the ocean.

Sometimes I'd make it to The Grand Hotel that my new friend Caesar's Dad owned down there, but only when I was sharp and brought my girl Celene along with me on runs. Yet more often than not, do to my lack of composure and loneliness, I'd wake up in a seedy hotel off Revolution Street where I cooked up K with a candle and a glass ashtray to the bewilderment of Mexican hookers. When I didn't have a place to stay or the time to cook it up proper… I just threw it in a gas station microwave with a damn hot dog!

Down in Mexico I found a dance scene that kept my attention and social life active during my visits with Caesar and the "Ohtli" rock band he managed. But I didn't push down there, or around them, just got fucked up with um'. So fucked up that I had to pay my way out of more traffic tickets, handcuffs and dog cage paddy wagons… that I began to think, TJ would be a good place to retire! There was no trouble I couldn't buy my way out of down there. And Caesar's dad was one of the most established businessmen in Mexico. So where we went together, the road was paved and safe. We met at a hotel party I crashed in The Baha one night. When I walked in, he thought I was from England and started chatting me up. I can't explain why he thought that, but we partied all night regardless. It was all such great party down there night after night, from the beaches to the bullring and further… very good times. That is, till I woke up with pimples on my dick!

Immediately, I ran to a Pharmacia that day looking for a barrel filled with the magic juice I could stick my junk into and cure the outbreak. I was sure they had it! I ran into the first drugstore ran in holding my sex wounds with both hands!

"Where's the wooden barrel of secret
sauce to clean my junk!"

The Revolution Street Pharmacist just looked at me weird. Then he looked behind me. As if to see if I was alone or my absurd request was being video taped by someone. I just stood there squeezing my Johnson over my sweatpants waiting for his answer.

"You know what I'm talking about!"

But in retrospect, I guess he couldn't believe that I actually was serious, but I was at the time. Defeated and reading his face, I understood that maybe there was no remedy just as I imagined.

"No barrel of magic for my dick zits?"
I squeaked out.

He nodded his head nope. It then sunk in, how crazy I sounded as I turned around to leave.

"You barbequed iguana crack-head,"
I murmured to myself,
about myself.

But on my way out, the counter dude finally spoke up…

"Check around the corner,"
he suggested.

"Buena! Where?"

"Right next door to the donkey show."
He said with a big grin.

"There's no donkey show,"
I responded.

"No cure for what you got either!"
he laughed out.

After he and his fellow employees talked a little more trash, they gave me some cream on the house and wished me luck. At that point, it appeared I might have finally got caught with something in Mexico I couldn't buy my way out of. The cream didn't work immediately; it gave me no relief at all! So I felt the need for other drugs to medicate my Mexican trick dick.

When I got back to my cheap hotel room to cook up some K, I caked more of the medication cream on my penis pimples, and took a handful of pills till the cream kicked in. Somehow, in that mix of medical mayhem, my body went on strike in my sleep! Much later, I woke up in the humid old room with a broken ceiling fan and stained walls feeling like a sand bag of bones. Something weird happened to me in my sleep. When my eyes opened, I couldn't move! My body was still asleep! But my right leg really numb! It was all very confusing and scary! It was like being in a waking dream of some sort where I was locked in my head, no use of my body, eyes wide open.

I must have lay there for nearly an hour, frozen in my sweat before my body began to wake up. When I could make it to the bed stand, I did some more coke to jump-start my bones, successfully; but my right leg remained numb and dead asleep. Then, numbness gave way to pain in my leg when I tried to walk around the room. But luckily I had some Oxycontin in my backpack. There I was, alone, on the edge of a raggedy worn out bed in a TJ hotel crying in pain. It was the first time that I couldn't seem to take enough drugs to take away most of the pain, but I kept trying till long after the sun went down before I passed out again.

Much later the next day, I tried to mask my limp with strut to the front desk to check out, before I made it to my wheels off Revolution Street. Once inside my ride I woke up on more coke and drove straight from Mexico to LA for medical attention. I thought if they couldn't help with my trick dick south of the border, my connections down there would be worthless reviving a dead leg. And I thought if I had to, I'd rather rest it off in Hollywood.

Once I got back to LA, I went straight to a medical center in Beverly Hills because I'd rather die than go back to another Emergency Room. I found the strongest name on the directory in the lobby, and then limped to the elevator. Up at the doctor's office the receptionist greeted me…

"May I help you sir?"

"I need to see the good doctor
Khan immediately."

Do you have an appointment?

"No I don't, but my leg is dead,
it won't wake up!"
I panicked.

"Sir, you're at a plastic surgeons office,"
she informed me.

Evidently, I missed that on the directory downstairs. I drove all the way from TJ, with…

"No problems."
I murmured to myself, confused.

"Sir, go visit the emergency room,"
she politely recommended.

But I couldn't do that! Just the thought of an ER gave me naked flashbacks of the leaves being fished out of my ass by the cartoon nurses trying to fit a little straw in my penis! I began to shake with my unresolved trauma.

"There is nothing you can do for me?"
I asked.
I'm fallin' apart here."
…like Ratso Rizzo

Sadly, and a little scared of me I think, the receptionist shook her head no. And she was so cute and Beverly Hills hot, it just made my dick zits hurt more!

Finally, after leaving there no better then I arrived, I found a doctor on Avenue of the Stars who would see me. I assure you, I will not go back to an ER conscious! This nice Doc examined my leg and concluded that it was probably the result of a stroke I had in my sleep, but more tests would have to be administered to be certain.

"In time, you will probably get back,
some use of your leg,"
he informed me.

"Ok,"
I said defeated,
"I see doc."

But I had more on my mind, so I whipped out my penis! It's what pushed me over the edge to begin with.

"What about this?"

He put on some science glasses, took a close look at it, and nodded his head yes.

"I can cut them right off,"
he seemed to boast.

"But will they come back?"
I asked.

"You'll never see them again."

I was immediately dumfounded with my recent actions when I thought of all the damage I'd done to myself in taking, the long way around, to this simple remedy.

Moments later the doctor froze, and cut, the Warts off. Warts! That's it! I assumed they were herpes, but not so. While he did the procedure, he schooled me on HPV's so I would not ever overreact in such a way ever again. Once more, a good doctor saved one of my limbs.

When I got home to Philly I slowed my roll, but I didn't stop. My strut fell to a limp for a year as my leg slowly came back to life after the massive Junky-Palsy attack in Mexico. During that time in recovery my mood was way off! And then, the sky fell! Fort Dodge Ketamine stopped exporting to Mexico altogether. So as the quality of the ketamine plummeted, it seemed my attitude did too.

As I limped around that year I found myself really wanting to be… someone else, anyone else. But I had no idea who. I was as lost as David Gahan stage diving in the 90's. And when my roll hit that dead end hopeless, I wrote more!

It was then I tried to do something a little bigger called "The Ways & Means". A story about a guy desperately trying to get out of the mix via measures I found in a book titled "NORJAK" I read once. But I was much too high all the time to sort out a solid storyline and do the needed drafts. It was easier to just ingest the drugs and dream about it over drinks, than to seriously engage the writing of it. And besides, it was hard work doing all those drugs; there was little time for any other recreation.

Around this time, I felt like my creative mind was at odds with cravings of my brain. It was truly deconstructing me, balancing them was impossible. I was falling to pieces!

"You just need to get on some
different shit,"
I'd murmur.

That was my short cut to thinking. I didn't think to stop using, only to switch my twists. When the chemicals I mixed together ceased to work at all, I'd break it all down, and do everything at once. But I couldn't get my fill on drugs, nor was I writing enough to complete anything to lift my spirit. In fact, I think my spirit began looking ahead knowing it may be out of work once the body shop went out of business. Then, my soul stopped showing up for work all together. It just kinda hung out near the ceiling in the corner of every room I wondered. I first noticed it happen when I had nothing to write about; and looked around the room for something, anything to say. But the words had no meaning anymore, the show was over for sometime now, and I was left all alone in the stadium called Earth. I couldn't think of anything but ending the sentence of life. And in that ultra hopeless moment, I wanted to end my story abruptly! Once the black hole of depression has you, the light doesn't exist anymore. Depressions gravitational pull can become so great it seems impossible to escape!

But I don't think I made the decision to attempt suicide in that moment though, I think the intention was planted years before I attempted to do it. It crossed my mind often over the years, and gradually gained support from different levels inside me. What ever makes intentions materialize was at work on me in a very dubious way this time. And at that low point, when all I wanted to do was die, I found myself on autopilot after years of conditioning for it. It seemed too natural and democratic between my mind, body, and spirit to think it was at all wrong to do or would hurt me at all. After all, I was in fact looking for relief at the end.

From way outside my body, in the corner of the room, my spirit watched me consume a death wish of substances in my nose, smothering what was left of my brain and stopping my heart. And then, it was over. No light, no blackness, nothing.

My girl Celene came home that night and found me blue and unconscious by the fireplace. She was too scared to call the paramedics because of all the drugs and money I had in a safe upstairs, so she called Richy. Then she dragged me outside to the snow to try and wake me up. When my brother got there, he could care less what was in the safe upstairs.

"My brothers fuckin' dying!"

He immediately called an ambulance to save me! Much later, I woke up in a dreadful emergency room once again. But "normal" doctors stood over me this time; the show was over.

"Do you know where you are Brian?"
a doctor asked.

"The hospital."

"Do you know your name?"
She asked.

"Braze."

My name is Brian Paul of course.

"Braze is his nick name."
Mom informed them.

"Was this a suicide attempt Braze?"
asked the doc.

"I wouldn't say that."

"What would you say?"

"I'd say…
God knows my name now.

Then my Mom stepped up next to the doctor. She was unusually optimistic when she found me in Emergency Rooms. As if the will to save me would be enough to do so, and always seemed too.

"You didn't want to kill yourself,
did you Braze.

"No Mum, course not.
Just had a bit of a pain in the gulliver,
and did too much.

…But no one got the Clockwork Orange reference.

And that was that. I was cleared of any mental health issues and advised to seek a rehab for substance abuse. A few days later… I was back on the street with the blinding sun on my green eyes over my thin, pale, desperate face looking to re-up!

For the next month straight I ducked my Mom and Richy as much as possible. I just got high and listened to Dandelions push through the cracks in the pavement of Center City. Rolling drums slammed inside me on Broad Street as relentless riffs filled my bones in back alleyways. Everywhere I turned the band of inner city wild flowers found me through the pavement cracks and screamed like Kevin Morpurgo to my vacant face…

"You're almost dirt,"
the flowers sung to me,
"You'll be pushin' us up, soon enough.
Pushin' us up soon enough!"

I loved those lil wild dandelions in Center City where I continued to play my pumping heart like an experimental jazz musician… flop house, after crack house, with strangers, ravers, strippers and freaks that come out at night like rap Whodini's. But eventually, even my good friends wouldn't get high with me any longer! Maybe out of love, but more because I brought them down I think. My girlfriend moved out too. She knew I continued to carry a death wish and didn't want to be there when it happened, again. So she packed her bags and took my credit card and new BMW and was out! The car was in her name though, but the credit card in mine.

Faded and lonely, I started ordering escorts to the apartment. But each time one got to the door, I'd lose my drive for the Kensington socialites and their services, and just gave them 20 bucks before I closed the door. As if I looked any better? I even tried ordering a set of twins one time. That was twice the mistake! I just can't to skank hoe; call me square.

"No thanks girls."

"Why not?"
they chimed in time with each other…
"we work."

"You's, work?"
I asked confused.

Where they robots I wondered very seriously. As paranoid and tweaking as I was, I thought, it's possible! And when I thought about it further…

"Maybe, you should find out Bee?"
I murmured.

And so I did so. In less than 60 minutes flat, on my back, those twins really disrupted any sense of reality I had left. They may not have been robots, but they worked like The Jetsons on lil boy Elroy!

Completely faded, but masking the shade of shit I was on, I showed up for Sunday dinner at my Grandpa's that weekend. It was a regular thing at his house on Sundays, though I wasn't there on a regular basis during this time. I went over there and had dinner with some of the family because in my head, I was saying goodbye to them all that night.

Afterwards, on a dead cold of winter night, alone in my loft once again, coke and dope mixed by second nature on my lap, and my goodbyes given earlier at

Grandpa's, I began snorting the pile that filled a coffee saucer I was holding; the powder was in a pile about the size of my fist. I can't tell you how many times I stuck my nose into that hybrid pile of smack, but I remember the taste of the barrel on my tongue as the sun began to break through the drapes I had drawn. With the break of dawn in my eyes, I put the gun down to make a note and write a line down. Not a suicide note, just a journal entry. The same old entry, but this time, it wasn't metaphorical, it was after after all, to my head at this time…

Guns to head since I was a child.

The led taste on my tongue is ever so mild

And then I paused with the pen in my hand on a line truer than ever… and, and began hyperventilating. In a panic I looked for my gun because I didn't want to die with the pain of a heart attack, but I suppose the .45 fell through the cushions of the couch before I could find it. Because then I faded, and, and… entered a dark, black, void. What a writer like me with a Depeche Mode weakness might call, an ultra flat black day.

Sometime later, could have been moments, hours or more, I remember paramedics racing me into the hospital on a gurney. Between the void and regaining consciousness, and despite the damage done to the brain, my heart and soul must have made a compromise and decided to hold on to the body.

When I woke in the hospital, I think I heard my Mom crying in the background while doctors hovered over top of me as I moaned with frustration for being, back! One of the doctors asked softly…

"What's your name?"

"Braze."

"Do you know where you are?"

"At the hospital again?"

"Do you know what happened to you?"

I took moment, gathered my composure, and realized I didn't want help, I wanted out! So I responded with what I thought might… speed things up.

"I did too much."

"Why Braze? Why!"
Mom cried.

"How did I get here?"
I asked.

I was supposed to be dead! Not there. Waking up coherent like this even dumfound me, not just the doctors who just saw me here a few weeks ago. It all seemed so unreal, as if I was a joke that everyone was laughing at, or a rat in a maze being experimented on in a lab disguised as Earth. My strings were being pulled by something! I couldn't take control of my life, and I couldn't even kill myself. I felt life, as I knew it, was a big charade. A game of chutes and ladders where I was just something being played with like a pet. But the fact was, my Mom saved my life this time. She felt it happening and raced to the city and saved me. And though there are more desperate details to that, I can't explain that any further.

The next day, still in Pennsylvania Hospital, it felt as if the circuitry in my head was really damaged this time. I tried to shake all the bad thoughts away, physically. I yelled at them too…

"Stop. Stop It!"
I'd scream, at nothing apparent.

I was just yelling over thoughts I didn't want to have but couldn't stop having. And then, my head began to shake violently from emotional convulsions that hit me with the impact of a car crash! These shakes and twitches would stay for years to come. But initially, the doctors sedated me on Lithium and more to calm me down.

Once I was knocked out there in a warm hospital bed, the Lithium took me elsewhere… where I found my Mom in a dream, outside of the building in the cold with Richy. He was squatting down in a fetal position with his feet to his chest, rocking back and forth…

"My brother, my brother, my brother."
Richy cried.

It being winter, I noticed a cold fog of breath come from his mouth when he spoke. Behind him, my Mom was a train wreck of anger.

"It's these damn drugs!
Why! Why do you's do them?"
she yelled with her fists clinched.
"What is wrong with you jerks!
I don't know!
I just don't know anymore!"

My Mom knew what we were up to. She found our money and drugs in her house when we were kids and before us… I hear Dad was dealing to stay high.

"I'm sick and tired of it Richy!
No one listens to me.
Not you, not your father,
not Braze!"

And she was right, we didn't. I wish we did. A little later, I woke up warm in a bed, with three doctors at my side talking to Mom.

"It's disappointing,
but no surprise he's back."

"What can I do?"
she asked.

"Well, you should prepare yourself.
He's going to leave here with
brain damage this time."

"Why?" He woke up fine!"

"It took a very long time to revive him,
his brain wasn't
getting the oxygen it needs."

But a few days later, they concluded that there was no, apparent, brain damage. So then, they assumed I was still breathing when the paramedics got to me, and that my heart rate must have slowed to a quiet, undetected, murmur. When I heard that, I looked up to my Mom and the doctors with more disbelief than a born again agnostic; a look only Jack Nicholson could outshine frozen in the snow! How could this be? Let me die already!

"You got really lucky Braze"
Mom said.

"But it really doesn't matter,"
the doctor said bluntly,
"The next time he'll arrive here dead."

I almost smiled, but I thought my mom was going to attack the doctor who said that! There wasn't any optimism from them this time around. None.

A week later when the sunlight hit my face and I emerged from the hospital, green was not just the color of my eyes but my face and random spots of my ill body.

When Richy got home to my brownstone, I went to the only thing I had in there to comfort me a little, my journal. Richy knew I'd probably hit the safe as soon as I could, so he took it to his place where he opened it up and cashed me out. My time as hustler, was over.

"I have your cash,"
Richy said,
"You need anything? Just ask me."

Evidently, I couldn't be trusted any longer.

"Go to rehab,"
he went on to say,
"and then we'll talk about you managing
your money later."

Then he left… maybe a little angry, but very disappointed, and incredibly stressed out! Alone, I immediately dove in my journal; noting most of what I'd wrote the last few pages. And after done with diary entries, I went to look for the Ways & Means story in another notebook; I found it laying on my Mardi Gras pinball machine.

The pinball machine was an antique nickel slot arcade game I stopped playing moons ago when I couldn't rock the machine like I could before my stroke in Mexico. But instead of picking up The Ways & Means story, I pushed the journal aside and put a ball in play, a few balls where waiting for there. I worked it around the table for a while and lit up crowds of people who threw Mardi Gras beads on the displays behind the games glass. When my last pinball finally went down the drain, I opened the steel door to the change bank because from inside there the pinball machine could be tripped endlessly to play without nickels. And when I looked inside it, boy, did I score!

"Hooray for the hustler,"
I said to my reflection on the glass of
the pinball machine.

For inside the antique game, on top of decades of dust, was a small pile of money! Some I hid and forgot about months ago. I pulled out the cash, and counted out 1,700 dollars on the glass. Then I took a step back… and looked at it all… The cash, the Ways & Means Story, the Mardi Gras pinball machine. Then, I put it all together as blood let oxygen to my brain. I took the money in my hand, stared the New Orleans game down, and then looked at my story title on the journal again.

"I have, the ways & means…"
I murmured.

But before I could finish my thought, something flashed in my mind that brought the hairs on my arm to attention! Then, I pocketed the money, grabbed my notebook and packed absolutely nothing. Not a damn thing!

Outside, I got in my Pathfinder and began heading south. As I left Philadelphia and continued down I-95, I spoke into a digital recorder I had stashed…

"With one foot on the gas, One foot in the grave,
One hand on the wheel, With the other I wave."

BOOK SAFE

And with that, I realized I was rolling dirty! I had a midget in the trunk! So I slowly exited the highway, turned the car stereo off and pulled up behind an Acme Supermarket. Then I parked and opened my hatch to discreetly throw a blue, three foot No2 tank in a dumpster. That is, after I hit on it like a psychedelic scuba instructor before I got back on the road with ways and means in my veins of bloodletting blues in to dusk. I didn't kill myself, my story continued. Playing a game of pinball would finance what be… a new life for me.

MAKING CHANGE

From slow nickels to Fast Dimes
And on to the French Quarter

Much later the next day I drove by mausoleums that rest under the I-10 before I took a French Quarter exit. The streets were packed! Intersections were blocked off, sidewalks full of folks wearing costumes, and no parking anywhere! Then, I noticed beads on people. Beads?

"Mardi Gras?"
I murmured,
"Naaaw!"

Then, a girl looked back at me as I was looking at her; she yelled over to me with a big smile…

"Happy Mardi Gras!"

Now, despite the fact that my old Mardi Gras Pinball Machine clued me in to take this semi-spiritual direction, I had no idea when I left Philly that it was actually carnival time in New Orleans. In fact, I was in such bad mental shape that if someone were to ask me what year it was, I wouldn't have been quite sure. My mind was blown like a boardwalk arcade pimp smacked by a title wave.

I drove around for a while with my lack of awareness on my mind, before I finally found a parking spot. I stepped from my truck and spit shined my snakeskin Pumas and then walked back to The French Quarter. Back then I thought why would anyone want to be anywhere else in this city but The Quarter? With my bearings off, and tired from the long ride, Check Point Charlie's looked like an Oasis! Inside, the bar was predictably crowded, but I found one seat at the end of the bar and ordered an Abita.

"Hew yi wa ta wene?"
asked a Euro-drunk.

Now I don't know much about Scotland or what Irvine Welsh looked like since Trainspotting, but to me, it sounded like he was sitting right next to me; drinking a pint.

"Who's playing?"
I asked.

"Na mooch ova a van er-yi?"
he laughed.

I just shook my head nope, not a fan. Turns out, the game on the TV he was referring to and wondering who my pick was to win, was the Super Bowl. I thought the only thing I had any references to in the world, was pop culture. But while getting so high, life just passed me by like that chick in the Pharside song. Disconnected from everything it seemed, I broke my journal out on the bar and began to make a few forgettable notes about my initial awkwardness in New Orleans. Then I finished my beer and went on my way down Decatur.

A few blocks later I walked by a Christmas Store where I nearly stumbled over a street artists' work that was displayed across the pavement. The pieces were an array of disfigured, mostly naked, slightly gross, highly emotional, watercolors of a man and or woman. The two characters this artist reinvented time and time again gave me the impression that they were highly strung out on life, and love. The pieces he painted where carefully loose and confidently wicked. I found some of my own naked life bleeding in his watercolors accented with the spray from a can of paint. I connected to it technically because I noticed no apparent rules or boundaries in any of the pieces. In the bottom corner of each piece was tagged "NEB" in a very legible, adolescent hand. As I admired the work, the artist spoke to me…

"All the pieces are
10, 15, or 20 dollars.
Whatever you can afford."

He was a disheveled man with taped up glasses and paint all over his clothes sitting on his knees next to the art.

"I'm Braze,"
I told um,
"I write MES. You're NEB?"

He immediately understood that I wasn't talking about writing books. Then he cased me, and became a little confused I think because I was so clean cut.

"Yeah, it's Ben spelled backwards.
You're a writer?"

I nodded yes, bent down and picked up his pen and notebook from the sidewalk, did a quick throw up and a Philly style tag. Then I handed it back to him. Impressed, he responded with eager eyes…

"I experiment with spray paint.
Do you paint in New Orleans?"

"No, I just got to town today.
You live here Neb?"

"Sometimes, I'm a traveler."

At that time I had a limited understanding of what a traveler was, but by the looks of him, there was something to it outside my own travels for sure.

"You wanna pop a squat?" he asked.

As I took a moment to respond, he gestures to the space available on the sidewalk. Then I understood…

"Oh… sure. Thanks!"

As I made the mental note that "pop a squat", means in this case "have a seat", I was happy to make a friend here. During our convo I continued to subtly adapt to the lingo. I'm not afraid to ask questions in classrooms. But I find that just listening when I want the answer to the question, in mind, on the street, an answer often surfaces without me looking naive. We talked art, colors, influences and style for some time before we decided to close up his shop there and continue over a cup of coffee up the street. On to the coffee shop Neb asked me…

"Where you crashin'?"

"My car."

"Meeee too,"
he disclosed.

Later, as we hung out and continued to talk about art at Café Envie, he introduced me to other dirty kids like him; travelers I gathered. Most mentioned… "catching out", "hot shots" "double stacks" "flying signs", "freshies" "busking" "spanging" and other terms that were new to me. But it was clear, that these were all terms they used around the "Train Hopping" scene…

"Huh, all these kids hop trains?"
I asked Neb.

"Pretty much."

"You?"
I asked um.

"No, I rubber tramp it.
You ever train hop?"

I just laughed…
"I've hopped more subway trains
then I can recall.
I loved those cars since Style Wars."

Yet they weren't the trains these kids were riding, but Neb knew about the Style Wars doc I referred to. So he and I talked about Subway Art till the coffee shop closed. We were far from similar on the surface, but under the skin, nearly the same. Later, we called it a night and walked back to our cars. And it turned out we were parked on the same street, by coincidence.

The next morning when I woke up in my back seat, I peeked out of the window and noticed a couple of dirty kids from the night before, hanging out on the corner across the street. Then it set in, I had nothing to change into, nor toothbrush or deodorant. My car kind of smelled, and I stunk. So I took my shirt and sox off to try and shake the stink loose and turn them inside out. I could deal with the shirt worn inside out, but I needed to find some fresh sox later! They were crusty. And at that moment, I assumed I knew what "freshies" could mean. So I put my sneakers back on and peeked out the back window again, and noticed those kids going into a big warehouse. I gathered myself in the back seat, then exited my car and rolled across the street to follow those kids. Why not? My behavior seemed to loose it's struggle between extraversion and introversion, and gravitate towards situational-ism, rising to each occasion.

Once over there and inside the warehouse, I noticed a few shelves stacked with old books under a sign that said Free. Next to that were some theater props, a few old bikes and some beat up furniture where those kids, who I followed in, were chilling out and drinking coffee. They were the same dirty kids Neb introduced me to the night before, so I gave them a nod. But they didn't recognize me. Or maybe they just didn't care too. Whoever they were, they were the faces of New Orleans that had my attention. It was from their personas, lingo, and attitudes that a story about train hopping sparked inside me. And though I was pretty far out of my element, I was comfortable in New Orleans, around them, and at that moment inside the warehouse, I felt at home. Maybe it was the free books inside there. Maybe the damp air in the building that reminded me of my Grandpa's cellar. Maybe it was the room that looked like the Space Available spots for The Goats, Dandelion and Gushing Red shows in Center City; I du-know. But the warehouse had my imagination flowing like old Rusto with the gusto, bold and dripping.

The dirty kids paid me no mind as I walked by them and into the black hole a little deeper; I felt like a ghost. Inside the next open door, I found a small library! Crazy. I thought I was in an abandon building, and then, I walked into a legit literary speakeasy of some sort. At the entrance behind the counter was a tall woman standing there with Diana Ross in a headlock, for lack of a better description. Ol'girl looked up in my direction with no hello or a welcome of any kind, but seemed to look right through me. A few more dirty kids were inside there at a table, looking at zeens and drinking coffee. Beside them was a coffee pot in the library which appeared to be free self serve coffee, so I fixed myself a cup and put some change in the tip jar; then went searched for diamonds in the rough. I like to parooz books because I'm a person who rarely finishes them. I'm happy to just get the feel and style of it, kinda gat it, and move on to the next. I mean after all… I only cared how I felt along the way! Not about the story I was leading, reading, or how it ends, and for me, it ends when I say it does. Libraries don't excite me unless they have a good feel. School libraries? I've been in one or two good ones. Public Libraries? Depends. But there's no library, like a vinyl library! …This space? It had potential. But it was clear it would not reach it in the state it was in. Unless run down and assed out was the comfort zone for everyone passing through. My poisons of choice are of a different nature than huffing asbestos. While assessing the joint, a kid eyeballed me, so I greeted him…

"How you doin?"

I got a nod from um' and finally, someone acknowledged my presence. So, I wasn't dead but found myself the odd duck out in a bookstore for outcasts.

A lil later, on my way out, I noticed a hand painted sign that read Iron Rail Anarchy Book Store. I popped a squat on the curb, finished my coffee, and scripted those experiences in my journal. And as I sat there, I had a feeling as though I was in the real world for the first time in a long while. I'd been in my own headspace for so long, I forgot what it felt like to be around people and just be present in natural, sober feelings.

For the next few days Neb introduced me around at Zotz on Royal. Locals passed through while travelers almost lived there, as did I the first couple weeks. There was a back room where you could sit and pass the day away, and a back yard where old timey hobo musicians would gather with tattooed "Know Nothing" clowns who dropped out of that circus years ago to pick at steel guitars for loose change long before Loose Marbles. Zots also had a big bathroom where I could wash up. For the price of a small coffee, I used that bathroom as if it were my own spa to manage better the few hundred dollars I had left in my pocket. I stole food and freshies from the grocery stores, and gave up soft drinks for free water. At night, I followed the dirty traveler kids to a homeless feeding line called "The Wall" at the end of Elysian Fields hosted by church folk. As I met even more travelers, I became aware of the slightly different personas they carried. Within this group of train hoppers there were subgenres within this subculture of new wave nomads… hobo's, gutter punks, house punks, old timey kids, each person projected a different message to the world by how they carried themselves. More then ever, after assessing their attention to attire, as well as the image priorities of my own as I looked down at my own Pumas that strutted uncontrollably when I was on the move; made me realize finally what Fugazi got in the beginning, discouraged often, and lived by it seemed. Even people with next to nothing seem caught up in what they look like and are willing to waste so much to hold onto the image they desire. I began to think how much time I could save if I could shake the importance of self-image.

Months later, my clothes were as grey as everyone around me. Neb, my first crusty friend in town, bought me a watercolor set so we could paint together and compare artwork pieces in the backyard of Zotz. Back there I became friendly with even more artists, performers, and musicians. The nicer gentleman of the gang was Stumps Duh Clown. During our first convo I found out that we both grew up in Philly; yet that didn't connect us. He hates Philly! At thirteen he hopped a train out of town to Atlanta and never seem to look back. Just the mention of Philly seemed to turn his stomach; as it did when I told him I was from there. I imagine there are some very heavy reasons a kid leaves home that young. But he said nothing more about it, other than having to often run errands to the corner bar for family. One time he left to get somebody a pack of cigarettes, and decided to catch a train out of town instead. By the time he and I connected in New Orleans, he was a semi-retired circus clown, and the oldest swinger in town with a steel guitar on his lap.

He and his dog Big Mama busked on Lower Decatur every day. Down there, they made enough dough to get by. And Stumps had more friends in town than anyone else! So when some of his friends became my friend, I felt myself in the middle of something exciting and… uncut. He began including me in all the happenings on the fringe of town.

"Hey patna,
wanna go to a party tonight?"
he asked me.

"Sure.
What's goin' on?"

"Good music. Cheap booze,"
Skinny-dipping, puppet shows, y'know."

Then Stumps wrote down the address, handed it over, and encouraged me once again.

"You should come Braze."

When I looked down at the address, I was very surprised to see the party was at… a country club?

Later that night, when I got to that address deep, deep in the Bi-Water, I found a hundred bicycles locked up to the short steel fence in front of "The Country Club" where the party was happening. There, with Stumps' invitation, I felt very confident walking in for whatever shenanigans he was hosting. It looked grand, southern, and far from crusty on the outside.

Inside, the southern style mansion was just as impressive! I immediately found my way past an old stagecoach to a swank bar with enough old timey hipster hobo's around it to over throw a train yard in a wino revolution. The stagecoach was well lit for a shadow puppet show being performed as I found Stumps at the bar drinking gin. One eye on the puppet show, and the other on a pair of bare teenage tits that had normal painted across them, I thought, man… this place is far from ordinary. Stumps just gave me a hug, laughed with me, and then he pointed out the open back door. Out there, dozens of people were naked, meandering about, and swimming in this very big pool acting like fools! Never a swinger, but merely a wishy-wash patron in the past, I found myself a little nervous and maybe even slightly, homophobic, despite the normal sign bouncing next to me.

"What kinda party is this Stumpy?"

He just smirked, as if it needed any explanation. In this grand old place with a beautiful puppet show being held in the front room and who knows what out back, I took a seat there at the bar and drank with Stumps and started a convo with the normal chick.

Around the stagecoach old timey musicians played everything from banjos to fiddles with spoons in between, and a suitcase drum with a washtub bass during the shadow puppet show I was privy to. In the back yard of The Club, 40 or more gutter punks could care less and were out there skinny-dipping in a bizarre escapade of acceptance, surrender and chaos not far from the rest of New Orleans. Since arriving in this town, the music and story overwhelmed me in some kind of lucid Fellini way. I'd thought I'd seen it all at parties in Philly, New York, LA and TJ. But at the time, in 2005, this place was not ahead of the times, and far from behind them, but I got more the impression that the people down here, at least in this circle, were turned inside out and timeless! Their bodies were merely their spirits' torn up and worn out dirty wardrobes! Their skin tattooed youthfully with black ink, scabs that seemed to never heal, and weeks of sweat that permeated the air like atomic stink bombs. Crusty wasn't cool to them, it was a side effect of an endless road where those on it crashed in this alternate universe known as New Orleans. They weren't druggies, not even alcoholics most of them, but more… incestuous souls partaking in good old mayhem behind gypsy music maybe… I'm not sure, it was all so foreign to me getting drunk down here. After all, a few months before this I was at a DJ's dance floor in Center City on gel tabs, coke and ketamine.

At The Country Club, my reality began to stretch like matter in an old timey black hole. Where life slowed down and the gravitational pull of steel guitars was stronger than the crack I could score just a few blocks away. In fact, drugs weren't on the forefront of my mind at this time. I wasn't trying to escape anything down here, but rather peruse new interests. My life began to mushroom into good old fashion fun with drinks, music & new friends. Money and drugs were never part of our conversations, where back home it was the center of most. The nights down here were too long with song to blow lines or worry too much about the rent or car payments of any kind. It was the best getaway I could have from the junk that was destroying me back in Philadelphia. Philly is a great city, as is LA and TJ in their own ways. But my relationship with them ruined, and nearly killed me. Where now in New Orleans, it seemed I was reborn in a new world far from my old ways and means.

Nights after night I found myself alone on my way home to my car from wherever in the Bi-Water I was drinking that night. Sometimes, still buzzed, I kept walking past the block where my car was parked, and stumble into The French Quarter looking for food. One night, as I rolled down Royal Street towards Viux Carre Pizza, I saw a couple wearing oversized Goth pants and velvet capes who appeared to be gliding over the sidewalk down the street as if they were just a few inches above the ground; just as I had seen ravers in Jenco jeans slide across dance floors years ago. Although I should have, I didn't feel as though it was an illusion of any sort at the time, but got the impression they were hybrids of some sort. These beings appeared more than human to me, but I was a lesser person on such late nights witnessing these experiences when I wanted to be bitten by a vampire in The Quarter or abducted by aliens after a Rave. I was a sucker for magic! Even when I meditated back then, I really wanted to levitate, not ground myself. Nights like those in New Orleans… I'd watch the sunrise with a slice of pizza on the wooden steps leading down to the Mississippi at The River Walk like the other wharf rats down there. Unlike my nights with jumping music, slick DJ's, fog machines and laser rays in Philly, the hobo's had my shoes nailed to the floor, not high. I suppose my new hobo friends drank me off the drugs, but I was still seeing things that didn't add up. And that was just fine with me. I took being a little delusional at times, big progress from being suicidal. I felt like a retired addict, and just wondered… why was I so crazy back home? Must have been the drugs. And maybe, maybe I wasn't crazy after all, just burned out.

I went back every Wednesday to The Country Club; I loved that place! Why they allowed those crusty hoedowns to continue, I'll never know.

Most other nights the hobo crowd would gather at The Slab off Press Street by the train tracks. The Slab is a large piece of concrete at the edge of a field once used as a loading dock, or something like that; now abandoned. To me, it was the stage of a great nucleus of talent. There, I became a little friendlier with people I met around town through Stumps such as Kiowa, Barnabis, Ean, Ratty, Kate and Stix. With all that talent there playing wicked music, I thought that spot by the tracks was how it may have been at 821 Sixth Ave in New York in the late 1950's. Drunken old timey music and gypsy jams flowed in New Orleans at The Slab like the high times of endless jazz nights I imagined at the loft of W. Eugene Smith's. Just picture those two era's of music, late 50's experimental jazz & new millennium buskers jamming on different sides of the wall… like RUN-DMC & Aerosmith.

After long and hot days busking on Royal Street that summer, these musicians would keep playing through the AM till the moon was tired and all the cheap drinks were gone. Many nights ended in an epic gypsy jam session with the musicians silhouetted by the one light hanging from the top of the warehouse behind a high barbed wire fence next to The Slab.

From afar, it looked to me like something foreign. It seemed very un-American, but more a Russian, Greek and Mexican mash up. Or, what the enemy sound track to Red Dawn should have sounded like, with broken fiddle string and groan box beats of debauchery on a straight "bublichki" diet. And everyone there could play music but me, I had nothing to offer but nobody seemed to care. My first friend in town, Neb, was manic about his painting and really didn't make time for anything else. Stumps and I became better friends over countless drinks and talks at the Slab. Then, I met a guy named Matthew Sepher at The Slab with a different kind of instrument than all the others; a camera. Seph shot the scene!

After introducing himself to me one night while he was taking photographs, Matthew asked about the notes I was making in my journal…

"What do you write?"

"Graffiti, short stories, and some poetry."
I uttered back to him.

A short convo between us followed, and I immediately got the impression Matt Sepher was a nice guy. He has a sincere voice, and is not a big drinker, like most of us back then. Maybe that's why he smelled better than everyone else. He was grungy but not crusty. He held down a job and rented a place in the 7th Ward. We began to connect frequently at The Slab, and continued to record things in our own way.

Soon, I opened up to Sepher a bit more than I did with Neb & Stumps, and gave him some of my background. When I mention the depression and drug use I lived with, as well as the overdoses and suicide attempts, he suggested I call home and let my family know I was OK. But I found a wonderful comfort zone down here off the map! No matter how selfish it was indeed, I was better than ever alone in New Orleans. Yet after a few more talks with him, I realized that maybe he was right. I was OK! Why not call home and give them some good news? So I finally made the phone call at a pay phone on Esplanade and Royal, to my brother. He answered with a familiar…

"Yo?"

"Yo Richy, it's Braze."

"Oh God man, you're alive!"
he yelled into the phone.

I thought he'd be angry, but no. He continued excited…

"Where are you B!
We've been lookin' everywhere!"

"I'm not in Philly bro."

"Where then man?"

"I'm… down South." …I murmured.

"Mexico?"
he assumed.

"New Orleans."
I clarified.

"What? …Just come home Braze."

I took a moment, then…

"Richy, I just don't know man."

"Know what Bee!"

BOOK SAFE

I thought about where I was, how much I've changed down here, and how little my old life seemed to mean to me, and told um…

"Bro, I may have gone too far
to come home."

Then, a few days' later, big bad winds brewed at sea and began to scare most everyone out of New Orleans as Hurricane Katrina approached. At first, I didn't feel the need to go anywhere. But when most of my hobo friends started hopping trains out of town, I decided to drive to Baton Rouge at the last minute to wait out the storm.

As I camped in my car and the weather passed with fury, I listened to the radio for updates. While sitting there, my head echoed once again with my Moms voice like it had on my drug binges before I left Philly, she screamed and cried…

"Why Braze? WHY!
Why Braze? Why! Why Braze?"
over and over in my head!

"Why, did I call home?"
I murmured.

I felt after calling home and letting Richy know I was in New Orleans, Mom would be worried more than ever thinking of me in that catastrophic storm! The news coverage was intense! And after the winds and rain finally ceased in Baton Rouge, the thought of going home brought on all the anxiety, voices, and depression I thought I left back in Philly. Those feelings are the glue traps of my life! I thought they were behind me. But pulling a geographic to NOLA was just a quick fix for my bad situation at home, not a cure for my crash after all. And now, according to the radio broadcasts I'd been listening to, New Orleans was under water? I felt lost and wasn't sure where to go from Baton Rouge… back home to Philly, or Mexico maybe? So I flipped a coin; Philly won. So then I flipped again. But this time Philly, or LA? As the coin spun in the air, I heard a train whistle closing in on me. Beside the service road I was parked on, a freight train suddenly raced by just a few yards from my parked car. After I caught the coin tumbling in the air, I just sat there watching the racing train and glanced at the graffiti streaking by. Then I smiled and found myself looking for people on boxcars. I never thought to look for hobos before! I was always one to look for UFO's in the sky; not tramps on a freight car. When the train passed, I looked back to the coin in my hand…

"Ahhh damn it."

Then I started up the car and headed north. And soon, I was numbing with anger and depression that seemed to intensify the closer I got to Philly. My bad mood seemed to pull my forehead over my eyebrows and my teeth grinded mindlessly as I drove hundreds of miles on autopilot. With some clean time under my belt, the drastic change in mood was more apparent then ever.

PHILLY TOWN

I wouldn't be this Writer
Had I not met her in that Dinner

A day later, when I walked in the back door of my Moms house, her shocked face raced from relief and surprise when she first noticed me…

"Braze!"
she sighed.

Then…

"Why BRAZE!"
she yelled.

Apparently, as I suspected, she'd been watching the news reports on TV of the hurricane aftermath, looking for my car. It wasn't until I got back to Philly that I actually could see for myself what the devastation looked like in New Orleans. Had I known how it looked, I would have called Richy again.

Beat from the drive, my racing mind, and storming emotions, I went to the basement for a nap after assuring my Mom I wouldn't leave again without notifying her first. But found myself not sleeping, but hiding down there for a couple days. Depression makes a bed, quicksand for me. Mom brought me down food, but eventually, Richy had enough and pulled me out…

"Come on Braze,
lets go out to lunch."

"I don't know Richy,
I'm kinda tired."

"I'll take you to the Melrose."

He knew that diner was my favorite spot, and it had crossed my mind since I returned. So I was game.

Later, when we made it to the Melrose and found our usual booth open, Richy stopped asking about me, and brought me up to speed on him over a couple of MP1 dishes.

"I bought a landscaping business.
And a house in Jersey."

"How'd you swing a house?"
I asked.

"Good credit and small
legit business made it possible."

Just before the Great Recession, the Real estate market was at an all time high with loose loans. Every drug dealer, stripper or car thief could get a mortgage.

"I'm looking into investment
properties in South Philly too."

"Just gonna flip them?"

He nodded yes, his plans sounded good me. And it seemed in fact that there was less drama in his life since I'd been gone. I was impressed by his sterling composure. And I should have been much happier for him, but coming back to Philly stirred my emotions. Before, I had my vices for escapes in the city. But now, just eating that MP1 chicken dish with gravy was not enough satisfaction or relief to settle things inside me. I thought about getting high, because I knew I could easily. But I wiped those thoughts away, and just ordered another MP1 dish.

Richy went in his pocket and pulled out a small knot of money in a rubber band and handed it to me. It looked like a few hundred bucks. I didn't count it, just put it in my pocket.

"I still have all your money Braze.
Anything you want to do with it?"

Not long ago money and the luxuries it bought motivated me. Buying this, paying rent, making this payment, whatever it was… really made me hustle! But at that moment, the thought of it almost sounded absurd. I realized at that point how living on the streets in the same clothes for a few months did a real head job on me. So I just told um…

"Hold on to it.
I'm good for now Rich.
Thanks."

As I sat there cleaned up in a classic South Philly diner with a few dollars in my pocket and eating lunch with my brother… I realized, maybe, I had all I needed for the first time.

Though not having a hustle was very uncomfortable back home. I felt like player, benched! You see, when you grow up street smart… having no hustle is like a steak without wiz. You're just plain without! I felt very self-conscious about it, naked almost, like everyone was looking at me all the time as if I was a nudist on a subway car, a freak! I even thought I noticed strangers laughing and talking about me out of the corner of my eyes because I was just another bum without a hustle. I was tripping. I just felt so bad about myself back home, bad for being a dealer for so long, and now bad for not being one. I just wanted to be someone else, and if I could erase my personal history in the process, better yet! Maybe that's why I wanted to get high and die for as long as I did. I was more than just unhappy… I was completely ashamed of myself.

Before I left Philly, as you know, I medicated myself constantly. This time around Philly, I was alone with my unmanageable emotions like never before. It sparked so many echoes in my head, and murmurs from my lips… I felt like I really had two heads at times, one crazy, the other observing the crazy.

My troubled mind got so bad that sleep didn't even protect me. My dreams were constantly haunted by horrible headlines barked by a newsie on the corner of a busy intersection in my brain…

"Extra! Extra!
MAN CAUGHT NAKED!
Dusted high and screaming on LSD."

Was that, what I was initially most ashamed of? Did that one night open the black hole that was to become the rest of my life? Was I dead? Alive? Are my thoughts creating all this, or is all this creating my thoughts? There was a battle for sure inside me. So to escape from this war with myself, rather than fuel the nightmares with drugs, I just dreamed of New Orleans instead. Down there, I was in the moment. The past was behind me and the future wasn't a concern. In Philadelphia, I was disturbed by all the mistakes I made and the stature I thought I lost. I was basically anxious, because I was always thinking about being anxious; thus I medicated back then. The thought of sorting the thoughts out never came to mind. But now, despite how heavy it all was, I was clearer than ever. Yet once again, I began mumbling like a schizophrenic. My head twitched and shook uncontrollably as it tried to physically remove the bad vibes. It seemed my "mumbling murmurs" over the years, were the result of me trying to burry thoughts I didn't want to think about. As if saying one thing, out loud, would silence the messages that were being transmitted from elsewhere; thus the war.

And on top of it all… Office friends of my mothers deemed me a New Orleans refugee. That was weird. She brought me home cloths and other donations given to her, by them. Although I felt far from a victim of the storm, I was perceived as one by some of her close friends. After I made that call to Richy, the word was passed on to everyone in town that I was alive and well in New Orleans. But when the storm hit, everyone got back on the worry wagon again. Throughout my desperate attempts to bring change, comfort and calmness in my life, I put everyone on rough seas. I never felt like a Katrina evacuee, but by that time I'd been evacuating from my own traumatic events for more than a decade. Seeing how uncomfortable I was at home, my brother dragged me over to stay with him at his new house in Jersey.

When I got there, far from anywhere we ever lived, and found that his big new home made our inner city lofts look like section eight; I was pleasantly surprised. I never thought Richy, nor I, would be welcomed, comfortable, or fit in at such a tranquil, suburban development. But like I said, mortgages where being given out to everyone, so he wasn't the only hustler on the block out there. But this place was palatial! And, he had no intention of downsizing what so ever. He was like… Mr. America over night. But everyone was going in that direction before I left, I was just to self-absorbed, nickel and diming, to notice it.

"I'm holding on to the
Center City address too."

"Why?
I asked perplexed.

I business down there,
I don't want anywhere near my house.
Soon,
I'll be done with the dumb shit."

Richy was moving into real estate and landscaping full time and just dealing part time it seemed. And it looked to me like he was on the verge of cashing out with a nice stack of paper, but I never asked him specifically. I suppose at this point, my Mom didn't either; I'm not sure. But when I stayed with him, he put me to work, that's for damn sure!

He got me up every morning to walk the goddamn lawns with him! I had to weed whack lawns from the break a dawn, till sunset! I never worked so hard! By the end of the first week, I had enough!

"This is bullshit Richy!
I walk with a weed-wacker while you
ride the lawnmower?"

Richy just laughed at me and kept working. He did it all, including, walking the lawns with a weed whacker. I hadn't put such long hours in since working on my habit. The longest hours I'd ever worked… were on my hustles and getting high. Working any harder than that, on a lawn no less, was ludicrous! But Richy didn't mind it. I think he really liked his new business, and I know he worked hard at it. But to keep going at such a hard and fast pace, Richy's whole crew stayed high on different pills all day. They were swallowing, crushing and snorting so many different pills… all had a various a-ray of colorful rings around their noses! It looked like they carried a candy raver flu; very contagious, but one I avoided this time around.

Yet not only I noticed the colorful rings around their nostrils, even some of the customers of Richy's stood in their windows with perplexed looks while these crazy junkie's ran loose on the their lawns in broad daylight! In an effort to be the most productive landscapers in the hood, they'd brought a junky apocalypse to the lawns of the suburbs! Nonetheless, Richy worked very hard, but his habits were just as heavy. He admitted it…

"The oxys are getting to me bro."

He went on to say that he had to swallow a couple just to get out of bed in the morning. And after work, he'd often run to North Philly for a bundle of dust. He began smoking more of that stuff than Rick Rubin in the back of the bus at one time. Richy said the dust helped him come off the oxys.

And though he had a beautiful home in a peaceful development in New Jersey, he only slept in it half the time. He'd more often than not, crash in his loft in center city, smoking wet. Then, after a nap, he'd get up before dawn to pick me up for work. Richy was still a player, but he was caught up in habit more than ever. I knew the life of little sleep and occasional naps as much and all that came with it. In between highs, he was usually angry or worried when he wasn't rolling on something to keep him going. I knew the life, but observing it rather than living it was new for me. And I was feeling so bad so often I think I would have eventually got high with him, if I didn't find someone to distract me one night.

One night, when Richy gave me the keys to his BMW, I found my way to The Melrose where MP1 was my new meth. The boneless breaded chicken and mash potatoes with gravy and a snowflake roll became as sacred to me as the Holy Eucharist on Sundays to the starved. But that night, just as I sat down at the counter, I noticed a younger waitress who instantly gave me the impression of a street kid in The French Quarter. Her energy brought on a collage of images in my head from The Slab, to The Country Club in New Orleans.

I hadn't been reminded by anyone in Philly, of anything in New Orleans, since I evacuated. But there was something in this young waitress's composure that brought back a rush of feelings. She carried herself with a carefree unglamorous confidence and limitless way I'd say was… ruinously attractive! I read her waitress nametag to her and asked…

"What do they call you Deana?"

She measured me up for a second, took a good look in my eyes, then noticed I was clued in before she responded…

"They call me Green."

"Why?"

She laughed, and responded…

"Once upon a time,
I had green hair."

"My name's Braze.
But some call me MES."

"Mes?"
she wondered aloud.

I nodded yes, and continued…

"Yeah."
Then I laughed and continued…
"People tend to grow into their names…

…So with a name like Green,
you better be careful too."

"Ssshhh-yeah."
she uttered.

"How much have you traveled?"
I asked.

I knew Green had some miles on her soles because she carried the same squat art orbs that many of the travelers I met in New Orleans were haunted and twisted with. If you can picture a Barry Mcgee piece dripping the aftermath of a misspent youth at a roadside of self-slaughter… you'd find Deana Green and her road kill kind dining on each others food stamps and ground scored left over crack, homeless, underneath a bridge, somewhere. I suspected Green was a massive attack of crust culture underneath her waitress uniform and cheap perfume.

"I'm taking a rest from the road."
she admitted with her youthful lips.

I could tell by the deep breath she took at that moment, and her crooked smile, that the miles she traveled weighed on her like a freight car. Her soul bled through the goose bumps on her arms, addiction filled her weathered Von Dutch eyeballs.

"How ya travel?"
I asked, but knew.

"I hop trains!"
she said with joy.

Later, I found out Deana Green didn't have a phone number, but she gave me her address. She was living on a ghetto street in South Philly not far from the diner.

The next night, as I drove down to her crib after work in Richy's BMW, I found her predictably living in what resembled an old-timey dosshouse where I envisioned legs going in and out the front window in a red light district of some sort. Green was seventeen and took to the road a couple years back when she got hooked. And it wasn't long before she found her way to Philly wrapped in dope. She was getting clean when we met because a close friend of hers named Kotton overdosed dead; heartbroken, she took it real hard, hard enough to get straight.

"Couple nights after he died
I woke up outside, on a piss stained mattress,
at the West Philly Oil Cans."

That's a hobo camp near some train tracks. Crying, she continued with her account…

"Without him around, I just wanted to die!
But then he came back in my dreams!
Singing, with a… fake,
English accent."

Then she laughed through her tears. I smiled, and shared that…

"I have vivid dreams that leave
great impressions on me too."

"I can't stop thinking, and dreaming,
about him singing old punk songs to me.
In this funny forced accent!
It's all I dream of!"

I shut up and let her enjoy his memory, and his sense of humor in the recollection of her dream…

"I love him so much
that I'm afraid if I die now,
I'll never hear
him in my dreams again."

Fearful she would overdose, and personally certain there was no heaven she could meet Kotton in, she decided to stay in Philly and tossed aside the needles filled with North Philly gasoline, to get clean. And I was as happy as I could be for her. She was down and out, but not dead. Her struggle made me more comfortable with my own, and we began to hang out often.

Green and I stayed up night after night under dying stars as she talked about her rides on trains less traveled out there in space, as I drove her around the city in my brothers wheels from the West Philly Oil Cans where we walked around the industrial caves she would sleep in on desperate stained mattress at one time, to the steps of the Art Museum where I've launched many of my dreams into outer space. We were comforted not by what we learned from each other, but what we already knew about each other.

I thought it was funny that Green never took notice to the slick car we were in or the freestyle music of Judy Torres, digitized off old five-dollar tapes from the ancient South Philly Record Bar when Fugazi was doing shows for as much. My dance floor blues music didn't bother her; she seemed to be comfortable everywhere but in her own skin. We talked it out till dawn and on in her South Philly dump as neighborhood drifters stopped by to get high in her bathroom. Although she wasn't using, she still hosted those who did.

"Anyone of these beat punks here
can take you down the wrong road again Green,
before you find a better path,"
I reminded her.

"Shhh-yeah, I know."

Later that night when the junky parade stalled and we where alone, we kissed; I guess I just got caught up in her story.

Days later, on a hot South side night as we chilled on her stoop brainstorming art projects, someone threw out half a cheese steak from an open car window before it came to a skidding stop in the gutter at our feet.

"I call it!"
she insisted.

And with the quickness, she went in the gutter, and swooped up the tossed leftovers. Then, she put the sandwich to her nose for a good whiff…

"Smells like chicken."

"Ishkabibble chicken cheeses,"
I clued in.

I'm a connoisseur of steak sandwiches, as are most from my part of town. And with no further ado, she took a big bite and splat painted her chin with whiz. Then, with her mouth full, she laughed…

"Some habits are just too
hard to break."

I think she said, but couldn't be sure as she devoured the ground score.

"I like having money in my pocket,"
she continued, mouth full,
"and still eating what I find!"

"What do you miss from the road most?"

"My friends."
she answered without hesitation.

"When I'll be somewhere
and I smell a traveler kid
pass me by I just
think… aaaaaaah, home!"

She was a gutter punk to her core! It was there in South Philly with Green, that so much of the story that was baking in me back in New Orleans, began to heat up! With ideas cooking inside me, I began to feel comfortable with my creative self like never before. I wasn't thinking in terms of pages or anything literary in fact, it was much more visual, like graffiti. But much bigger than anything I'd ever tried to paint before. I wasn't sure what I had in mind, but it was moving!

Green and I both had some hard times and a love for trains. She found all my stories of hopping the Subway and climbing the rooftops along the EL as exciting as I found her ducking the bull in the yards and hopping freight cars on the fly.

"Your trains take you from one end of the city
to the other."
she pointed out,
"But mine go from coast to coast!"

"What trains take you that far?"
I asked.

"I got an old friend
dropping me off something,
I'll show ya soon!"
She said with such excitement.

Her sporadic enthusiasm was sunshine to me like the Dead Man Street Orchestra singing off key.

The next day, on the lawns with my Brother, I was wrapped in memories of New Orleans, The Dead Man Street Orchestra, Stumps Duh Clown, Neb, Sepher, and others I met down there. Where were they now? The conversations with Green about the trains seemed to connect all my daydreams and recent history, together. I hadn't felt this good since the first time I stole the Henry Chalfant's book from the Springfield Mall. Whatever had its hold on me, had Subway Art for a heart!

While in my head with these thoughts of New Orleans, I couldn't edge a lawn to buy me lunch. The only thing that sounded good to me was being off the map down South. And by the looks of the hurricane aftermath on TV, it appeared like a squatters paradise. I was pretty sure a lot of people I met down there had returned to squat, if in fact they had evacuated; many of course were squatting down there before the storm. So at the end of that day, sunburned with a touch of poison ivy, I retired my weed-whacker to organize another retreat to New Orleans. Enough is enough!

Later, I raced to South Philly to ask Green if she wanted to travel down to NOLA with me! I knew she would! When I got to there and knocked on her door, a couple of knuckle heads where arguing over a parking spot across the street…

"You cant park dare!"
said some dude
standing on the sidewalk.

"Fuck I can't!"
barked the driver back.

She didn't answer the door, but it was unlocked. So I let myself inside and waited for her to come back as the dispute outside continued…

"You can't fit Cheech!"

said Dude.

"I'm a parallel park Olympian!"
the Driver bragged.

And before I knew it, I fell a sleep. My brother worked me hard on those lawns for weeks! But moments or more later, not sure, but it was dark now, I woke up to the same nonsense coming from the street…

"Yo Cheech! You got dat Cheech?"
asked Dude.

"I got jack fa-you Chal-uch,"
Cheech yelled back.

As I went to the bathroom, I remember mimicking the Pope of Queen Village retards outside…

"Yo cheech,
you know where it hangs?"

"No!
They took my wang Charlie!
They took my
wang-chung tonight Charlie."

In South Philly a lot of people goof and called each other Cheech, not because they are fans of Cheech Wizard like I. But I think because they can't remember each other's name all the time. It's a big neighborhood.

As I looked over to find the light switch in the bathroom and sang Wang Chung Tonight, I kicked something that startled me. I shut up, looked down to see what it was as the light flickered off and on… then, when it came on, Green was at my feet slumped on the floor! Needle on the toilet, and an ink pen by her side. I immediately went to my knees to help her, but her body seemed vacant, eyes soulless… her once pale teen skin and lips I once kissed, now dead calm and sea blue.

Call it shock, or curiosity, but I froze there looking at her not in a panic, but momentarily curiously, projecting myself in her situation…

"That's what it looks like?"
I murmured softly.

I thought of myself coming back from such states. Then it occurred to me, she might not be dead! I then immediately felt her chest for any sign of life! I tried to find a pulse in her wrist, but what do I know! So I put my ear to her mouth to listen for a breath, but nothing! So then I picked her up, put her in the bathtub and turned on the cold water from the shower as if that would help. I breathed, looked at her, and took a few more conscious breaths. Breathing is something we take for granite all day, and most of our lives. You don't tell the body to do it because it just does, until it doesn't anymore. In every situation my mind is racing! Breathing speed traps it.

Helpless, I brushed her hair back, wiped the water from her face, away from her open eyes, gentle mouth, and flawless skin, as if it would make her more comfortable. But at that moment, I felt for sure she was dead and there was nothing that could be done. I took a deep breath, closed my eyes and fell against the wall, head to my knees. I thought in terms of passing through, and of how much of a rental the body is, vacant space where souls and matter merge. Alone there, with my eyes closed and head down…

I envisioned myself above her, sitting in a cypress tree growing out of the water in the tub. Drops of water rolled down her face and from her open eyes like tears as if she were just sad and couldn't sleep. Then, she gently touched my hand… when I some how found her sitting on a branch beside me. We sat up there together wishing we could do things different below. Wishing we could both start over again and create a new history for our selves to delay such early epitaphs of our kind. I could feel the wake of her energy next to me in the tree from her dead body on the thick cypress root in the tub water below… the tree, she and I, all the same. Produced on a blue island in space blanketed by a delicate atmosphere; everything else is ancient idiot story telling before Hubble orbited. But at that moment, time felt negotiable and travel felt possible in either direction. It was evident to me from the hands of a wristwatch dripping from my arm at that time. The running shower made it appeared as though it was raining on her below. And in the water, were tiny mirrors of life balled in each drop. As we held hands on the translucent branch we were sitting on, below us, a perfect garden of wetness surrounded her material body.

Sometimes I find myself in dimensions I gather will always be there, because they've always been in the boundless creation of the universe according to some. These are places that are so fertile I won't dare plant a seed other than love because whatever intention I plant out there, will grow in that deep space. So I looked to her spirit next to me and told her, whole heartedly…

"I love you."

I hope she got the message, somewhere in time. But below in real time, I was a few hours late. I will always ask myself… was she still alive, when I first arrived?

Back in my skin and hopeless on this lonely planet, I gathered myself when I opened my eyes and reconnected the wires in my dented up box. Then, I did what had to be done. I phoned it in…

"Please send an ambulance to 1209 Annin,
someone has overdosed."

We both had miles behind us we couldn't forget. What she used to bury the bullshit, buried her; it often does. All her traveling led to an abrupt dead end with a little diesel in a needle.

I stood there numb for some time thinking you can't out run your history, because it passes you every time on our way to the same place. Junkies kill some time with a rush, while those who commit suicide are just in a much bigger rush.

"Safe Travels,"
I wished Green.

Then I closed her eyes, and kissed her on the forehead. When I rose to my feet, I noticed a lil booklet on the sink. Underneath the booklet I found a poem that I wrote for her days ago. I thought it would comfort the withdrawal from the traveler fragrances she fancied that passed her by on the streets occasionally.

Not wanting to leave her just yet, I kneeled back down next to her and read the poem in the dark silent morning…

Stained Earl Grey

Such were the joys tasted in poisons
From the bottom shelf...
With a future branded in condemnation,
Where bodies shook on clotheslines of washtub bases,
Young tramps danced mindless,
Souls bunny hopped searching for sane skin.
In this lot of recklessly tattooed crusties
Inked in black with punk rock needles made of
Steel Guitar strings gunned by bastards with
Dirty blue grass fingers tips.
Folk filled lungs of marching dead men screamed to
Gutter maze minds where cannibal rats feasted on
Themselves long after the brain cells seasoned with
The music of Left Over Crack lovers went on
In song, out of key…
About the one and only sunshine being theirs!
Happy on stilts, Easy Biscuits rose a mile high
With a bamboo pole and paper cup on the hook
As he fished for loose change…
While a riff raff banjo, mindful fiddle and a
Guitar Named Desperation…
Outshined on the edge of New Orleans.
There I stood with my earl grey pen,
Crust punked,
Brazen.

Then I looked over to the lil booklet on the sink she left with my poem. On the cover was printed: From Birmingham to Wendover "An alternative travel guide to camping places and obscure urban hiking trails throughout the United States and Canada." Just below the pamphlet fonts on the cover it was signed: For BRAZE, safe travels! I looked over to her, perplexed, but smiling. Then I heard an ambulance in the distance, and quickly climbed out of the broken window into the alley. The front door was open, they would find her; I had outstanding warrants and couldn't deal with it at that time.

Later, when I got home to Richy's in Jersey, I found my brother still awake in his basement smoking dust. When he noticed me, he whispered…

"Excuse my dust,"
and forced a smile.

I just smirked and shook my head.

"Just trying to keep the stink out
of my new crib."
He continued softly.

"I see.
But why you whispering?"

He shrugged his shoulders; he really didn't know why.

"How many jugs you cop?"
I asked him.

"Two bundles."
he whispered.

We never half stepped. It was all or nothing, always.

"You wanna hit Bee?"

Other than basketball games and numerous dance floors and deals, Richy and I connected over little more than getting high on drugs as adults. And after the night I just had, this time… I didn't say no.

We emptied all those jugs he copped and whispered to each other the rest of the night. Why whisper? I don't know either. The world just gets delicate and softer on different shit. After an hour or so, he opened his arms and asked…

"Give me a hug Bee?"

So I gave him one.

"See,
doesn't that feel good."
he said.

He held me for a minute or more; it was kinda weird. But the more he held me, the more apparent it became he was in need of some comfort that I was unaware of. He needed to be touched. Or maybe just needed to touch me. But I'm really not sure.

The next day, when my eyes cracked with bliss before my mind had yet to sum it up, I found the lil booklet I brought back from Green's crib on the nightstand next to me, and read the cover aloud…

"Birmingham, to Wendover?"

I couldn't crash at my brothers any longer, or hide in Philly now that Green was dead, I felt too… alive! So I got out of bed, wrote Richy a thank you note, took that booklet with me and got in my car and on the road for New Orleans once more.

BIRMINGHAM TO WENDOVER

Was on the Cover
But inside was a crew change oh my Brother

While the crust punk Dead Man Street rendition of "You Are My Sunshine" played from my car stereo (Recorded pre-Katrina in the laundry matte next to Zots on Royal.) I drove into New Orleans where the flood lines were high above my head underneath every train trestle and byway I drove through on the interstate. Then, the stain of the storm became more apparent on the side of countless home.

When I finally rolled off the I-10 at the French Quarter, there were no celebrations as I remembered the last time I exited here; pre-K. No laughs, parades or celebrations of any sort, no one, nearly a ghost town by comparison prior to the storm. It felt more like a hunted movie set to me, rather than the birthplace of jazz… No musicians busking. Not even homeless panhandling! Nothing but mud filled cars underneath the highway and refrigerators lining the streets. The city was nearly dead, but some of her souls were exposed like never before in desperate graffiti such as "Please, God Help Us" asking the storm to pass with help from a higher power. Most of the rooftops where patched up with blue tarps and all the streets were lined with refrigerators duck taped shut and mysteriously decorated that said to me "Art is not dead." in New Orleans. But what was inside of them certainly was by the smell of the contents dripping from most.

Each message on the wall, piece of aftermath art, and miles of blue tarp led me to believe that this city was beginning to rise from the mud it was under. Seeing the city barely survived made me feel more alive with a Carl Jung sense of self-destruction. In New Orleans, I was no longer an empty Iceberg Slim Death Wish! It filled me with life and that was why I was drawn back to it! I had no home here, but it was where I felt most at home. As I drove back through all this, swerving around countless rooftop shingles with protruding roofing nails and other tire land mines of many kinds, I parked my car in the Marigny on Frenchmen Street by Washington Square.

The Washington Square Park looked like a refuge commune, or a Lollapalooza sideshow of some sort. Camping tents were pitched and shelters made of blue tarps that lined all the pathways around the park. Food was being cooked up in there and given out like the old days at the homeless feeding line down the street at "The Wall". Returning Katrina refugees played the guitar and sang familiar songs while girl's hula hooped barefoot in the grass. Pick-up trucks came and went all day loading and unloading volunteers to help clean out flooded houses for the elderly and others in the need. Survivor stories were traded like high currency and all those who weathered the storm, no matter how long they had resided in New Orleans prior to the catastrophe, seemed to feel grandfathered in and called the city their home now.

A squatter told me,
"The water came right under the floorboards.
My home was good,"
as if it had always been his.

Though I didn't say it to anyone, or even to myself, I felt home too. Within most of the stories of those who stayed during Katrina, were shocking accounts of panic, survival and drastic measures to enforce a state of order and protect and save whatever one could.

A Resident recalled,
"I swam out! Then walked through water up to my chest to the Navy base! Y'know, thinking we could get help. But when we got there… the MP's turned us away at the gate with guns!"

A hobo complained,
"I waited in line and tried to get some FEMA money after the storm, but they couldn't help me because I didn't have a social security number."

A hero said,
"I canoed around for days,
rescuing whomever I could. We set up camp where I lived in the Marigny and BBQ with my neighbors. We carried shotguns and helped everyone."

An old crusty yelled,
"I got shot with a salt gun for
looting food bro!"

And a Gutter Punk bragged to me that,
"It was the best two weeks
of my life!"

Many of my train hoppin' friends had stories of shelter mishaps and lack of FEMA assistance. They were mostly turned away from FEMA because they didn't have a permanent New Orleans address, while other travelers were just not from this planet. Then I found Matthew Sepher! He shared far out stories of 7th Ward mayhem and lawlessness freedoms. He stuck around! And at one point Matt said to me, quietly…

"The anarchists were waiting for this one."

Matt was wise enough not to say that too loud, well aware it was the worst event for everyone else in the city, punks and thieves aside. What I came to realize was that the lack of food, water, electricity, protection, and the absence of any other comfort, necessity, or human right that outraged most when it all disappeared after the storm, was not all that unusual for the outliers of society I made friends with here in New Orleans prior to the flood; but maybe, more the norm for them. They did without all the time! Being resourceful with low standards may have helped them survive easier than others. In fact, I would go so far as to say Katrina, did not put many young traveler kids out of their comfort zone, but deeper in it. It's a truth that would anger some but I didn't pick a side because I didn't quite know where I belonged. After catching up with Matt Sepher and some others that day, I went for a walk down lower Decatur Street.

And as soon as I approached the Christmas Store, it was like nothing happened. I found Duh Clown and his dog in a doorway, busking!

"Show-enough. Stumps duh Clown!"
I yelled out.

He was there, buskin, with his dog Big Mama who was wearing new sunglasses and had a smoke in her mouth.

"Hey there Mr. Man,"
he laughed.

"You making money out here today?"

"It's kinda slow,"
he admitted with a smile.

As I stood there looking at Stumps, I noticed he didn't have a Katrina story in his eyes. Stump's was the first person I met upon my return to New Orleans who didn't seem to be looking back.

"Have you been writing?"
Stumps asked me, like an older to a younger.

"Indeed my brotha!"

Then he mentioned,
"My man Eddie Joe has a book.
You should read it. It's called Hobo."

Then he handed me that same book from his back pocket.

"Hobo? Hobo! Can I borrow this?"

"You can have it.
It's not all true, but what is?"

"Thank you Stumps."

Then I went into my back pocket to retrieve the booklet I got from my now, dead friend, Green, and handed it to him, asking…

"What's this?"

Stumps kind of snickered, and asked…

"Where'd you get that?"

"A friend left it to me."

He looked at the folded paperback booklet and examined it a little closer, before remarking…

"Hmm, it's current."
he remarked.

"Current train schedules?"

"Yes sir.
It's a crew change my brother.
You gonna travel with it?"

Then he handed it back to me.

"Hop trains?"
I wondered aloud.

It was never something I thought of before New Orleans. But there I was… Crew Change in one hand, Hobo in the other, Stumps was looking at me and Big Mama chilled on the sidewalk, as an October breeze blew a flock of phoenix in the wind.

"The rails have a story,"
Stumps expressed,
"Put an ear to the track and listen Braze."

Stumps made my soul stir with that! Because to me, it was like Led Belly himself telling me to write, hop trains, and let what ever it was the tracks had to say to me, be said.

As Halloween 2005 approached, the spirits in New Orleans were in no rush to leave; they stayed near their loved ones to answer their prayers around their most recent, decorated graves on Day of the Dead. I could imagine by the stir in the wind, that this holiday would be a busy celebration for Lady Catrina to host in New Orleans. The air was filled with those in transit like a downtown rush hour!

I decided to put my personal journals on the back burner and write about the new pictures I had in mind; feeling a freedom in the winds of travel and a desire to move forward and chase a future no matter where it would lead me! For the next few days, I wrote a story about a girl who lost her boyfriend. The girl was based on Deana Green and her boyfriend Kotton. But the story I was writing wasn't about them dying on heroin, but one of broken love in New Orleans and train hopping across the United States.

"The winds of travel got between them,
Now she hops freight trains to find him."

…Were the first words to fall from my lips, and be scripted with my blotting ink pen. From there, I closed my eyes and opened up. Just like my journal entries, I decided to only move forward and not look back, reread, or rewrite anything. Not until it was all out of me. Whenever I get filled with ideas, I have to peruse them, or crush them with any means available. Some call it manic, I call it trying to live with myself. Drugs & spray paint flushed them out most of my life. Now, it was just me myself and I.

I flowed forward with the confidence I acquired from blue coral fat caps long ago when I first became a writer. A writer who went outside in pitch-black danger zones with a passion to share that a school can't teach. All the voices in my head, the untamed emotions in my heart, and the courage I acquired as a criminal, was useful to me to write how I pleased.

And as I did so, I found myself stopping from time to time and pacing with racing thoughts. My emotions have always moved me, physically, for better or for worse… uptown, downtown, TJ, LA and now NO-LA. The challenge wasn't to come up with a story; I'm filled with drama. But to focus on letting it move my hand with the pen, and not to the bar for a drink, or to the corner for a bag, a bathhouse for a blowjob, etc., etc. All of which come to mind when I roll through the pages. I've wasted a lot of time copping highs in the world, but there is nothing more available to me than writing. Had I known earlier I might have a knack for it, I may have gotten over the paint cans much earlier.

Be it writing about getting higher than city rooftops as an adolescent, forging deep into the subway tunnel of life, finding myself in Mexico with trick dick, or a crust punk pool party in The South… writing makes me an egotistic historian, a scientist of sorts, and as you'll see when we get there, a tour agent in the heavens to places no one thought could ever be in transit with one another. But in 2005, on Earth, I had trains on the brain! I've just always wanted to see how far I could go. As I sipped on hot tea at Cafe Envie I called the piece I was writing… "The Art of Train Hopping." And in it, I wanted to see Green again.

Everything in my head has always felt so real that getting closer to someone who died seemed possible to me through my writing. I was driven to write it out of pure desire and nothing else, with no hope other than writing a good little story to maybe share with my friends at The Slab. But at Envie, I crossed the line from writer to train hopper with one seed of intention.

"If you can write it,
You can live it."
I murmured.

It occurred to me that this story wasn't a new idea of mine, but one I planted years ago when I walked out of The Ritz Movie Theater with Richy in Philly. It was then I desired to live out My Own Private Idaho. And now, it was happening? In fact, it had been unfolding since I first came to New Orleans. Seeing that connection between what I wanted to do long ago, and it actually beginning to materialize in this covert cosmic way, was very interesting to me; I soberingly thought. If I were high, I'd think it was probably the work of David Blaine or Deepak Chopra in my life. Although, for the sake of magic, I felt my storyline might have been the result of something somewhere between intensions and trajectories where ideas grow and evolve in a way that science has yet to grasp. Some think it's a universal consciousness at work, others say such ideas are merely a temporal occurrence. Although I grew up inspired by spiritual stories, science has since grounded me.

A few days later with a 3rd draft done, I went to The Slab to connect with Matthew Sepher. When I found him, I immediately handed him my beat up journal and opened it towards the end of the book where my last draft was (many more would follow) and he began at the beginning, and read the title aloud…

"The Art of Train Hoppin…"

Sepher laughed and continued,
"What exactly is this?"

"A movie!"

"A screenplay? Hmm.
So… what's it about?"

"It's about a girl lookin' for her
boyfriend on the rails."

Sepher began reading.

"Why out there?"
he asked.

"They're squatters who split up during
Katrina evacuation.
She hopped out,
he stayed behind in the squat."

Then, he noticed his name in the script, and asked…

"Sepher?"
he wondered aloud,
"With me?"

"Yeah man!"
I said with uncontrollable enthusiasm,
"She evacuated with you and me…
Sepher & Mes! But her boyfriend,
Kotton, stayed behind to guard the squat!"

At that point, instead of reading it, he just kinda shrugged it off and said…

"That's it?"

"Well…"
I took a breath,
…not exactly."

Then I gathered myself as Gypsy music was being played behind us on The Slab and I felt the picture I wanted to shoot vibrate through my bones. Matthew stood there smiling, slightly infected by my idea, but needed more than my quick synopsis. As I stood there buzzing with in my own personal mania, I took a deep breath and explained as calmly as I could…

"I want to fuse the
fiction I wrote here,
with documentary coverage
we acquire, while hopping trains
across the country."

He took a moment; I think to digest the idea some more, not sure. But that's all it was at that point, an idea shared between a couple friends on Press Street by The Slab in the Bi-Water.

"Does that make sense now?"
I asked 'um.

"It sounds interesting,"
he admitted.

Then I suggested that he just take the journal home with him and give it a good read. He obliged and said…

"OK,"
very calmly.

And I was my regular aggressive self, and immediately suggested…

"We'll continue the conversation
after you read it. Ok? I'd appreciate it Matt!

"Sure,"
he added,
"it's good to see you so excited."

The next day, I went to Matt's house in the 7th Ward where the water came just a few inches below his floorboards, so his house and neighborhood were relatively much better off than most in the city. He was a late sleeper so when I got there at noon, he was drinking coffee and finishing the screenplay.

"It's pretty good,"
he told me.

"Good enough?"
I inquired.

"To go this far,
coast to coast on trains…
I would say that good,
isn't good enough!"

And that was my introduction to Seph's good taste. He was definitely on another wavelength than I, but he never looked down on me, not once. He continued…

"What I like most,
is what I don't know… exactly,
how you're gonna pull it off?"

"What's that?"

"When you want to jump from the narrative,
to interviews,"
he said perplexed,
"That's not clear to me.
How are you going to do that?"

"That's the cool part!"

"Doing something because it's cool,
is never good enough."
he told me bluntly.

To the sneaker pimp that I was, a comment like that takes on profound sounds. One that Puma pimps would snicker at, but not I. At that point, it was clear I was talking to the right person. From that moment on, Sepher elevated my ideas. So I shut up, and told him…

"OK Matt,
I'm listening."

So he continued,
"There are a few things on my mind.
Who's shooting the movie?"

"I shoot the moving picture,
you shoot the stills."

"Have you ever shot anything before?"
he asked sarcastically.

"No."
I admitted,
"But in the story the camera is bought by an
amateur with some FEMA money…
At the end of the first minute of the movie…
I fall and break the camera!"
I said laughing.

"Yeah, that's weird.
Why?"
he asked.

"To dumb it down
and shine later."

"I'm not sure
how you're going to pull that off,
but I get it.
But how do you plan to blend
the doc, and the drama?"

"That's pretty easy,"
I told 'um,
"the audience just can't
know we're acting."

"Have you ever done any acting?"

"Well, I a… hung out in
Hollywood for a while."

Then I handed him the crew change…

"Get me on those trains Seph.
And I'll make it all happen."

He took the crew change from my hands. Matt knew what it was without even opening it, he squatted and spanged in New Orleans with travelers long before I arrived in town.

"I've never hopped trains before,"
he indicated.

"Me neither,"
I admitted,
"Not freights!"

"Not freights?"
he asked,
"What do you mean Braze?"

"Well, I've been hopping subways
since grade school.
And in West Philly
that counts for something."

I stood there staring at Sepher with Subway Art eyes, a graduate of West Philly rooftops and Center City Cinemas with pawnshop ways and means to New Orleans plotting a coast-to-coast feature film! A masterpiece so big, it'd make a SABER piece in the Los Angeles River look like a drip on a Jackson Pollock!

"I want to paint
this motion picture Seph?
Do you?"

He took a moment, before he answered…

"Yeah. Yeah I think I do."

Matt had more questions than I could ever imagine one would have about a story that was only 45 pages long. It was obvious to me that he was the smartest guy in the room. While searching for answers to all his questions, I was growing. But was he? I had to know.

"Why are you doing this with me Matt?"

"I think you're a person
who can finish things,"
he conveyed,
"that's big to me right now."

As I was flipping through a portfolio of his photography on the kitchen table, where shots included a few models he shot back in his hometown of Baltimore. One model caught my eye in particular…

"Who's this?"
I asked 'um.

"That's Sara Ruin."

"Ruin?"
I echoed with wonder,
"Great name!"

Sara Ruin looked glamorous in Matt's photos, but she had an edge I found interesting. Each photo bared a confidence and slight reinvention of her persona from shot to shot. I'm not a casting agent, but I do know what I like.

"Call her up Matt!"

"I was thinking the same thing,"
he responded.

Moments later, Sara and I spoke on the phone, but I needed to meet her face to face. So I mailed her a draft of the screenplay to see if she was interested in connecting with me any further. Turned out, she thought it was one of the more interesting stories she read in years.

And just a week later, Sara Ruin found her way to New Orleans! We walked The Quarter and chatted up the script.

"Why is the project both
a drama and a doc?"
Sara asked.

"I'm not the voice of this generation.
They have to speak for themselves."

"What happens if we get into
trouble out there?"

"Just don't fall off Sara.
Everything else is a luxury problem."

"Well, what happens if
we do get caught?"

"No worries,"
I said with a smile,
"My Dad's a bail bondsman!"

Everything Sara brought up I had discussed with Sepher, so I felt good about it. Quite confidant.

"I can make this picture,"
I assured her.

Then she said she read the script a couple times, and was certain after meeting me, I could indeed make the movie. And I felt she didn't come all the way down here to say no, so as we walked down Charters Street I asked…

"Will you play the roll,
and hop trains with us Sara?"

"How long will we be shooting Braze?"

"All summer."

She paused, and thought about that for a moment before answering…

"I'd have to give up
my apartment."

That perplexed me. I didn't see why she would want to do that. She'd need a place to return home too.

"That's not necessary,
just sublet it Sara."

But she was, serious, about the character.

"No,
I think it's important for
her to be homeless."

And with that, she had me beat. I mean, with commitment like that, maybe playing the roll wouldn't be such a stretch!

"I'm in Braze."

And with that, our bond truly began.

"But Braze,
why is her name Green?"

"Because she has green hair."

Sara looked unimpressed by that idea, and then she nodded her head no. So I just went with it, despite my connection to the name.

"Ok, I…
love your hair Sara."

She looked like she wanted more. This wasn't going to be as easy as I thought maybe. I swallowed, and suggested…

"And maybe,
we should call her Ruin,
not Green."

Then she smiled and walked into a clothing boutique in control of the character she committed to play, and me it seemed. After all, she was the main focus now. Before I followed her in, I looked up at the storefront sign hanging under the French Quarter Balcony above; Drugstore Cowboy taught me to read the signs whenever possible. This one said "Trashy Diva". I gently laughed to myself.

"What gutter funk starlet
wouldn't shop here?"
I murmured.

Or even shop lift if one prefers; crossed my mind.

For the next few months I'd continued to shadow my friends and acquaintances in the traveler circle of NOLA. Loose Marbles & The Dead Man Street Orchestra still caught most of my attention. As well as Stumps duh Clown who played hard on the streets blocks away from Marbles in the afternoons. Locking down certain locations was an art in itself. A band member would often be designated to hold a spot after the sunrises and shoo other musicians away that morning till the rest of the band showed up around 11 am. This was how business on the street was handled, and it worked most of the time. Though I've seen some arguments, no guitars were ever broken by my account.

As newbie train hoppers and old timey kids with banjos began growing in numbers around the city, old crusties and some new-gen gutter punks continued to show up and spange on the sidewalks, fly signs at intersections, and began just sleeping in the common grounds rather than pop squats. While the musicians continued to make music and went on tours playing coast-to-coast, and even further! When I found out some of these musician cats were flying overseas and bicycling around to other countries to make a living at busking, my plans to hop trains around The States to make a movie seemed much easier to me.

Eventually, to raise cash, I parked the car I was living in on Rampart Street and put a for sale sign on it. From there, I phoned Sara Ruin in Baltimore and asked…

"You ready to roll soon?"

"I'm out of my apartment the 1st of June!"
she responded.

"Did you find a location to shoot
the first scene?"
I asked.

"Yes.
It's an abandoned factory over a creek.
At the end of some train tracks."

"The end of the tracks?"
I reiterated,
"Nice!"

And with some bites on my truck, I began shopping for video cameras at Seph's house. He suggested a website for a store in New York called B&H, but I found a better deal in Philly. A few days later my truck sold for $4,000 and with some of the cash I bought a Panasonic 100B 24P that I had my eye on. When it arrived in the mail days later, it was time to roll!

SANE & SOBER

Hopping trains was my Solution
With cohorts named Sepher & Ruin

I was ready to hop trains as Mes! And took on a graffiti punk persona of sorts. With me, Sepher and Ruin were my cohorts in crime or, "road dogs" as the cool kids say in the scene. When Sepher and I got to the yard to catch out to meet up with Ruin in Baltimore, we found a train with a blinking F.R.E.D. on the main track heading north as soon as we got there.

"Does that looks like our train Seph."

"Well,
the crew change says our ride comes
in twenty minutes."
he informed.

Thinking these freight trains run on schedule, as the crew change implied, we waited. And watched that train roll out moments later, making room for our train we thought. Probably an hour passed before Matt admitted…

"That was our train that pulled out."

"It was waiting for us,"
I chuckled out at our lack common sense!

We were just too "oogle" to hop on that first train as quickly as we should have. Feeling a little dumb but determined, we camped by the yard to catch the first ride out in the morning.

When I woke up the next day… the tracks were empty at 7:30am. We were expecting a train to arrive and do a crew change at 8:45, so I went for some coffee at the gas station near the yard. When I returned, Sepher was just waking up 8:15. At 9:30am, our train had still not arrived.

Then we started talking about the next train. That according to the crew change was scheduled to pass through later that morning. Seph could decipher the jargon in the C.C. much better than I in the beginning. With no help of a glossary, the language and abbreviations were a bit of mysterious to me.

Although I trusted Sepher's knowledge of the book, we missed our first two trains at this point. So at noon we found ourselves waiting on another train long past the noted arrival time. Much later, the sun began to set and before we knew it, we decided to stay another night and wait on yet another ride… the next morning.

If we don't catch a ride tomorrow,"
Sepher suggested,
"We should consider taking a bus to Baltimore."

"I don't know. Maybe."
I blew it off.

My success hopping subways when I was a kid didn't get me off to a great start on the freights, but I wasn't thinking about a bus yet like Seph!

When I woke in the yard on day three, I went for some coffee again; I became a morning person in New Orleans. After a long sleep or even a 10-minute snooze, I'd be up and on the go. Once a veteran under the sheets, I was now on point first thing every morning. I just simply stopped hiding from myself I think. When I returned from the coffee run, Sepher was still sleeping. I tried to wake him up, but he rolled over and just blew me off.

Our train was once again scheduled to pass through the yard at 8:45am. It was maybe 8:30 when I was sipping my latte and Seph was snoring as our freaking train finally rolled in the yard, stealth like! But I was ready like Radar when choppers approach.

"Wake the fuck up Seph!"
I whispered.

Alert to the scene, he began wrapping his bedroll and gathered his things.

"Hurry!"
I urged.

"Fuck off."
he told me.

And I thought with a smile, it's about time I bought one from this guy! After all, I'd been pretty aggressive and persistent with him since our first meeting at the slab! But what I was to learn later during our travels, was that Sepher was just not a morning person, not at all.

As we rushed to gear up and catch our ride, the middle of the train came to a complete stop right in front of us. Right there sat our first ride we were to hop, a grainier with "THEORY" painted wild on it.

"That car there?"
I asked.

"Looks good, it's got a bottom,"
he pointed out.

So we took a few steps from the woods toward our first hop, but just as we did, a white workers truck pulled up on the side of the tracks between us, and that grainier car! We dropped and chewed rocks with the quickness!

The train was right there! It sat idling only 15 yards away from us, but just out of reach; we were cut off by two workers in a truck having a coffee break it seemed. And we had no cover because the woods were behind us! The workers were so close, I could hear them talking inside the cab, but they didn't look over in our direction where they could easily spot us. All we could do was lay there on the ground, and not move an angry inch.

At that time, lying there with Seph, I recalled playing kick the can when I was a kid. And that the rule of thumb was if you could see them, they could see you! And those workers in the truck were in clear sight!

Maybe ten minutes passed, belly down on the rocks. To hell with being scared at that moment, I was angrier than ever! I'm committing a crime of passion I'd planned for months by now, and these guys were in my way talking trash and drinking cheap coffee. Those guys were so damn close we couldn't move back into the woods and regroup to find another car farther down the tracks because they would surly hear us moving around down there. So we were forced to stay chameleon on the ground, time ticking away, and soon our train would be on its way. If I had more money in my pocket, I would have just stood up and offered these guys a bribe.

So while frozen there on the ground, I tried to think of a way to talk Seph into staying in the yard to catch another train. Because the night before I agreed to catch a bus if we missed this train, but now I knew the crew change worked to some degree. Our train sat there, on time, ready to pull out any second. I was really sweating each second by now!

And then, the worker truck got a call over the radio and rolled off! And at that moment, the train became ours once again. We dashed across the tracks to the main rail where our train sat heading north. While I ran across the tracks in the bright morning light, I kept and eye on the truck that had nearly foiled our efforts. But those guys just kept moving forward. As I reached the grainer and struggled up the ladder with my pack, hoping neither one of those guys in the truck had their eyes in a rear view, we made our way on board! Seph and I immediately stuffed our bags in the grainer hobo-hole, got on the floor, and waited for the train to get going. And hardly a moment later, the train jerked, rolled, and drove from the yard pushing my big picture plans forward with full force. This path began to take control of my life experience like I'd never imagined for my self. I always just wanted to make money in a rush, now I was broke and driven by wanderlust? Gus Van Sant made me do it; damn him.

Sepher retrieved his camera and shot stills as I enjoyed the ride like I did on old Brooklyn E Bombs. It wasn't a rush or a high I felt, but a pure feeling that shared undiscovered keys on the piano of my emotions. As those keys played on while the train rolled forward on the tracks at different tempos with my bones and heart in the rhythm of the ride, I wrote as I rushed forward…

Speeding over screaming of train tracks,
My dreams merge with utmost pining,
Intentions colliding.

Within a flash,
Everything's in hand.
Everything I wanted ahead,
Now behind me instead.

As I raced forward over the tracks and all the rocks below me, the rails became a resurrection, and the rocks below turned to stone roses. It was more than a feeling, more than a party, and more than a high but a cosmic connection. The first time I ever sat back and enjoyed a clean ride in my adult life.

"Do you have flip-flops on?"
Seph asked.

As his dreads twisted wild style in the wind, my "MES" character, surfaced bold and cocky like a rooftop burner and answered…

"I train hop in leisurewear.
Flip-flops are my Reeboks out here,"
Said me, as Mes.

The character I set out to play was never intended to roll like an old timey hobo, or a totally belligerent gutter punk; that had been done. But more a cocky hobo-sexual food stamp pimp with the charm of a butterfly knife; I'd say.

Two days later when Sepher and I made it to Baltimore, we walked to Ruin's after stopping for breakfast. When we arrived at her apartment, the place was empty. The only things in there were her backpack, some toilet paper, and a box of tea next to a trashcan. So I boiled water.

"Do you have sugar?"
I asked.

Ruin shook her head no. Then went into the kitchen trashcan and pulled out an old bottle of pancake syrup and handed it to me. I think Deana Green would have done the same thing. So I washed out the syrup bottle with some hot water and sweetened our tea, as Green would.

Later on we got to the old factory Ruin scouted where we would begin our shoot. The place was an old run down mill of some sort with industrial architecture, gears and steel ladders. And just outside was an old train trestle that came to a dead end into the concrete factory over a creek. In the script we were there to shoot, Mes climbs up a tree to get a big movie "Crain Shot" with his wanna-be filmmaker attitude. But very small trees surrounded the factory. So it was impossible to shoot what I wrote. Inside, was a solution, maybe?

There were steel ladders going up to a walkway near the ceiling that looked like a good substitution, maybe even better than the tree I had in mind. I imagined the camera could fall from the hands of Mes, tumble down the ladder, and crack the lens on the way down with some simple movie magic in the edits.

Excited about the prospect of shooting picture now, I began moving quickly around the building and started doing tests with the camera, casing the environment, and walking through the shots a number of times.

Sepher continued to shoot stills of me on the go as seen above. He was just as driven to get coverage and knew what he wanted all the time.

BOOK SAFE

"Braze, carry the MD 20/20,"
Mes should always have it in hand."
Seph reminded me.

I in fact kept the MD 20/20 bottle filled with orange soda to stay sober out there. While casing the joint, I noticed some possible danger to be avoided in the next room and pointed it out to them that…

"There's a big hole in the floor.
Be careful guys! It's a straight drop
to the creek below."

If someone fell down that hole, we'd be in trouble! But they were smart and I'm sure I was just being over precautious. So with that hole out of mind and all the shots scouted, I moved on and began going over the script with Ruin once again on my laptop.

After the read, and doing some last minute changes to the story to make it more our own, we began shooting the opening scene. Where I got the guts to begin this project, I'll never really know. Who the hell did I think I was? Certainly not a filmmaker, hardly a writer, just a guy looking for a reason to live I guess.

And so take after take we acted out the first scene smoothly, a number of times, a dozen maybe; each take ending with Mes climbing that steel ladder inside the factory and "dropping" the camera like a drunken fool. The "camera drop" and subsequent breaking of it, was created in the script for two reasons. To gain the trust of the audience in that what's ahead was not scripted. And, with only a broken camera left to shoot with; I imagined experimental transitions in the edits would be possible.

"I really don't get
the broken camera thing,"
Ruined remarked.

Rather than explaining it further, I just downsized the idea.

"Well, if nothing else…
it leaves the production to go
nowhere but up from there."

But in fact, I envisioned layers of video, like fading spray paint on a wall making up an old weathered graffiti masterpiece on bricks via a flickering broken camera effect in post-production! But that was beyond my vocabulary at the time to clearly articulate. Though I had it in mind all the time. I knew I was a first time filmmaker, and decided not to hide it, but let it be known immediately in the movie though a staged mishap. It gave me the confidence to move forward and do my best to surprise who ever might watch the movie, if I ever finished it.

As the sun fell… I lost light inside the building. So I moved even quicker with sound tests and choreographing more shots, which takes a lot of time even on a micro budget shoot like mine. As I raced around, Ruin suggested that maybe we quit and come back tomorrow. But being the junky I am, I wanted a little more!

"I think we got it B,"
Seph tried to assured me,
"lets quit."

"Yeah Braze"
Ruin continued
"let's call it a day."

They were both tired, I knew that, but I kept looking for more. As I did Ruin began doing yoga to cool off while Seph shot a few more stills. Then as I was running around, I… screwed up! …SMACK, FALL, SPLASH!

"Help! HELP ME!"
I screamed from the creek below.

Yelling up through the hole I just fell through! Up there, I found Sepher above taking pictures of me below through the hole above. I yelled up at Sepher…

"Don't Shoot this!
…This! This! This!"

…this, echoed around in the cavern below the building I was swimming under as Sepher kept taking shots and laughing at me. I unwittingly fell through "the hole" I asked Seph and Ruin to avoid.

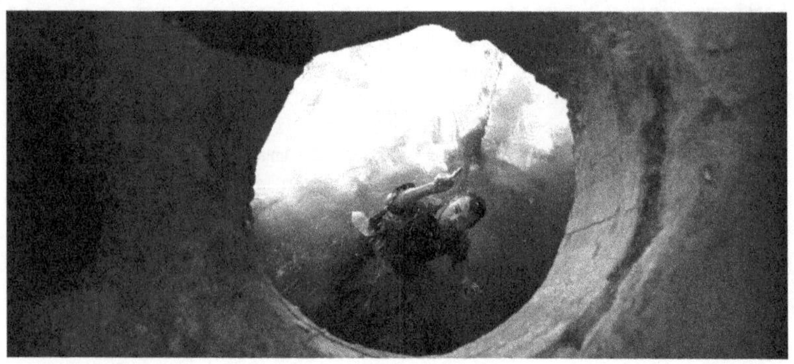

We avoided that damn hole all day, until the moment I fell through it in my haste. And I fell in it with my camera in hand! The camera smashed on the ground before I let go of it as I fell through the hole to the creek below. Up there, the Panasonic 24p was in pieces. I was OK, but the camera, not even close. Sepher was the first to examine it…

"The lens on the
camera exploded Braze."
he assessed,
"It's everywhere!"

That hit me like a train wreck!

"Did any fall into the creek?"
Ruin asked Sepher.

"Maybe."
he continued flatly,
"It's in a dozen pieces,"
I heard him say to Ruin.

"GOD DAMN IT!"
I screamed.

It echoed around me and in my head like a racquetball bouncing in my box! Other than breaking a leg… I don't think I could have felt any worse at that moment. But at least if I broke a leg I could have scored some painkillers to numb what appeared to be the end of my project just as it began.

As I stood in the creek like an actor in between takes of a Vietnam War movie… I could hear The Doors in the back ground singing about the end of my movie, as military choppers raced low, just above the tree lines, dropping napalm bombs on my hobo dream. I was so far from making a good movie, that I could only dream of other good ones.

I shook the Apocalypse Now flashback from my head and climbed from the creek to pick up the pieces of my camera, only to find Sepher assessing the damage with curiosity. I assumed it was unsalvageable, but he started putting the barrel of the camera back together while Ruin was on her cell phone talking to her boyfriend. I wanted to step away and call Richy, but I didn't know what to say? Instead, I just went for a walk and let Sepher try and pull a miracle.

And, a little later, truth be told, I called my Mom. She reminded me that whatever it was that I was doing now, I was miles away from the Emergency Rooms that she nearly lost me in time and time again. And she said the cost of a camera is nothing compared to the loss of a son. She assured me, whatever I needed, she would provide; and she always did. I felt like a chump, but with encouragement like hers, I could live with it.

Though, when I returned to the old factory, Sepher had the camera back together; minus the lens that was crushed.

"The camera, looks good as new!"
I rejoiced.

"I think the anamorphic lens
worked like an air bag,"
Sepher concluded.

"To hell with that lens,
I didn't know how to use it anyway!"
I admitted.

"It's together,"
Sepher continued,
"but I think it has a problematic
focus issues now."

And he was right about that. The focus was really screwed up, yet, somewhat manageable. But I wrote in the story that the camera was to break! So, I just decided to do another rewrite to the script, and immediately suggested to them…

"Tomorrow,
we come back and shoot
what just happened."

"What?"
Ruin asked.

"Why?"
Seph wondered.

"I got this guys.
I can make this work!"
I assured them.

The next day… I brought them back to reshoot the end of the first scene with my rewrite. In these takes, rather then fall from the ladder, I spiked the camera into the ground and had Ruin & Sepher run around the corner to find me gone, and the camera on the ground broken next to the hole. I had them run right to the camera and pick it up, only to find me below in the creek, soaked, and screaming drunk in the take! And with that, the ladder scene I shot the day before was no longer needed.

How did I create the appearance of a broken camera for the movie? I just stepped on a clear filter lens and screwed it on the camera in between the spike and the camera rolling on the ground; simple movie magic.

"How are we going to edit in?
This, broken camera effect Braze?"
Seph asked.

But I didn't bother to answer him because my answer was more visual in my head than grammatical on the tongue. I could see the cuts and fades just as I had in my black books since I was a kid painting graffiti along the El train rooftops. Despite my lack of experience with video, it was all clear to me. I had been a writer/painter since the age of twelve; the movie was just another canvas to me. So after assuring them I knew what I was doing, we completed the takes I needed upstairs before I climbed down into the muddy creek below. Once in place below the hole, I had Sepher pick up the broken camera upstairs and videotape me down there in the creek as I did what actors do best… yell, scream, and act drunk.

When that day of shooting wrapped, I was pretty optimistic again. But I got the impression Ruin didn't share my optimism, when she started calling me Mes off camera…

"So Mes, are we going to shoot the rest of the movie with an out of focus camera?"

"I'm going to exchange it for a
new one when we get to Philly,"
I replied with no doubts.

But they looked very doubtful!

"What?
I got the receipt,"
I said in defense.

"Do you think that's possible?"
she asked Sepher as if I wasn't right there.

"It's possible.
It does look good as new,"
he responded.

"Yeahhhh, but?"
Ruin said with hesitation.

I was standing across the room in front of what was left of a crumbling wall by the steps as I looked at the camera, pretending I wasn't listening. Then Sepher spoke, and tried to reassure her in his own way.

"I think Braze can talk
anyone into anything."

"You think?"
she asked.

"Sara,
look what he has us doing."
Seph pointed out.
"I mean come on,
he's kinda a sociopath."
…He said softly.

Then Ruin turned to me as I stood there "not" listening to them.

"Mes, are you afraid of snakes?"
she ask randomly.

"What? I hate snakes."

Then, she suggested calmly…
"Braze,
I think you should stay cool,
and just walk towards me.
Very, slowly."

Then, my prehistoric instincts kicked in. And like a lil bunny rabbit, I felt a predator behind me! But my dumb human nature had me glance back, and look for it. When I noticed it, and its tongue taunting me, I felt a sudden rush of blood to my head! This huge snake was on a stack of bricks a few feet behind me! Then, I cried out with the fear of jailhouse rape upon my back, uncontrollably…

"Snakes in my ass!
Great big black snake in my ass!"

I felt like naked lunch, on a general population fork! My white ass was grass. And it must have come up from the creek I was just swimming in! It was maybe 4 or 5 inches thick, and over 6 feet long. When I got to Ruin with the quickness I spun her like a dance partner! And though I was impressed how Sara handled it with me, I knew she was getting less and less impressed with me. And that concluded the shooting of our first scene together. It wasn't pretty, but we completed it; I think. I didn't look at the takes.

Next on our shot list, was to get coverage of our train hop from Baltimore, to Philly. A short but exciting one because it would be Ruin's first ride on the rails! But the next day, as Seph and I packed our gear before we all went to the yard to catch out, Ruin approached with other plans…

"I'm going to Bus up to Philly Mes."

"Say what!"
I snapped.

"I need a day alone
to connect with my boyfriend."
She decided out of the blue!

Sepher noticed my pupils turning red and came to my aid, answering for me.

"That's fine Sara."

"Here's his West Philly address."
she handed me it, then added
"We'll just meet there."

Then she just split. I wanted to, to… bite her! And I don't remember how, but I stayed in my skin. Then Sepher reminded me…

"Listen man,
the camera is busted.
Getting good video on the train is
impossible anyway."

I'm really not sure what was exactly going on in her head, but I felt she was giving up on the project. Or maybe she wanted to see if I could actually return the camera for a new one before she took a ride and the risk on a train with us. Though I actually have never been to the store I purchased the camera from, I had to move forward to Philly where I mail ordered it. And she knew that. The possibility that she told me the truth and just wanted to see her boyfriend… didn't come to mind at the time. Ruin took a Chinatown bus to Philly. Seph and I caught our train, as planned.

Later that same day, out there on the rails, despite all the reasons I had to be discouraged, not one picture Sepher took of me along the ride from Baltimore to Philly shows anything less than joy. Somewhere out there life eased, the weight of my ambition shed, the failures that tattooed my spirit washed in the wind like a beautiful losers baptism. The sad epitaph I began to chisel myself years ago began a brighter rewrite. Out there, suicide became a sickness, not a solution. But that's easy to say when you're not in the danger zone of depression.

BRIGHTDAWN

When I'm alone in the badlands of my mind, I'm not thinking whom I may hurt in the wake of taking my life. I'm self-absorbed and uncontrollably thinking about a permanent solution for my temporary problems. I have to remind myself of that, often. I just kept telling myself then, that my bad moods were just passing clouds. And that bought me time, and helped me not to pick up a gun and put it to my head, like an addict trying not to pick up the needle and put it to the vein.

"You can kill yourself,
just not today,"
I murmured.

I opened a door to suicide and I couldn't close it. But I never thought I was a victim of any kind, I felt as if I brought it on myself. I just couldn't see the brighter side of life unless it was wrapped in a rush of blood to the head. My highs made me euphoric dependent and notebook hooked. The volumes of notes I've penned about it all, are just materials I'll use ahead I guess. I'd pick up a journal and draw some graffiti, write a poem, or drop my emotional science on a page to medicate me with the success of placebo sometimes. My journal took the stress out of writing, but not from my life as easily. Writing is my self-medication to an illness I'll probably die with; I think my sadness will always be there. But while out there on the trains, I thought I was going in the right direction, from it!

After those thoughts passed, I was once again determined to exchange the camera for a new one as soon as our train got to Philly. So when I started to recognize familiar neighborhoods as we came up on I-95, I gathered my gear. I wasn't exactly sure what part of the city the train would slow down in, and where we could hop off, but when we began rolling through Southwest Philly; I had my shit together; but not like back in the day when I rolled with pride on city streets like the freestyle singer Noel. And at that moment, I relieved in my mind… when I cruised the streets with my kicker box where the back seats once sat, booming club music in my Suzuki Samurai jeep. I sported gold Gucci G's holding my big ass blockbuster name in place on my chest, and fat shoe laces that held relaxed weaves through my slick suede Pumas. I'd roll down your block like I owned it. But this time, I was hoboing through the hood. And as the train slowed to a stop, that really hit home. I stopped daydreaming when the train let us off somewhere near Woodland Avenue. It was time to jump off and walk it, when it occurred to me…

"You gotta tramp through your
hometown kid-o."

Then I emerged from an underpass with Sepher, and on the street where we began the slow trek on foot with our oversized pickle packs. I carried a graffiti bombed steel camera case as well, and was really far from the kid that first cruised these streets years prior, but so were the people I grew up with in them parts. If I ran into a familiar face in the neighborhood, chances are they might look worse than me. Or even worse, they hadn't changed at all.

Despite my insecurities, my ego still pushed a strut that could ward off a creep from across the street. By this time in life, my eyes said more than my strut, my mind said less than my heart, and my soul spoke softer than my dreams. Day after day, I began to put more good ones together despite my emotional problems. But once in my hometown and off my pink cloud of trains, I began to psychotically relapse and lose my composure, talking nonsense…

"Had guns to my head
since I was a child.
I don't know.
Stop! STOP IT!"
I murmured loudly.

My head tried to shake off that nonsense as I found myself once again physically jerking with uncontrollable emotions. So I talked to myself over my shakes and murmurs to try and overpower the unwanted thoughts. Often I would even read random signs around me to distract me from these uncomfortable notions passing through my head.

When I noticed Sepher next to me realizing some of this going on with me, I began to rap as if it's all part of a rhyme inside me…

"Once lost in the sauce, no taste no flavor.
Lost in my cause both devil and savior.
Lost in a cause I pawned all my favors.
Graffiti's the cost a being lost in my thoughts."

He was amused, and didn't seem to be aware of what was really going on inside me. At least I hoped he didn't.

A few blocks later we made it to a 108 bus stop to 69th Street. I have an uncle between Southwest Philly and Upper Darby in East Lansdowne. He was the first person to really coach my game. While my Mom gave me some dance moves, my uncle Jack gave me a good pump fake. What I got most from him about playing basketball was how to warm up, and get into a rhythm to sink shots.

I was usually pretty busy being careful in my reckless years leading me to the trains. Now, I was a warmed up outlaw. Train hopping was the same game I played on the streets with no rules and where anything goes that you can get away with. I though about all this along the bus ride before the 108 would let Sepher and I off on Long Lane; where my parents initially met. While on the bus I thought of them too. I envisioned… long ago, when my Dad went to The Five & Dime that my Mom worked at on Long Lane to ask her out on their first date. They were just teenager's back then.

I'm told that my Grandmother (his Mom) told my Dad, that a nice girl worked the register at The Five & Dime and that he should go ask her out. So, per his Mom's request, he did. When he got there, sure enough was the beautiful girl his Mom said would be there. So after a short conversation, and Mom getting a little excited Dad shared the name of her favorite Beatle, he asked...

"Would you like to see
a movie with me?"

"Sure,"
my Mom said,
"there' s a new Al Pacino movie
playing I'd like to see!"

They went to see Panic In Needle Park that weekend. And Mom said he was sweating and scratching himself a lot in the movie theater. Though at the time she didn't know why, later she'd find out that heroin was my Dad's drug of choice. We all have first date stories and that's what I know of theirs. I love that movie!

When we got off the bus and stepped onto Long Lane in East Lansdowne, I got out of my head and we went on to find my uncle Jack who tended bar at a dive on The Lane in the neighborhood we grew up in. Uncle Jack is a regular guy, just like the neighborhood. He drives a pick up truck and decided to stay in the small town he grew up in, like his father. And I'm happy he's there and that I still have family in the neighborhood.

When we made it to the bar, Seph and I rolled in and found a couple empty stools. It was lunchtime, when roofers knock down cold ones and the neighborhood bums milk afternoon two-dollar pitchers. A moment later my Uncle Jack noticed us, and he was happy to see me.

"Two cokes Jack?"
I asked.

"Look, at, you!"
he laughed,
"Fall on hard times Braze?"

"Maybe Jack. But I never
felt better."

I went on to tell him what I was doing, but I don't think it registered with him. Or maybe he thought I was just bullshitting him, or I stunk, because he cut me off and told me…

"Braze my back door
is open if you want to
go and shower up."

His back door was always open, or at least it was until this book. I wanted to stop by and see my Mom who lived just a few blocks away, but I knew how worried she might be seeing me in character hopping trains. She knew what I was up to, but no need to make her an accomplice! So I made my way out of East Lansdowne quietly after I made plans to connect with Ruin Downtown to exchange the camera. I was enthusiastic to return to Center City. I always loved the energy of that part of town!

Later on the three of us connected just before I made the return of the damaged video camera. I left Seph & Ruin on a corner after I double-checked it on the city street before I got inside the store; I had to make sure the camera didn't fall apart again!

"Good luck Mes,"
Ruin wished me, laughing.

My concern was not being unable to exchange it for a new one, but for the camera to come apart in the shop owners hand like a Jenga stack before I could do the swap!

"Just wait here across the
street guys."

As I ran through traffic with my camera case in hand, a late 80's Corvette jammed "No Reason To Cry" as if it were Green, saying hello. Last time that song crossed my radar I was with her in Richy's car a few months back.

Once across the street I entered the Zoom Monster Camera Store on Walnut Street. Inside there, from the corner of my eye, I could see Seph and Ruin watching me as I introduced myself to the Pakistani guys behind the counter. The Beastie Boys rocked Slow and Low from a new, but "old school looking" boom box behind the counter with a first generation Ipod plugged in it.

"Hello gentleman,"
I started the convo with,
"I have a defective camera
bought from here.
It won't focus!
I mail ordered it a month ago."

They looked skeptical, but didn't say a word yet. We just all looked at the camera. Then, after a quick inspection, one said…

"Was the camera dropped?"

"No.
It's fresh out the box."
I responded.

Then they examined the camera further, and thoroughly. But found nothing wrong! They were puzzled by it, and that was just what I wanted. I stood there playing just as puzzled.

"The camera was not dropped?"
asked the other guy.

"No.
I've been fully pro-plexed by it,"
I mispronounced.

But when that came out of my mouth, I felt my Don King coming on strong! So I went with it, and continued rapping like a two-bit street preacher leaning toward Muhammad in their presence.

"The whole first day
I thought it was my fault!
But God is good,
and I had faith you sent me
a good camera. But that's NOT what I got,
so help me God."

They just remained silent while I continued with my product return sermon…

"Don't worry,
I don't want my money back gentlemen.
Just a camera that works."

They looked at each other and seemed to be on the same page without saying a word to each other.

"We can take it back
and do a return no problem."
I was told,
"But the time it may take
to get the repair done,
or a replacement?"
he wondered and looked to his partner before
speculating…
"Thirty to sixty days."

I gasped!

"Good God, what!
I need one of those off the shelf
behind you
today my Arabic brothers."

"No, so sorry.
We have to
ship it back to the
Panasonic distributor in Ohio."

It appeared that these guys had been through this before. So I took a moment to gather myself, looked these two guys over, and slowly… lost it.

"Under other circumstances,
I could wait in peace.
But I'm in the middle of
a movie shoot right now!

But they were not moved by my situation. Not enough to reach behind them and give me one of those new cameras just yet. A new camera, the same as mine, was right there on the shelf as close as that snake was to my ass in Baltimore! So, I went on to tell the guys all about my train hopping project and said…

"Gentlemen,
you are in the presence of the next…"

As I went on to say that I was going from the rags I was wearing, to film festivals some day, Ruin and Sepher where outside still watching me. And as I began to really animate myself in the window and inform the guys inside about how much of a badass rebel I am, who needs a new camera! Outside, my peoples where trying to read my body language…

"What's he doing in there?"
asked Ruin.

"Looks like he's playing charades."
Seph laughed.

"It looks like he's really trying hard
to make his point Matt."

"Well…
he can be quite emotional."

Back in side, I was standing at the counter out of breath, when I finally just told the guys…

"I got
emotional problems fellas!
You really have to
help me here!"

The guys looked at each other again, and then back to me, just rolling their eye at this point, fed up. So, I made them an offer. In God We Trust…

"Listen fellas…
we all know this camera is defective and the
replacement is sure to come in!
So, you give me that replacement behind you, NOW.
And I will give you…
two hundred, cash money right now,
just for your patience!
Two hundred dollars…
just to wait for the other camera to come back from
Ohio. Then just put that one back
on the shelf for sale."

I held up two hundred dollar bills. And then it seemed I had their attention again. So I continued…

"It's worth these two notes to me,
so I can move forward. Is it worth it to you?"

They looked at each other once again and, and once again communicated without saying a word. Assuming these guys were spiritual people, I went on to say…

"I'm just trying to buy
some peace of mind here.
Can I get some peace,
for two hundred dollars!"

I felt I was near the close, but it looked like peace was going to cost me a little more. So, I upped the offer…

"How about giving me some peace for
two hundred and FIFTY dollars?"

"Ok!"
one blurted out, to the others surprise.

"God is good!"
I exclaimed.
"But not great,"
I murmured softly.

Then we made the exchange, and I was back on the go!

After taking care of that piece of business, I went to see my brother and got buzzed into the lobby entrance of his Center City apartment building. Sepher and Ruin nodded goodbye to me and went back to her boyfriends, as I went inside to see Richy.

"I'll see you two in the morning,"
I told them.

They went to Ruin's boyfriends' in West Philly because the last friend I brought to Richy's crib was a mobster who got knocked off a week after we stopped over together. Since then, I didn't have a guest list at his loft. I understood that. I mean, who wants someone on a mob hit list in his home, or pseudo-hobos stinking up the crib in this case? Not my brother.

Upstairs, when I knocked on Richy's front door, I noticed him turn off an alarm system inside, releasing locks, dead bolts; it sounded complicated. But then, the door opened and he greeted me…

"Alive and illegal Braze!"

He immediately gave me a huge hug that reminded me how much bigger, my little brother actually is. Then I asked sarcastically…

"Please bro, call me Mr. Mes.
I'm in character."

"You're a weirdo Bee."

His loft had ultra high ceiling, lots of technology, Italian furniture, saltwater fish tank, gas fireplace and a huge painting of baby angels over it; the painting was new. I was instantly reminded of the good life that I left behind when I jetted to New Orleans. And then, as I looked around, I found more paintings… of angels on every wall.

"You've become an art collector?"

"I du-know.
I just like angels Braze.
They make me feel good."

He enjoyed his music too, usually trance and other club genres, but that day he was playing something out of charter for him. He had Mary Wells singing from an old record player? So I asked…

"Sup with the oldies man?"

He just laughed, and was kinda excited!

"Mommy gave me her old
Caliphone record player.
And her albums!"

I laughed with him and listened to the song. I recognized it easily, and murmured the title…

"My Guy?"

He shook his head yes, with a big smile.

"My guy."
I said again, charmed by it.

Moments later I couldn't resist rolling outside to his balcony where I could look over most of old city from the penthouse view. There was a time, not long before I hopped trains, that Center City was my love and heartbeat! Where the hairs on my arms would often tingle from the tags I recognized on the walls, the childhood packs I rolled in down the streets, the bars we would rage in, the coffee shops I chilled at, the restaurants Richy & I frequented, and of course the traffic that boomed beats down city streets from underneath the back seat as they so often do in our part of town. My days residing in South Philly and Center City were some of the best days of my life, despite the dark days I write about.

Up there in his lofty life, Richy had all the comforts and views I was finding on the rails at that time. We both seemed pretty happy in our skin for once it seemed. Then, Richy came outside on the balcony, took me from my flashbacks, and brought us some ice tea.

"Yo Bee,
your clothes are pretty torn up.
You good?"

"It's a roll I'm playing bro,"
I reminded him.

"You play the roll 24/7?"

I didn't care to explain because he wasn't really asking me, but kinda kidding with me. So I just changed the subject…

"What's going on with you Rich?"

"Investing in more real-estate.
Everybody with a hammer
is flipping houses."

"You can actually
invest that much money legally?"

"Not exactly,"
he said,
"but the Russians are
giving away mortgages like lap
dances at Delilah's Den."

I knew the Russian guys he was referring to, old "KGB" nightclub hustlers, so an explanation wasn't necessary. He had it going on and figured out. But he didn't think I did.

"What are you doin' Braze?"

"I'm makin' this movie."

"You think you're gonna
be a movie star?"

I didn't dignify his sarcasm with an answer.

"You gonna make money off it?"
he asked.

"Yup."

"How?"

I took a deep breath, and shared what I thought…

"Magazines will write about me.
Then I'll sell the movie."

He shared a somewhat sympathetic laugh. I added…

"I've already seen it happen,
and much more…
in this head of mine."

"You're a fortune-teller now Bee?"

I didn't answer that one directly either. Getting spiritual or talking about vision was to big a convo to have at that time. So instead, I just said…

"I'm following a hunch."

Apparently moody, he then shared a bigger laugh! I guess he could read my mind…

"You're a visionary Braze!"

I realized that I was being a little vague with everyone at that time in my life. So I didn't blame Richy or even Sepher & Ruin for doubting me often. Rather, I just joined in on the laughs…

"I'd call it more,
a spark on insight Rich."

What I was embarking on was rather uncharted, and I knew it. I felt I was creating an opportunity to become an outlier entrepreneur in storytelling. Yet explaining this to everyone, all the time, was a waste of time.

Later that night… I brewed some hot tea and sat by a burning fire at his place. It was cool that night with a nice breeze coming in from the open balcony doors. Richy kept spinning some of Moms' Billie Holiday records while he was in the kitchen, patiently cooking up ketamine over the stove on a Pyrex plate over a boiling pot of water; an outlaw chef with a secret ingredient…

"I like putting a dash of vanilla
in the K to flavor the drips."

Then he scraped the ketamine off the glass plate with a spatula. But to me, it sounded so… natural! Like pigeons cooing in the morning by the window, a very familiar sound in the city. And though I was comforted by it, I had to block it out. It made my mind loose focus of my bigger ideas. So I enquired…

"Richy, what's up
with all the dead bolts on the door.

"I had to do it.
They tried to rob me."

"What!"

"They knew I was a saver."

"What happened man?"

"Peter Gaten's boys made a
move on me."

"Gaten!"

I was shocked! Gaten was in jail for MDMA manufacturing at this time, but his soldiers, BTS, where ruthless! And then Richy, with an apparent balance of fear and anger in his voice, continued to say…

"They broke into the house.
Tied me up with the telephone chord.
And put a gun to my head…
Told me to open the safe."

Then he stared off, maybe shocked by the memory, I don't know. He just stared at the large angelic painting over the fireplace. He was frozen, not even blinking. It was as if it was all flashing before him. For a moment, I briefly wondered whether he got the angel paintings before or after the robbery happened.

"How much did they get off you?"

Still in his head, somewhere else, he then came back and answered…

"Nothing.
I told 'um to kill me."

"What!"

"Yeah, told 'um to kill me,"
he repeated,
"I knew they weren't killers.
But they beat the shit out of me!
Beat me till I blacked out.
Then they tried to take the whole safe.
But that's impossible,
it weighs a ton."

I took a deep breath, took a step back, and bent over. This kind of shit was out of my league! Peter

Gaten was one of the most successful street hustlers to ever come out of Brooklyn. He got his start by essentially stealing the American Dream, than hording as much. Later, he went on to own a string of clubs in Manhattan. Now that Gaten, the "BTS" cash cow was locked up, his clubs closed, and the scene was dead, they were back to robbing homes. Richy continued…

"When I woke up,
and opened my eyes,
I found them trying to
drag the safe out the house."

"That thing weighs a ton!"
I recalled.

"Yeah-up.
While they struggled with that,
I made it to the fire alarm in here.
It woke up the whole building."

"They jetted?"
I asked.

"The safe and I are still here Bee."

"Who was it Richy?"

He seemed to shake his head in disgust.

"Who was it?"

Richy told me specifically who it was of Gaten's "BTS" gang, but those guys aren't part of the legacy I'll leave on this page. But their leader, Peter Gaten, is sitting in jail today. Without him around, his BTS gang got desperate and where back to robbing homes, banks, and probably car stereo's sometimes; they're just animals in the concrete jungles. Richy some how made it on their "hustlers to rob list".

The next morning I left early to meet Seph & Ruin, so I just wrote a Thank You note and placed it on the dining room table for Richy. He always slept in on Sundays. On my way out, my two road dogs called and said they were waiting for me just a few blocks away at… "The Last Drop Coffee Shop down from the Cop Stop." A line I'd drop in a poem much later when editing the movie.

Once the three of us connected, we shot our second scene in a local alley filled with graffiti pieces just a block off South Street. But after numerous takes, I felt it just wasn't going well at all; Ruin & I dropped line after line. Seph and her felt the same way. I just thought that maybe our chemistry was off and we needed to bond some more. In that scene we were discussing whether we should hop a train, or take a Chinatown bus to New York. But we just couldn't find a natural flow. So I told them…

"We'll get the scene later,
lets call it a day."

But we never did. Other than scoring the camera in Philly, which was necessary of course, and letting Ruin connect with her boyfriend, my hometown did little to further my project. So I decided to just move on and thought about hopping out. But so they didn't get discouraged, I pointed out…

"It doesn't matter what city
we shoot this scene in because locations like this
are a dime a dozen in cities ahead."

"How are people going
to know where we are
in the story?"
Ruin asked.

A solution came to mind immediately…

"I'm going to write the cities
we're in on boxcar with an oil pastel.
We can cheat this
scene later, elsewhere."

I had moniker art on my mind because Old Bill Daniels was on tour screening his Bozo Texino film while we were on the road shooting our picture.

Instead of sticking around Philly any longer and trying to get the scene done, I decided to move on to our next stop, New York City. Although our shoot didn't go well in Philly, I was excited for us to ride our first train together as Mes, Sepher & Ruin, or The ICOP Camp, as I began to call us. I thought the trains could bring us together and get us on the same page. But once again, it was a slow departure on the rail.

After missing a train during our first try to hop out of Philly, we decided to camp in the woods that afternoon by the Schuylkill River under the South Street Bridge and wait for the next ride the following morning. We hung out safely on the duck and in the brush that night.

Later, while Seph and Ruin slept, I watched a game of bicycle polo at a park not far from the tracks. While it drizzled that night, the cement was glossy from the lights above the playground that reflected a glare on the wet concrete as the bicycles moved at half speed. It appeared Yuengling Lager was the unofficial sponsor; but I was still honest with myself and didn't partake. Instead, I just wandered around that part of town all night watching fucked up people "sketch out" as I held on tightly to my camera. It still felt odd being home and not trying to sell or cop something, but I was starting to be fulfilled with all I needed inside as I enjoyed my charade on the rails. In fact, I was buzzing so much I couldn't sleep.

Early the next morning… with my hot tea in one hand, camera in the other, I stood on top of the South Street Bridge looking over in the direction of 30th Street Station. I was comforted by the glow of the moon just before the sunrise as cars on the other side of the river ebbed and flowed through metropolitan arteries. As I pulsed with the city, I found myself thinking of Richy, and relived one of his near death episodes, when years ago…

His white Chevy Beretta flipped over after running up a median coming to a skidding stop in flames! I could see it happening across the river as if it just happened, and not years ago as it were. I could see RA

A much younger Richy climbed out of the car wearing a white Sergio Techieni Suit, looking around to see if anyone had witnessed what just happened, before retrieving a school bag from the trunk, and quickly running from the scene! …And fading from my waking dream. My mind frequently plays tricks on me and blurs timelines in this world, sharing past and future events, in the present. Images that appear like Ghosts, or UFO's, or even Flying Crosses over Europe hundreds of years ago to the bewilderment of those around me on the ground who where unfamiliar with the airplane at that time, I visited; once bitten.

Back in the present world, and out of my dangerous headspace… A train approached below me, very slowly, rolling under the South Street Bridge, creeping over the rails just enough to wake me from my time warp.

"That's a silent mutha,"
I whispered.

I stood there clueless, with hot tea in one hand and my new camera in the other. Before it occurred to me, that…

"My train?
That's our train!"
I yelled.

I dumped my tea and quickly picked up some coverage of the train from atop the bridge, before I raced down to wake Sepher & Ruin! When I made it to them by the tracks, they were up and gathering their belongings. The train pulled up right there next to our camp sight, as if we planned it! Soon, we found a grainer and boarded it. The spot we camped near was considered by what some graffiti artists call a lay up, a spot where trains park, or in our case, do a crew change… but not in an actual yard. Hopping or graffiti bombing a train is easier here. Ruin didn't have to experience the frustrations Sepher and I had, getting to Philly. So maybe she was more than our actress, but good luck!

After sneaking on the train we sat idle for a time long after the sun came up. The whole time, Ruin didn't say a word, but simply meditated. Eventually, with no hassles, we rolled down the rails. And as the train picked up speed, she continued to sit as still as a statue.

Then, down the tracks, she finally opened her eyes and seemed to be communed with the train. Ruin rolled on a level all her own.

As for me, now on my third freight train, I was feeling better and began to interpret the sound from the rails below as 3rd Bass beats dropped on My Own Private Style War. Seph was taking still shots, Ruin was chilling, and I was as excited as a kid with a new drivers license!

As we raced forward, my future blew through my hair like ketamine on the beach in The Baha of Mexico. All my screw ups, all my near escapes, all my get mine all my life… came crashing against my face with the wind and left behind me in diesel exhaust like an industrial rite of passage. With my Camp and new camera in tow I was on top of it as I picked up coverage from Philly to New York while forging on with the evolution of my own artistic style. If my project was in pieces before, it felt as if it were coming together slowly, at 60 miles per hour in the Northeast. This, the 3rd ride, was filled with all the thrills and uncertainty of the first two rides. Each mile was a beautiful balance of being there, and wondering what was just ahead!

I had my plan, wrote my script, and was traveling with two smart & resourceful people, but anything could go wrong… such as one of us falling off. And then there was jail, but my Dad's bail bonds business card was in my pocket in case of that.

Much later, as we continued north and the graffiti evolved, it was obvious to me we were on the right track and getting closer to a New York State of mind. And soon enough… we rode into a sketchy north Jersey yard! Trains were being pushed around on several tracks, gangs of workers were doing construction, and it was broad daylight no less! The yard was big and we were newbies on high alert! Getting off the train would be easy, but walking out of the yard unnoticed would be challenging, if not impossible it seemed. It was a prison of a train yard.

"Do we get off here?"
Ruin asked.

"Yes,"
Sepher replied firmly.

"Well, how do we get out of the yard?"
she asked.

"Follow me,"
I told her. Certain I could manage it.

I quickly hopped off the parked train and headed in the direction we entered the yard; my pack was just too heavy to do the fence quickly in that daylight. But within just a few moments after we climbed down off the train, a worker crossed our path! I saw him, before he saw us. Immediately, without hesitation, I called for his attention; politely…

"Excuse me, hey buddy?"

The worker gave me the "what the hell" face, but that's often just a Jersey greeting. When I motioned to Ruin and Seph to give me a second, they looked at me like I was crazy. So I expressed to them very softly…

"I can handle this."

Then I walked towards the worker who was a track over, and asked him with a friendly smile…

"Please, can you tell me
how to get the fuck outta here?"

Approaching someone like this just comes natural to me. Growing up I learned when someone is looking for me… to go to him first! I always felt it gave me the upper hand, like a cordial sucker punch. And with a smile that says, "I'm not afraid of you," never hurts. But the worker was a tough guy who just stared me down. Some people always need someone to look down on, and I was just the guy for him that day. So I told um…

"Listen buddy,
I know what this looks like.
It is what it is. …Y'know?
We'd just like to get out of here
in one-piece man."

He was a man of no words, but nodded towards the way we were already heading. I nodded back in appreciation. I really didn't want any directions from this dude anyway. But I had to say something to him. Just like crossing the Mexican border with Ketamine countless times, I've found a small sense of entitlement goes a long way with authority!

Eventually, my cohorts and I walked out of that yard with no troubles. And then took a subway across to New York City. From there we found our way to St. Marks, and to our slated location, Tomkins Square Park to continue our shoot. It's a place where you find travelers like us popping squats in the grass, playing music on the sidewalks, and waiting in food lines. We instantly connected with some stray cats like us on some benches and chilled with them for a minute. Two stood out… Dan'o and Dougie Fresh. We got Dougie and his boy to play along with our script as we passed a photo of Kotton around and asked if they'd seen him or not. They played it off as best they could; I was grateful. Dan'O was the brother of a New Orleans old head named Church who I met in my initial stretch down in New Orleans. So I asked Dan'o if he would meet us there the next day, and sit down and give us an interview.

"Sure, bring some beer!"
he said.

Then we left Tomkins Square and headed back to the subway to go to one of Ruin's friends who agreed to host us while we were in town. There's nothing like a mattress with clean sheets.

BOOK SAFE

The next day… I asked Sepher about his boy Ian, a connection he said he had at C-Squat, but no word there. So after the interview with Dan'O and a few others, the three of us split up to breathe and do our own things. I took the subway over to where the World Trade Center once stood.

Once I got over there it appeared as though the foundations for the new buildings began. As I stood there, I thought of Richy's friend Joey D who did time in Iraq and ate dirt in Fallujah. There I was in life, trying to shoot a movie about the American hobo, and Joey put his life on the line for the America way. Joey, Richy and I all played on the exact same streets when we were kids, but our roads from them led us to be very different adults… one an American Hero, the other an American Hustler and I, an American Writer. There was an enthusiasm on the streets of our neighborhood that since died. Death was on my mind at Ground Zero where souls stirred in the wind. At that point, I had to bring my spirit back up from where The Towers were leveled. To do that I went over to 5 Pointz!

5 Pointz is a graffiti mecca where writers from everywhere come together and paint the walls. In so many youthful and passionate ways that building spoke to my spirit! To me, the walls told stories of high risk and outlaw lifestyles such as mine in The Art of Train Hoppin. I felt so young again on the rails!

My train-hopping project was becoming my personal Ponce de Leon. A pursuit to get back in touch with the kid who started writing his name on the rooftops of

69th street back in grade school. The movie I was making was about hobos, but I was still the same undercover writer I was way back in the day.

At the 5 Pointz I daydreamed of being buried inside a stone mausoleum in Saint Louis Cemetery. The outside of my grave would be pieced like the artwork on the walls of that graffiti mecca in NYC. I imagined any outlaw could die happy at 5 Pointz, but I gravitate towards the hustler Marie Laveau.

The next day, with our coverage in The Apple completed, we found our way out of New York City and back to a train yard. The work we got done thus far on the movie was minimal. I got one good interview with Dan'o, a few bites from other crusties, along with some coverage on streets to establish that we passed through NYC, but that was it. My camera was together, but my script was falling apart. Then it occurred to me, the story may not be taking shape, but I am. I wasn't sad or depressed, angry or violent. Nor was I certain of anything, but pretty close to comfortable with nothing. I often forgot I was making a movie because I was too busy being present in it. But I wasn't about to let any kind of spiritual awakening be a substitute for an incomplete project.

"Science over spirituality,"
I murmured.

Our next destination was West and halfway across the country, in Chicago! The focus from here on was to continue in that direction and make it to The Coast. Making it coast to coast would be a great accomplishment. After all, this was the big stunt in the movie! It was those trains that kept us all in the project, we all wanted to keep riding! So if the movie fell apart, it wouldn't matter as much to Sepher & Ruin because they would still have the experience of train hopping across the country. But for me, going this far to make a movie just put pressure on me to finish it.

I had no intention of going that far for anything less than a good picture. I was in way too deep to do anything other than find my way out of it, just as before when I found myself in over my head everywhere else. Like a 49er on the frontier digging holes to fulfill his dreams, I always thought going a little farther or deeper would bring me all I ever wanted.

With a slight drizzle, it was pretty wet out when we arrived that night in the yard, it stayed damp like that throughout the night. Hollywood would bring in water trucks to glisten a street, so why complain about a little water on the rails in New York. The yard was dead, there was a little train movement, but I don't remember seeing any workers. As I scouted cars, Sepher took still shots whenever he could pull some light from somewhere…

With our train not there yet, we crashed on the ground by the side of the tracks as trains moved around us. Again, I felt like a movie soldier on set. I thought hiding in the yards was like playing war, snipers or kick the can when I was a kid… just some friends and I sneaking around from the enemy bull.

And the coolest part was that Sepher was our photojournalist! The photos he was taking broke down another wall in the project. I was making a movie, about making a movie with a "broken camera" as Seph documented everything with still shots. It was wild style filmmaking with few rules and no boundaries.

As it continued to rain and got even wetter that night, we crawled from the damp grass and onto a dry train to wait for the ride we were expecting to pull up on an adjacent track. But as we got comfortable, the train jerked forward! Alarmed, we all looked at each other for answers!

"Do we want to stay on
this train Seph?"

"We can stay on the train,
but I don't know where it's going,"
he said, all smart.

Talking to Sepher was like speaking to Spok sometimes, all logic! But then, I felt the excitement of the moving train I was riding as the scream of the wheels from the rails shook my bones and began to rock my world just like a good hit of any street poison you can think of, dope, rock, etc. The kind that makes your knees give and your jaw grinds. At that point, I was in!

"Lets roll with it my peoples!"
I called out like a raver on a good record.

Once you're in on a heavy high, you're along for the ride, and the train was my fix at this time! So jumping off after a lil taste was not possible. I found the trains as comforting as a bottle of Ketaset. The ride made me breathe deep and be much more present in the moment. Yeah we may be on the wrong train, but we had to be going in the right direction. The only thing that could have thrown me for a loop was if we ended up in Canada and certain that was not going to happen, I decide to enjoy the comfort of the ride and catch some winks before figuring out the next ride in a yard ahead.

Hours later… pouring rain woke me up at dawn and I was alarmed when I found the sun rising next to our moving train in the east. So I yelled over to Ruin & Sepher…

"I think were going north,
not west!"

We were way off course! But they were too soaking wet to care as we moved forward for about an hour not even knowing exactly where we were. Then the train paralleled a road where I could read the license plates of a few cars…

"Massachusetts?"
I read off license plate.

Sepher noticed too…

"We can get off in Boston!"
he suggested.

"Let's just go to Canada!"
Ruin joked.

I was very tense about it, but I stayed in my skin, just as I somewhat did when the camera broke in Baltimore. I was nervous, but the rain hid my concerns as I got soaked and hustled to keep all my camera gear dry, everything else I carried got wet by default. I remember having dramatic thoughts of marines in Vietnam getting drenched while in the thick of it all in Hamburger Hill.

"If those actors can do it,
So can you man!"
I encouraged myself aloud.

Then I got into damage control mode and into the fetal position around my camera case like a scared marine sitting on his helmet to save his nuts. If my camera got wet, I'd have nothing to shoot with in the field.

A bit later, when the rain stopped and the train began to slow, I peeked my head up and felt more discouraged and lost than I'd been in a long time. All I wanted was to keep Ruin & Seph in the project and move forward. But they didn't look to enthusiastic any longer.

BRIGHTDAWN

It all weighed on me… Sepher & Ruin quitting, my camera being functional, getting back on track, shooting my script… the more one thinks about things, the more they become real!

"Your problems aren't heavy.
They just feel like they are,"
I remind myself.

For years prior to this, even the slightest bit of uncomfortable boredom would have my cells calling out for a fix of some kind… pill, powder, pussy, something! And whenever a very desperate situation came up, I felt like a sucker, suffered and thought of suicide. That's where my mind went on a weekly basis since I was seventeen. But while rolling north instead of our intended west, I thought of all the bad things that happened to me and realized for the first time that within much of it, were some of the luckiest things that could have ever happened. Had there actually been good luck, within my terrible times? I suppose it's possible, luck-n-all. Something was saving me from myself.

Such as when I almost lost my arm when I was a crazy kid on acid, only to have a world-renowned nerve doctor who was passing through town giving a lecture take a look before they amputated. And in doing so, saved it.

Or the morning I sat there overdosing in my Center City loft, and a window washer with his ladder being right there next to my address for my Mom to borrow and save me from another suicide attempt.

And little things… like breaking my camera on the first day of our movie shoot, which saved me from acquiring coverage through an anamorphic lens I didn't know how to use.

Emerging from those sparks in my headspace and back into the world, we continued going the wrong way on a speeding train when I realized I wasn't emotionally broke this time around. Instead, I was OK in a big mistake for the first time in a while! I did panic at first, but it passed. I felt some growth in me at that point. Thoughts like, how can I get out of this? Flipped to… how can I work with this? So at that point

I decided to just keep my mouth shut and hoped Ruin and Sepher could enjoy the ride. I'd worry about the movie later.

And soon, the train came to a stop in a layup right outside a yard, where we carried our wet gear off the train and headed into town with our packs heavier than ever, looking for a Laundromat. Turns out we jumped off short of Boston, we were in a place called Worcester.

On the streets of this lil armpit I found myself on the outside looking in, while everyone just passed me without much of a glance. After the ride in the rain, I looked more haggard then ever! So much so, I think people tried to not make eye contact with me because I just might ask for some help or loose change.

In that skin, I noticed people with different incomes spending their money on very similar things… nice shoes, frothy coffee, etc., etc. I come from that culture of frivolous luxury and knew who made the shoes they were wearing and could smell the flavored coffee in the air as they passed. Just as Green knew her kind when they passed her in South Philly. While traveling cheap, finding tap water and fresh sox took priority over designer lattes and Italian shoes.

When we found a laundry matte, we stripped down to our underwear, put everything in the dryers, and just didn't care that we were the only ones there, in our underwear, and nobody else did really; the town had the atmosphere of a Gimbles dressing room. Afterwards, we fit in better and bummed around town a bit, then got some food at a mini mart before we rolled back to the train yard and camped out.

Out there in the woods while waiting on the next train with Seph and Ruin, they hit from a handle, but I didn't. I've had pretty long stretches of sobriety in the past, so I didn't feel much different than then. But I knew I was changing just a little. Underneath the persona of being an assed out punk in the movie, I began to feel comfortable in my own skin. Out there while carrying my backpack and managing a troubled motion picture, I had no desire to dig myself a hole; not a Dandelion song on my mind. Though I did miss that soundtrack that was the anthem to my recklessness… I wanted The Art of Train Hopping more!

The next day, we still found ourselves in the woods, on the side of the tracks, waiting for an afternoon train where we hopped off the day before. Waiting, as train after train passed us by since yesterday.

"Are any of these trains
going to stop Mes?"
Ruin asked.

How would I know? And she knew that! We waited all day for just one to stop, one! We just wanted to go south at this point! But nope, they just kept rolling by like women past losers. Trains rolled up, but none of them stopped next to our camp. Although they did come by slow, catching on the fly with our heavy packs didn't come to mind, yet. And before anyone started talking about a bus, I made a comfort run for us…

"I'm a get us a pizza!"

We all needed to stretch at that point, so we went for a walk together to get pie. As we looked for a pizza shop, I attracted attention this time with my backpack, steel camera case, and good attitude.

"You people on a hike?"
asked some old dude.

"Hoppin' trains,"
I told 'um.

"My old lady hopped out once.
I dared her too!"
he bragged.

I really didn't want to hear that. I waited all day and couldn't catch a train out, and this old dude was trying to tell me his old lady hopped out? Old fart! When I found us some pizza, I quickly ate my anger. Later, we gave up and crashed.

The next day was just another one filled with missed trains, and pizza. And to kick what was left of my strut in the nuts, an old lady stopped to talk to me while I was on a solo comfort food run. She knew I was riding the rails. I embodied it.

"I hopped out years ago.
Got lost out there for years!
Loved it!" she told me.
Then added,
"I had to shake a creep here in town."

…As she said that EMF blasted from a passing car…

"Ohhhhhhh!"

…It was so "Unbelievable", I didn't even bring it up to Sepher and Ruin when I got back with the pizza. Now on day three, we found ourselves out of the woods and waiting on a parked train, as "our" train, rolled by on the main track next to us. After waiting three whole days in one spot, I was getting really, really impatient! So as Ruin, Sepher and I stood on the back of a parked double stack, I climbed to the edge of the car and announced…

"I'm a go for it!"

And neither one tried to stop me! So I thought, that maybe, maybe it was a good idea. I mean, the train wasn't going that fast. And I guess they wanted out of town as much as I did. So leaping over from a parked train, to a moving train, was about to become our way out!

I waited as a couple of cars passed me by to time my jump. It was only two feet away, but the fall down was maybe seven or eight, between cars. The thought of falling under the train never came to mind; I felt capable from my leaps for graffiti back in the day. But I'd soon find out that the spray cans I carried back then, didn't have the drag of the pickle pack on my back now. I reached over, my hands clenched on passing ladder on the passing train; then…

"Screw me!"

It yanked me forward much, much harder then I anticipated it would! And with no choice my feet followed fast! If I slipped I'd become salad for sure. But I hung on! Once I got a good footing on the moving train, I immediately feared for Seph and yelled back…

"Don't do it!
DON'T DO IT!"

…at the top of my lungs! But they couldn't hear me through all the train noise! I wanted to jump off and stop them, but I couldn't do it because the parked train I came from was right there next to me! If I leaped off I'd have probably bounced off it and under the one I was moving on. There was just no room to jump off between the two, so I waited it out, till the last car of the parked train beside me, passed me by. I then jumped off to stop them! And just as I did, Sepher leaped to the moving train. He made it! But that complicated things even more.

"Ruin noooooo! Ruin!"
I cried out.

I really created a pickle here! Sepher was on, I was off, and Ruin was next to jump! Without having time to think it out any further, I dropped my backpack and ran towards her screaming…

"Jump Seph! Don't Sara!
Jump Seph! Don't Sara!"

Sepher looked really confused, but I didn't stop to explain as I raced towards Ruin!

"Sara Please! Hear me!"
I screamed,
"Sara! Ruin! Don't!"

Standing on the edge of the bucket, timing her hop, just as we did, she was preparing to jump! And that was the first time, in a sober minute, where time went slow motion… Her arms opened and closed like an accordion. Then, she extended her arms to grab onto the train… when my yoga-mind-whammy connected with her! She noticed me. I nodded my head no. Confused, but getting the message, she aborted.

Back in real time the train raced forward as Ruin climbed down, and Sepher walked up behind me. I stood there with my camp safe, but defeated once again, in Worcester.

.

Later that night we finally went to the other side of the yard to try and hop out over there. We should have tried it days ago, but the "crew change" led us to that initial spot. But it wasn't going to work unless you wanted to "catch on the fly", which I scrubbed after my attempt. Never again!

From the beginning of our efforts to hop out, I was the one scouting the trains in the yards. I would sneak around to search out "units" on the front end, and "F.R.E.D.'s" on the back. It was just necessary, and I had the energy, so I didn't think to ask Sepher or Ruin to ever do it. But they didn't see what I was doing as thoughtful, or necessary.

"Why are you always
running around Braze?"
Sara asked.

"You're taking unnecessary risks!"
Sepher added

"We have to confirm it's the right train,"
I said in defense.

But whatever patience they had with me thus far, had come to a boil. But I was just as frustrated!

"You're gonna get us all caught Braze!"
Seph yelled.

"Yeah Mes.
You suck at waiting,"
Ruin added.

My posse turned their guns on me. I knew nothing of Revolt at this point in my life, other than he was a founding artist in the New York Subway graffiti movement in the 1970's. Other than on the dance floor no one ever really challenged me! So I lost it on these two modern ass hippies…

"I'm gettin' things done,
while ya'll sit on your ass
eating granola bars!"
I queered.

"You can't make a train appear
just by looking for it,"
Seph pointed out.

"He's right Mes,"
Ruin added.

Their mutiny made me so angry! I stood up in the brush on the side of the tracks, and screamed from a dimension I've yet to chart in my mind, that…

"I assure you.
The more I chase anything,
the realer it gets!"

I was serious, and they knew it. But instead of understanding me, they blew off my quantum explanation for racing around the yards, and together, they continue with an intellectual analysis of my behavior that attacked my character. Finally, out brain powered by them both, I blurted out…

"You… granola-heads!
I don't wanna be a granola-head!"

If someone gave me this kind of beef prior to this conflict, I would have cracked them over the head with something in reach… beer bottle, mug, a bar stool. But I knew I couldn't do that with these nice people. Instead, I listened to them and stayed in my skin. I just backed up, took it on the chin, and let them laugh at me without flinching. I realized nothing I could say, or do, could fix things at that point. So I shut up. The longer I was sober, the more I had to deal in many new ways, with everything. In defense of my own emotions, I let my mind wander elsewhere…

To where for the past few days, I'd been noting in mind an alternative ending for the movie. My new idea involved chase scenes on foot between Mes & Ruin! With smooth pans and long dolly shots that were far from the hand held nature of the entire shoot leading up to this… finale! My new idea was fueled with an explosion of action, a bigger production, and some creative cuts and fades I yet knew how to create; but had in mind nonetheless. This dramatic transition was to fully expose my doc hoax and call out myself in the end that in the movie, there were no doubt scripted moments. With a full-blown choreographed scene at The End of a "documentary", no telling what the audience would think in the end. And maybe they'd watch it again! Or at least spark a conversation.

Eventually, Seph & Ruin stopped complaining long enough for me to share this whole idea with them. They listened, and watched as I expressed my idea to change not only the ending of the movie, but its location by hundreds of miles.

"I was wrong to end this story in Seattle,"
I went on to say,
"It has to come full circle
to New Orleans!"

The aftermath of Katrina still had an extreme presence in the city and to overlook the apocalyptic resources to shoot in, would be an artistic mistake.

"In the new ending…
Ruin gets locked in a
boxcar and dies!"
I declared.

Sepher and Ruin were mute. But I was all-smiles and continued…

"Kotton's ghost
will lead her to that death!
Joining them forever,
in the afterlife!"

It made gothic joy division sense to me! I couldn't understand why they didn't get it? I summed it up like this…

"It happens all the time."

But they weren't into it. The three of us sat there in the brush on the side of the tracks while crickets sex it up in the grass. Loosing again, I murmured…

"Green would understand."

Then in an attempt to shoot me down further, Ruin asked…

"How do we shoot me
hopping a moving boxcar?
And,
close the door on me?"

And without a second thought, my solution was…

"I'll rent a train."

And the crickets went on with their thing in the grass. Maybe I should have thought that through.

"Rent a train Mes?"
she chuckled.

"With what,
your food stamps Braze?"
Sepher added.

They came together on a big laugh! I joined them, Seph & Ruin were all I had. Before them I was pretty desperate and a little passionate. Now I was pretty passionate and just a little desperate. If I totally lost it at that moment, I'd be on the outs quick. I controlled my anger because I didn't want to start all over, once again. And besides, how pushy could I be only paying them the small food per diem I was to go the distance with me on the rails? I just had to move forward no matter what crap I had to eat. As my teeth grinded with anger within my smile… our train finally pulled up slowly on the track behind me, and stopped! I dropped the conversation. A train came to my rescue!

THE HIGH LINE

Slow but strong as a Glacier
I gained my composure in Nature

We hid on that train for an hour or so in Worcester waiting for it to roll. When it did and we moved towards The High Line… my anger, fears and bleeding emotions, gave way to another outlaw train ride. A high one can't purchase. As we picked up speed on the rails, under the radar, free riding through all my issues, I felt a rush you can't jar and sniff in a john. A simple rush to the head does not compare to such power beneath your feet and oxygen in your face! I felt as if I was racing from my problems like a locomotive and becoming… Supersoberman! Or, pink clouding perhaps.

Creatures of comfort stay close to the milk that feeds them. For me, comfort was always at a cop corner. But on the trains it was just down the tracks! The difference between rolling to the corner to settle issues, and a journey down the tracks, is that constantly turning corners brings you in circles. The rails are one way, forward! I was a victim of my own life for some time before I became an adventurer to it on the rails. Everything was almost perfect out there. I know that feeling quite well, and how fleeting it had been in the past.

BRIGHTDAWN

As the train rolled on, I found myself a character on a page of an unfolding story. Chaptered with small towns found in an atlas with clues from water towers we passed that landmarked our rolling journey.

Watching the country pass me by was the show in my focus as the rails cut through the backyards of America that brought me to such euphoric heights I couldn't help but surf through!

And sometimes we just found ourselves stopping and waiting for other trains with higher priority to pass. While other times we hid there while they did crew changes in the yards, or in them being pushed back and forth as they built trains. And despite the hassle Seph & Ruin gave me in Massachusetts… I found myself still running to the back of the train during those long stops in the yard to check on the F.R.E D. at the rear! Once, pressing my luck out there in a yard, I had to catch a ride on the fly as the train rolled off when I was on one of those scouting runs. I lost a good paper hat on that hop when I climbed down the side of ten or so container cars to get back to the bucket where my backpack sat. It was a sweet paper hat too! Stumps duh Clown loved that hat. But I still had my Gucci glasses, of which Stumps could care less about. He's an old timey hobo who gave up the butt flap long ago. I was more, I'd say, a… metro-hobo-sexual.

Nonetheless, now hatless… Ruin, Sepher and I got back on track with the rhythm of the rails as the steel wheels electrified our enthusiasm over rolling stones below as I kept on shooting like a rockstar!

In this countryside, as on the moon, you just had to point and shoot to capture the moment. But what I experienced across our heartland was not as natural as that of the eye of Ansel Adams whatsoever. But a land of funk, folk and blues on a temporary, coal birthed, electric-grid with Rockstar Americans going out on the world's stage in a blaze of glory! I came to suspect out there that humanity is a terminal condition the planet must have acquired recently. Seph, Ruin and I ruffled like cancer cells with contagious containers in the arteries of the railway on the surface of what we call, The Earth. Some can read about it to get the message, others like me have to hop trains and make decades of mistakes before the gravity of the situation can sink in; as my overpriced exploited labor silk scarf blew off in the wind.

Across the country we passed busy intersections with occupied parked cars and dazed pedestrians who never seemed to notice me with my camera. I felt as if I was an alien on a UFO making a movie in the wild for the friends back home on a neighboring goldilocks rock. And later that night, in my mind, as we entered The Chicago Barr Yard… Saturn glowed and eclipsed the moon as Montana spray paint dripped from her rings in an aerosol art production.

Once parked in the yard, I climbed from the train like any other street artist from a crime, sneaky. Trying to find your way out of that huge train yard at night was like being on a football field while trains play flashlight tag while lugging a backpack! Ruin was the smart one; her pack was as lite as a teddy bear while mine was as heavy as a keg of beer. She found time to meditate on the trains, and packed like a pro, while Sepher and I always struggled to lug our weight and not be pissed off at each other along the way. And we were the ones bringing her along? I duh-know. As I struggled out there just to make sense of my life in this journal, Ruin made everything appear very easy! But I wasn't using over it, I was just jealous.

Later, when we emerged from the Barr Yard and into the Ghetto, as often happens when exiting a yard; we came across a cheap hotel.

BOOK SAFE

"Wanna shower?"
I asked the road dogs,
"I'll cover it."

There were no arguments. Yet they were too proud to celebrate by giving in to the luxury. They just rolled with my idea. Riding a train differentiates most from a gutter punk and a house punk, but I think we all missed our homes so much that we broke our vowel of homelessness, in silence. We showered and went to bed without so much as a peep. But my guess is that Mark Singer didn't spend every DARK DAY in the Freedom Tunnel.

The next day we took an el train downtown and bummed around Chicago's China Town. After lunch at a Chinese joint we went across the street and picked up the script to shoot some picture. But Seph & Ruin were in much too good a mood to shoot the darker story I was trying to paint. During every take they were laughing and smiling, not looking the least bit concerned about our missing person, Ruin's boyfriend, Kotton! And all the suggestions I made to curb their carefree enthusiasm, fell on deaf ears. Finally I just had to surrender the day to them when the story I wrote had improved into a political conversation that brought on combustible laughter at just mention of the name… Colin Powell. I got the impression they were giving up on my story. And I felt as though they were laughing at me, and the movie! Maybe they were at that point. I duh-know, but my self-control was tested again. I just reminded myself that whatever I'm feeling is in my head, and not in the world. I rolled with it. They just kept laughing. And that was the last shower and an MSG buffet for them.

"I'll get what I need,"
I murmured,
"just not today."

You can't move mountains with food stamps, only people at Wal-Mart. My talent was in charge out there and I had to roll with them. In Chicago, I gave up trying to shoot the script entirely. I told them I was going to shoot scenes in Seattle and cheat all the locations in the edits. Other than that, I was just going to get camping and train ride coverage of us along the way. I downsized the entire shoot because I wasn't getting what I wanted, and felt I was in no place to be insistent. I let it all go and rolled with it because I was a first time producer with a little script who paid his talent $15.00 a day while hopping trains homeless across the country. How much more could I ask of them? I had no room to get pushy out there. I think it was the little bit of time I spent in LA that I caught this passive aggressive approach to getting what I wanted.

On our second night in Chicago, two out of three of us dragged our big packs through the city streets once again, as Ruin made traveling look effortless. With no place to go, we decided to set out for "The Beach" by the lake to camp. And just as we did so, we crossed the radar of some Guy and a Lady sharing a bottle of wine on a brownstone stoop. I made eye contact with him and asked…

"Is this the right way to the beach?"

"Yeah, but it's a walk."
he said, and continued…
"Where you coming from with those packs?"

"We're riding freight trains.
I'm making a movie about it."
I said nonchalantly.

"How do you finance something like that?"
he asked me.

"I'm selling graffiti watercolors on the road.
Are you a collector?"

And then from my journal in hand, I pulled out a few watercolors and offered the pieces over to him to take a look. Ruin snickered, but the Guy looked at them. I wrote selling watercolors into the script in part to give some character development to Mr. Mes, but not to actually fund our travels. We were living off my money I made from selling my car back in NOLA. But I was so into shooting this movie; I often believed what I wrote in the script myself. I got the watercolor hustle from Neb and set up in New York and Chicago in the afternoons.

I decided being in it, was the only way for me to act it out. Some go to class to study Stanislavsky, in this project, I just gave up acting all together.

"Hopping trains, making movies,
selling graffiti… you're a renaissance man."
he laughed.

"A pseudo-hobo."
I responded.

I stayed in full on MES mode. The couple drinking wine laughed, while Ruin was somewhat charmed I think.

"Where does this talk of his
come from Sepher?"

But I had a prospect there, interested in my watercolors, which took president over flirting with Sara.

"So,"
I continued,
"I work on a sliding scale.
I ask 10,15 or 20 dollars for each piece.
Whatever you can afford."

"I can't decide. I like them all."
he said.

But he wasn't going in his pocket yet. Instead of being pushy, which was what it seemed my dogs expected; I just played it cool…

"Well my buddy,
just let me know what can I do,
to help you make a decision."
I said with a charm.

Ruin shook her head in disbelief. Sepher wasn't surprised at all. Then the guy made a decision.

"I like these three.
I'll give you forty."

Then he handed me a fifty.

"Take all five for fifty.
Thanks! My pleasure."

Then I looked over to Sara and raised my eyebrow to tickle her as she stood there with her mouth open, shaking her head. And then we all talked a little more about train hopping, which was included with every purchase. Then, after our train talk was exhausted, he asked…

"Why are you going to the beach?"

"To camp."
I responded.

"That's not a good idea."
he informed us,
"They patrol the beach."

It was late, our bags weighed us down, and I didn't have a plan B. I looked over to Seph & Ruin as I thought of finding us a rooftop somewhere. Then my collector there made me an offer…

"If you teach my kids how to paint like
this at breakfast,
you can stay in my basement
while you're in town."

"Sure, that's easy! But are
you sure about this man?"

I mean… I can't imagine that we looked like good houseguests. None that my Mom would have over!

"My wife will love it,"
he giggled,
"She's a hippy!"

I looked over at my camp, shrugged my shoulders, and it appeared we where all open to his offer. And it was obvious to me, that the woman he was having wine with on the stoop wasn't his "Hippy Wife". So I cleared the air.

"This sound great man! Thank you.
I said gratefully,
But just so we're all on the same page
when we're eating breakfast tomorrow…
does your wife,
know about this lovely business woman
your having wine with tonight?"

"Ahwwww, you're sweet,"
she said softly.

"Not really."
Ruin added.

"No need to fight over
my hobo-sexuality ladies."

Moments later, I found myself in the front seat of his AUDI. His bucket seat nearly put me to sleep after a long summers day in the beginning of July in Chicago where my toes began to overlap each other halfway across North America. I was making the trek in a pair of old shell top suede Pumas.

The next morning I woke up in the "basement" of our host's house; a finished downstairs apartment with an entertainment center, full bath, and a back door for us to come and go as we please. As always, I woke before Seph & Ruin. So I found my way upstairs to the kitchen where the family was eating breakfast and I was introduced to the kids. After some cereal, I schooled them.

"Ok kido's.
I'm Mr. Mes!
And the coolest thing
about graffiti is…
You get to name yourself!"

They liked that a lot!

"But you want to be very careful
picking a good name,"
I continued,
"You just may grow
into the name you choose."

As I gathered my watercolor supplies, I let the kids discuss, look at the person in them, and pick a handle, while halfway across the country I felt the High Line indeed. Not just because a stranger opened his door for me, yet because it seemed every wrong turn eventually opened to the right one. Redirecting me on a road that seemed paved for me, or I was paving, depending on my mood. Then one of the little squirts pulled on the fabric of my shirt, to gain my consciousness.

"I can't think of a name.
You name me Mr. MES!"

"How's bout… Kid Kismet!"
I suggested.

"Kismet!"
he screamed,
"I like that!
What does it mean?"

"Fate."
I schooled.

"What's fate?"

"Something nobody can beat."

"Wow!"
he roared
"I'm Kid Kismet!"

BOOK SAFE

I understand how out of control my life is and that people like me are always looking for signs to make meaning of it. But signs of destiny seem to surface often during my laps around our local star. The camera that broke in Baltimore was just another brick in that path. I took that occurrence at the time, as even more than a sign, but an intervention. By whom or what, I know too much to thank. My temporal understanding of kismet is a spiritual concept, and maybe just a symptom of my obsessions; I won't argue that. And my suspicions of the power of my own idea's, dreams and intentions are even more outside the realm of what most people think possible. But I can tell you at that point, whatever it was at work in my life, had my attention, or depending upon my mood; was distracting me. …I was a moody man! And boy did those drugs regulate things at times.

For a short week we stayed there with our hosts and made our way downtown on The EL every day after I gave the kids a graffiti lesson in the morning. Now in my fifth city via freights, and halfway across the country I remind you, I had little accomplished from my movie script. Other than breaking the camera. Though I did have some train ride coverage, I had no idea how it looked! I refused to play back the tapes on my camera because I feared accidently taping over the footage. By forcing myself to wait till I got back to New Orleans to digitize the work, I exercised my discipline and played it real safe; like when you're stepping on ounces with Bulavar Incense to make bundles. Which in retrospect… risking my life on a train and in the drug trade, but not messing with the DV tapes? Speaks volumes for my screwed priorities at the birth of my sobriety! Priorities that would need some adjusting if I were going to achieve all I had in mind down the road of life. When we finally decided to catch out of Chicago, I found myself still caught up in thought.

For most of my life, I was an undercover bad ass just seeing what he could get away with. And in the beginning, this entire Art of Train Hopping project was based on that. I knew I could get away with shooting a picture like this. My life was always filled with short cuts, from the start. Since the days I hustled at the neighborhood Acme in fact. I'll relive some for you now. Come back decades with me when I was The Acme Kid…

"Short cuts are cool,"
I acknowledged at five.
"The coolest thing ever!"

…I said in the wind as I pedaled as fast as I could on my Mongoose freestyle bike while I raced a Chevy Camaro RS blaring the "Ace of Spades" as the driver taunted me with the gas pedal on a long stretch next to a golf course.

"Why go around the golf course?"
I continued to myself,
"When I can just cut through on my bike!"

And off I went tearing up some green grass as the Camaro peeled off. And then there'd be times when I'd be running down the street away from some big kids.

"Why go all the way around duh block?"
I asked myself,
"When I can just hop duh fence!"

I could acrobat over a fence like an Olympian. Big kids couldn't keep up.

"Short cut suckers!"
I yelled back, with a finger.

And then came… why do my homework at night, when I can just play sick tomorrow. Why study for the test, when I can write a cheat sheet instead. Why wait till I'm old enough to get my own paper route, when I can subcontract a few blocks off a kid who already has one. Why pay for all this gold, when I can just steal it. Why just do these drugs with my friends, when I can sell it to them. Why sell it myself, when I can pay some of them twenty-five bucks out of every hundred to do it for me. Why pay full price for the car stereo, when I can buy a hot one. Why use all this money I'm making just to give it back to my drug connects, when I can buy counterfeit bills to re-up with. Why admit I'm a piece of shit, when I can play one in a movie and sell it to keep my stomach full. Instead of growing out of it all, I somehow seemed to grow into it like Cobain buying his wardrobe at Sunday swap meet.

On the road with Sepher & Ruin I couldn't implement my usual short cuts as I had for decades leading up to The Art of Train Hopping; I had to adjust. And I think the only reason I could, was because I was far away from the streets & drugs that had fueled the gusto of my ego. Some people drink and drug to get comfortable. But I had to get comfortable to drink or drug! So getting high on the road while carrying all my gear and rolling with non-users made things way too uncomfortable for me to get twisted out there. It was both a physical and emotional detox I unwittingly created for myself! And in the process, forced me to grow because I just couldn't find a short cut. I was out there on the rails in the middle of the country equally as far from everything I knew in every direction… mind, body and spirit, when I realized *the rails became my rehab*. When I was not on the pink cloud of a train, I often felt the weight of the world on my shoulders. But this time, I didn't think to kill myself. I still had a hustle at work through wanting something in life, and going for it! The game just changed.

In perusing the project, I created my own intervention and imprisoned my inner junky. And the weird part was I felt, that this was truly not my doing! What I perceived as good luck, and bad luck, had my undivided attention at times, enough for me to get to the other side of everyday thoughts on it. I realized on this movie shoot that I could not be in full control all the time, and was happy when it appeared I was. I settle on a basic understanding that this is the balance we all strive for everyday. But when all you want is a drug, or a drink, and you get it day in, and day out. It makes you feel that in fact your in full control of something. And if that something is really all you want… fulfillment, no matter how fleeting, is yours! That's what makes it really hard to walk away from. Not to mention the physiological circles and physical addiction people endure before they find a cure. There's only two ways out of this kind of trouble… If you're simpleminded, surrender. If you're daring, dream bigger! It will all be over in time and I'll meet you at the finish line so in the meantime, believe in kismet, live fulfilled but don't die to prove it. I suggest you do like Wham, Welsh and Myself… choose life, this, that and whiffle ball bat; keep swinging! When some truth reveals itself you won't kill yourself. Just believing in belief can be a good thing in itself, and optimism creates a higher chance of successful recovery; studies show.

So as my mind seemed to get back on track, the keys that struck the chords on my piano of emotions challenged me. I knew the deep anger key at one end as well as I knew the very high and often racing key at the other end, but trying to make music and enjoy all the other notes in between them was a horrible endeavor on the rails; as is in any other rehab I'd imagine. I realized out there, that my childhood hustling days should have been over long ago. And because they weren't, I was very unsettled inside, and wanted to make progress over night! In the beginning of your recovery, no matter how hard you work at first, if you're still reminded of your problem by stiches, an ankle monitor, crack lips, etc., etc., don't expect too much too soon. For me, my burden seemed to be the emotional piano I was ill equip to play. And rather than backing up, getting lessons, and having it tuned, I continued to alternate between the two keys I knew, and hide from the rest, just as I always did. But at least I knew what I didn't know; most don't. To mature, I needed to learn how to play this complex instrument, the piano of emotions. But where do I learn how to play it? And what in fact are the names, chemicals, and energy origins of each emotion that make up the keys that trouble me so? Sometimes, I wish I never took this leap. It too appears bottomless.

On the rails, beats transitioned with the steel wheels beneath my feet as other notes of my emotions became clear, and evident to me for the first time. Familiar with Joy, Depression and Anger… shades of Sadness, Disgust, Anticipation, Trust, Surprise and Remorse surfaced and could be identified, embraced and let go in the wind like never before, and oh how I knew there was so much more ahead! In the meantime, the awareness of these new keys (new to me) gave me much to work with. I wanted to learn how to play them better! And if I could…

"I'd be happier,"
I murmured.

How I made it this far so reckless and out of tune, is beyond me! But I knew contemplating these thoughts on the road while shooting a movie, was sure better than writing a book in jail about it all. I found myself thinking about how to thoughtfully react to situations for the first time, while working with Matt & Sara. And I came to believe the best I could do, was often, just not make it worse! But holding it all in would create bigger problems down the road, though at the time it worked as a tourniquet for my anger. Deep breaths cooled my stew as I reflected while we prepared for the rails once again. I needed another train to ride to get out of my head, and Chicago!

We had a head start on vagabond technology with our phones, laptop and cameras in 2006. From public transportation to tracking trains and ducking the rain, the phones and our trusted hard copy crew change provided all we needed to make decisions from coast to coast. There was not a question in the universe Sepher's cell phones didn't have an answer for as we departure Chicago. After we mass transited to a location across town to hop out of, we quickly made our way to a moving train and rolled out of the light pollution of the big city, and into some real country dark under diffused moonlight from the clouds between us.

I find cities lights touch my bones and pulses through me in the evening, keeping me awake. When I reached the city limits, and further past the suburbs, flashing red lights at the small town intersections are not enough to keep me going out there in the country. So I hung the hammock in my bucket and swung myself to sleep as my double stack moved forward though a brisk dark North American chill.

BRIGHTDAWN

When I woke at dawn, I was back to work with my camera in hand and my dolly beneath my feet moving at 60 miles per hour. Pictures raced bye and the wind stole my face as my skull came to surface in morning paradise on the rails like a deadhead showering in the sun after a long night out on a limb.

"Who knows better but them?"
I murmured.

I just had to point and shoot to capture the story. My only rule when shooting on the rails was to get a piece of the train in the frame while I danced to her beats beneath my feet.

I made it more than halfway across the country on my 6th train shooting my outlaw movie with no troubles from the law. Before I got cocky and decided to scale the side of a double stack from the back to front, on the side of it, tiptoeing on top of the three-inch thick steel wall that held the containers in place on the train, that raced at full speed. Overconfident, taking a tumble never came to mind, nor being spotted in broad daylight.

Hoping for the best I could get, I strapped my camera on my back and recorded video as my open hands and thin body grazed the container as it raced forward. My body and feet carefully inched ahead because my eyes told it so. It was like surfing a steel two by four, knees slightly bent to absorb the occasional shock from the repeating, but unforeseen, moments of thrust from the tracks below.

As I danced like a devil with the double stack, friendly with the wind that blew in my hair, and met every little dip beneath my feet with a smile as if I knew it was coming from my partner. I was into the groove the entire way, walking forward in the wind on a very thin long board riding a mighty wave across an ocean with BMW land sharks at my back.

High on my own adolescent ego, I made it to the front bucket just as I expected! Then I did a little jig in it like a spin-doctor to celebrate, before I started back up the other side of the container with the guts of Evil Knievel and the discipline of French parkourist. On my way I passed a few intersections as we rolled through a small town and wondered what the faces of the drivers at each intersection must have looked like when they noticed me walking up the side of a speeding locomotive with my camera strapped on my back, Or, if they noticed me at all? Hobo's are like UFO's. Some see them, others don't notice. When I returned, Ruin was meditating in the bucket, and Sepher was just waking up…

"What were you just doing?"
Seph asked paranoid.

And with that, the train began to slow and enter a yard on the other side of the small town I was surfing through. Before I ducked, a dick in a white truck noticed me! He continued to shadow the train car on a dirt road next to our tracks. I immediately hid in the bucket, but it was too late. It appeared that he didn't want to loose track of what car he noticed me on.

"He spotted us!"
I told Seph.

"You!
He spotted you!"

"What do we do Braze?"
asked Ruin.

"Gather your gear Sara.
It's about to go…
Emperor of the North!"

As the train slowed down, I noticed the white truck continue to keep pace with the bucket we were hiding in. The bull kept an eye on our car as I scrambled to put my camera away. When train stopped, Ruin asked…

"Should we run?"

"Like Carl Fuckin' Lewis!"

But before I could swing my bag over my shoulder, the Bull was climbing on our car, screaming…

"Let me see your hands, now!"

…And pointed a gun at us! It was over.

As we climbed down from the train, four Bulls surrounding us with their guns drawn. And though we all had backpacks on, they zeroed in on the one piece of luggage that was most important to me.

"What's in the steel case?"
Asked the Bull who looked like a marine.

"My camera, sir."

"Am I going to find a weapon in there?"
he asked me.

"Weapon? No sir! I'm just a film student
making a video."

"About what?"

"Dangers of train hopping."

"Who has the firearm?"
he asked.

"We have no weapons."
said the three of us, all together.

But I wanted to keep the conversation between he and I, and said as much to Ruin & Sepher, with a glance. If they split us up, they may get different stories from all of us. And that would complicate things.

"We have a witness says differently."

"Witness? I doubt it."
I responded.

"Someone called in…
a man on the side of a train
caring a machine gun on his back."

Then I thought of myself scaling the container car through that small town with the camera strapped on my back, rolling through intersections by parked cars waiting at the crossings. I knew then what happened as these guys looked through my camera case, and all our packs. Seph and Ruin looked worried, and angry. They knew that my stunt stopped the train.

The Bulls didn't find any weapons of course, and once the air was cleared… I thought they might let us go. But then one of them made a phone call, and was told…

"Office said to turn them over.
They're on their way now."

"What are they going to do with us?"
I asked 'um.

"That's up to them."

Soon enough, our train continued on without us just as the cop showed up; my stunt was leading us to jail. I felt so stupid! But I did so much wrong shit in my life, riding trains never seemed like much of a crime. In my mind, they were a ride to redemption! And at that point, whatever I could say, couldn't make things any better, but worse. So I didn't say a word. The Galesburg police officer immediately said…

"I need all your ID's."

He went to run them, and we continued to stand with with bulls while the officer did the background checks. It was much more relaxed now that we were cleared of carrying any weapons. And I began to hope that we'd just get a ticket for trespassing!.

"How long have you been doing this for?"
I asked the bull.

"Nine months.
I'm retired military."

"See much action in this yard?"

"You're the first hobo's
I pulled off a train."

Then officer came back with our ID's and announced to the bulls.

"No warrants, no attachments."

And then told us to…

"Put all your gear in my trunk.
And get in"

Inside the police car, Sepher sat next to me as Ruin was in the front seat while we rolled through a soy farm I think.

"Do you bums have money for a bus?"
asked the officer.

"Yes sir."

Then, the nice old cop dropped us off at the bus station. It couldn't have worked out any better! When he let us out of the patrol car, he wished us…

"Good luck."

"Thank you officer!"
I said with relief.

A soon as the fuzz rolled, I got back in Producer Mode and quickly brought up to Sepher & Ruin that a bus ride from here, wasn't in the script! Nor bus fares in the budget. So I told 'um…

"We can hitch a ride."

"Where is hitch hiking in the script Mes?"

"Why you gotta be a smart ass Ruin?"

She blew me off. Sepher looked over the crew change. Then he pointed out…

"If we get to the highway,
we can hitch to the next yard."

"Exactly,"
I agreed,
"Lets do it!"

But in reality, it's nearly impossible for three travelers to get one ride with big backpacks. While they were trying to figure out who was going with whom, I notice a Good Ol Boy in a pickup truck waiting on someone, and asked 'um….

"Heading west man?"

"Yea-up."

"You got room in the back for us?"

He measured us up, and then looked to his old Lady.

"Please sir,"
and then I shifted focus to her,
"We're just trying to
get on the highway mam."

They were cool, and people of few words who dropped us off a few exits over. There, we split up and caught other rides. Sepher & Ruin rolled together I went solo.

I found hitching for the first time that it took me a long while to get anywhere, because each ride only took me an exit or two down the highway. By nightfall, I decided to camp next to a truck stop where I found a couple trees and some tall grass to hide in. It looked like a small oasis. I walked through the tall grass and hung my hammock between the only two trees in the middle of it all. Then, I jumped in the hammock to catch a wink. The hammock stretched down to about a foot or so over the ground, with grass maybe four feet high over my head. It was great cover from the road and truck stop! But when I closed my eyes, I couldn't count sheep, because all I heard was hissing. Immediately, I acknowledged the possibility of snakes! Snakes French kissing my ears and slithered down my shorts between the cheeks of my skinny white ass.

"Snakes? SNAKES!"

The paranoid feelings I had during the endless nights riding high on cocaine, resurfaced in my hammock the moment the tall grass tickled my ear. I was sober, but petrified with symptoms of years past.

But unlike those occasions in Philly, when I couldn't run from where I was because I was just too paranoid up to move… I was straight now and able to jet with the quickness! So I slung shot from the hammock and ran out of the tall grass swatting at myself and screaming with the passion and urgency of Richard Pryor on fire! After I put the flames out, I then looked around, confused and paranoid like a…

"Stupid ass!"

And though I was alone out there, my heart continued to race with flashbacks of me running down that street high on acid, cocaine and bloody youth. I began to hyperventilate, shake and twitched violently. And I knew, it was all in my head,

"Stop it!
STOP IT! STOP!"

Then, I heard her say…

"Why Braze?
Why!"

Mom's cries echoed through my paralyzed body as my head shook demonically! One hand with a fist full of hair, the other held my dick to protect it from the snakebite of a catheter! Then, my spirit left me below and aborted this troubled vessele of mine. I was freaking out down there… And I really don't know why?

"I don't know! I don't know why!
STOP! STOP IT!"
I screamed like a lunatic.

I couldn't stop this paranoid jones in my bones! And once again, I was run over by emotions to the point I was a tortured victim of them.

With that point of view from a few feet over my head still available to me, I continued to watch myself act mindless below… just a brain that was regurgitating data and creating an episode out of a horror picture. I was told in Mexico once by a rock guitarist named Alex from The Baha, that he thought there was some sort of separation between my mind and spirit that he found special, and readily available to me. He then handed me an old paperback and said…

"I think you should read this."
I read the cover aloud and thanked him.

"The Teaching of Don Juan.
…Ok.
Thank you Alex."

"That book is a treasure Braze."

And maybe it is, but I'm not open to the *Yaqui Way of Knowledge* any longer. Or, that heavy drugs can expand a mind without possible consequences. I think I've done damage to my brain, and or something is now missing up there because of my use and engaging such stories on "higher states of consciousness" I grew up living out. If you've seen what I've blown out of my nose, felt the hopelessness, and fully experienced the disconnection I have… you'd see why I can't trust what I feel! In these potholes in my brain, pop culture, flashbacks and visions accumulate like acid rain water from chemically seeded clouds. The slightest thing can create an uncontrollable ripple of suffering in these pothole puddles in my head. It's a condition that concerns my doctors, friends and even "Medicine Men" along my path. Such as the one that approached me on Frenchmen Street when I was watching a couple girls work their fire burning hula-hoops. This self proclaimed Medicine Man tried to put the zap on me! After singling me out in the crowd and introducing himself to me with his mystic charm, I tried to blow him off…

"Listen man,
I'm kinda fucked up right now."

I was just drunk and horny for one of the girls.

"You think you're fucked up now?
You really gonna fuck up!
You're going to take the leap man.
I can see it."

"So, what if I do?"
I shrugged.

"So no telling where
you're gonna end up then!"

Turned out later, the leap took me on the High Line.

As I let all these thoughts, flashbacks and emotions pass, I began to regain my composure by the side of the truck stop. When I gathered what was left of my headspace, I stood there with an open mouth and still evacuated soul. But so far it stays close enough to give me an outside perspective of my emotionally crippled self. Then I let go of my hair and my nuts…

"There are no snakes.
No catheters."
I pointed out to myself.

Then I consciously jerked the webs from my box! When my wires get crossed like that, info flashes like channels on a broken TV. Reconnecting my wires always takes a little time.

Once I shook it off, I found a picnic table far away from the tall grass and slept on top of it till the sun came up. I can't say I slept to good that night, but can say I never saw that hammock again.

The next morning I caught a long ride from a crazy trucker who agreed to bring me down to the fork in the highway near my final destination. Inside the truck, his cab was clearly as disheveled as his mind, but I find it comforting seeing others besides me just getting by sometimes. It makes me feel a little less alone with all my own… quirks.

He didn't want to talk much. In fact when I asked for the ride and explained where I needed to go, he just nodded yes. But after being on the road for maybe fifteen minutes, he spoke to me and said…

"I'm not very social."

"How long you've been driving a rig?"
I asked 'um.

"Two years."
he said,

BOOK SAFE

"I got the job when I got out of the
the mental institution."

I waited for him to laugh, but no. He was certified.
"How much time you do in there?"

"A few years.
…Ten."

And still, not even a smirk from him. Whatever his mental state was at one time to get him institutionalized, truck driving seemed like a good fit for him now. He seemed very comfortable and competent behind the wheel. Then, he went for the visor over the steering wheel. Three bottles of prescription meds fell on his lap. He opened each bottle with his teeth, and swallowed pills like he was taking a shot at the bar. Now I've done my share of pills before, but this even shocked me. Me who've bumped K from my fist behind the wheel like a rocstar DJ's between the decks. Hit crack at red lights beside cop cars like Jerry Garcia. And who blew lines with a bill in one hand, a cassette tape case in the other, and steered the driving wheel with my knee like a drug crazed Geek Love amputee following the Arturo circus act.

But in the rig with this guy… who didn't even look at the bottles from which he was swigging (I guess he didn't have to), and who opened each bottle with his teeth, and swallowed them with the enthusiasm of the Cookie Monster after counting the pills with his tongue like crack dealers in downtown LA… I met my match!

And honestly, I couldn't help but fantasize what was in all those pill bottles! And wondered if he'd share some. I thought about asking, maybe buy a few off of him… and then, without actually reaching for my cash, I began counting the money in my pocket. But, my saner head prevailed, squashing the monster.

As he put his medication back in the same spot above his head, I noticed the fork in the highway I was trying to get to. We were heading to the right of the fork; I needed to catch a ride to the left!

"This is me.
That's me over there.
I'm going that way buddy!"

And without further hesitation the truck veered left and cut over three lanes to make the fork. Despite how much this guy was medicated, and him making a move fit for a Porsche not an 18-wheeler, I felt safe in the big rig; it was everyone else on the road I was concerned about.

After he dropped me off, I set up camp in the bushes behind a supermarket where I waited on Ruin & Sepher to catch up with me; napping in a shopping kart like did when I was a kid.

Later that same day, we all reconnected and went for some food & water inside the store before going to the train yard to hop out. But even shopping takes a little management when you're on the road. A traveler can't fit down the isles with a big pack, so one of your people is usually left out front to guard the packs while the others go in to make purchases. So Ruin & Sepher went in, I sat with the packs.

Out there, it wasn't long before a soccer mom leaving the store with her daughter and some groceries caught my eye. Since I was five years old I've been connecting with people at the exits of grocery stores.

When I was a lil kid, we would ride our bikes to the local Acme and offer to carry the bags for shoppers from their carts to their cars in hopes of getting a quarter tip, sometimes two quick quarters. Other times… one slow nickel. Way back then, I would stand in the grocery store entrance and ask shoppers as they exited…

"Do you need help
with your bags mam?"

They'd often shake their head no. But I'd move on to the next person…

"Sir, can I carry your bags sir?
Can I please?"

Since then, I didn't take rejection personally. I figured out early on that the more people I approached, the more opportunity I had to make money. I never saw a NO as rejection, but rather just not interested and closer to the next YES.

Decades later I found myself at the exit of a Super Market with not much more than the loose change I had in my pocket back long ago. And this time, I wasn't trying to work a program like I was when I was a lil kid; I was just waiting on my road dogs. But I figured… what the hell!

"Good evening mam.
Can I help you with your bags?"

But her response caught me really off guard…

"You're riding the rails!"

I was perplexed for a second, but then I looked down to the three backpacks I was guarding and my filthy dirty hands. She noticed me adding this up and continued…

"You do look the part."

I felt slightly sucker punched! Along the way thus far I remind you, few care to make the slightest eye contact with me! She continued with more fervor…

"Is it fun!"

She was so eager to know, eyes wide, mouth open!

"Well, most of the time!"
I replied.

"My husband's an engineer.
Need a ride to the yard?"

I kid you not!

"Yes mam! Can my two friends
and these packs fit?"

"Nooo problem,"
she said with a smirk,
"I have a minivan!"

I looked down at her little daughter hanging on to the shopping cart Mom was pushing and thought, my Mom would never pick up a stranger!

Not that my Mom is a mean or an uncaring person, but where we come from offering a ride to a dirty guy and two of his friends, while with your little daughter, is Crazy! As well as… giving the key to your back door to a crusty crew like us to come and go as they please while the family rests upstairs, as was the case back in Chicago. That's absurd where I come from! But out there on the road, I found some of this kindness and blind trust for the first time, ever. Some call it "Road Magic".

As soon as Ruin and Sepher came out of the store, I introduced them as Sara & Matthew. Then we loaded up the minivan and drove into the country dark… Mom at the wheel, daughter in the passenger seat, transients in the back, down dark roads to an out of the way train yard. It was so freaky to me that I thought for a moment that she might be the one preparing to slash out throats! But I don't think this crossed the minds of Sepher & Ruin. All of them chatted it up, while I was scared in the back seat of the mini van with all these crazy upper middle class people! Evidently, it's some secret society or something where people don't mug each other.

When we got to the over pass where we wanted to climb down to the yard, Mom decided to go down the road a ways to a darker parking lot to let us out. She was fearless out there in Middle America! Generous too! At the drop off point she went through her groceries and packed us a bag of supplies… fruits, juices and other snacks to see us on our way.

I'll tell you now that this lady was not as naive as I had just alluded. She seemed to know me better than I knew myself at that point… a higher self, not a high one. It's not until now that I can think of it this way. Back then I thought if she knew the reckless asshole I was, she would have never!

BOOK SAFE

When we got back to the spot below the overpass, we held up there for a few hours before our train came through. When it did, we found our way on a couple double stacks with Ruin and Sepher in one, myself in the bucket across from theirs. We rode out of there just after dawn, heading west for certain but exactly where, not so sure. As we finally rolled out of Illinois, and stabbed westward through Iowa, South Dakota (I think, I felt lost.) and then into Montana to our uncertain destination ahead, time and space began to queer…

Big barns passed slowly
Like ocean liners far below an
Airplane over the sea.

Miles of tunnel stretched through XL Mountains
Like wormholes from deep forests to open ranges,
Painted rivers, endless pastures,
Cooperate farms, UFO runways,
And passed countless hills as we pushed
Northwest speeding forward!

I sat between the cars happy to breathe,
Untroubled in my journal,
Content with water and jerky,
And in awe that my outlaw ways had led to such
Freedom so far off the map!

I realized when I was a kid that going after the money made me grown up, and as an adult I found it necessary to chase. But there are so many ways to create a career for ones self, why did I ever think such low roads of mine would pan out? Maybe it was the entrepreneurs digging tunnels from Mexico that kept my low riding dreams alive. But as I became a parasite on the back of an industrial dinosaur pondering how I could spend my time more wisely, time and space out there on the edge continued to lift me with more clarity. As we rolled by Glacier Park on the trains I believe I found it all, not just there in front of me, but inside me! It felt like everything in life was in reach. I just had to choose what it was I wanted. *The rails had truly become my rehab* because out there I had nothing to hide, no image to up hold, no status to chase; I was free! Sure I felt the pressure of the project, but that gave me something harmless to chase. And I knew my joy found on the trains would come to an end, but I was determined to find a *cure for my crash* once the ride was over. In the meantime, I felt I was healing.

Rolling forward, I always found myself the observer as I watched Sepher & Ruin commit themselves to the rails. My big idea of a train-hopping movie had initiated the journey, but these two souls stayed in the project not because of my script, but for all the unscripted moments in between.

We began debating which city we would hit on the West Coast. I was banking on Seattle because that's what I envisioned in the story, but Seph pointed out that Spokane was a good possibility while Ruin could have used a bathroom and other resources in either city; she began to fold up TP squares on the regular. She was real strong out there and much too proud to ever complain. Not to mention bold enough to hang off the side of the train, as if it were a boat, and piss off the side at sixty when she had to! When I pointed the camera at her while she was in the middle of "the act", she shook her head and smiled…

"Mes,
what are you doing?"

"Workin!"
I yelled over.

"But you're shooting
picture of me

going to the bathroom!"

She did all her own stunts! I turned the camera off and passed her some toilet paper, but she preferred to air dry.

It was hours later in the afternoon, when I decided to once again look at the world through the camera at 24 frames per second. The environment cried out with winds smacking the microphone as tape rolled and found the Earth patched with greens, browns and gold of a midsummers cooked land. It was so perfect I just sat the camera down on the edge of the bucket, out of my hand on the edge of the train all by itself, and just let picture roll as we "dollied" forward. My heart was filled with fresh ideas as my face blistered in the sun. I felt freedoms out there I can't write into a script. I found a land that birthed a name long before I began making one for myself! As my third eye protracted, I wrote these experiences down in my journal very, very slowly, at 60 miles per hour. Out there in the present, I became what I wrote in the past, as was my intension. Hopping trains was the leap that the Frenchman Street Medicine Man foresaw in me; if indeed he saw anything. Power exists in their vagueness. Nonetheless, I concurred with him…

"No telling
where I'm heading."

As my third eye was detached with wings above me like a Von Dutch illustration on an early 1980's subway car, euphoria pulsed inside me with the slow flow of Rakim and a twist of Mac Miller. Then, abruptly with a crashing force, my inner lyricist was choked with panic when the lead-unit pulling us down the tracks found its way in front of my camera! Our train was in U-turn? …U-turn!

"Oh my gosh!"

My five-year-old self stood at my side looking up at me with some youthful excitement that only he could muster. Together, we had a moment neither one could have ever imagined! My Von Dutch spirit flew home as my bliss bent with the train. Because just in front of us… the train continued U-turning!

"She's…
comin' round the mountain,
here she comes,"
my lil self sang.

"I see that!"
I told um.

I was split in two but holding it together as our train did a 180 and the front end of it became parallel to the back end we were on! I picked up the camera from the edge of the bucket, rolling picture, and began to capture the turn as it pulled us… round the mountain! When we hit that bending point, the full immensity of the train hit me even harder. We were speechless, Seph and Ruin too, as if being present in outer space for the first time. To my left, and my right, was train! We were smack in the middle of it all, where it looked like for a brief moment that we were part of train infinity! Once again, I was left with a frozen Jack Nicholson face in the hedge maze!

My mind remixes that event often with heavenly planets and man made satellites floating with the gold sunlight above. As if H.R Giger & Dali dusted an Ansel Adams photo. It's an industrial, surreal and organic mash up in my memory. None of which I could ever recall the truth of, but only a true message from memories of a grandest fulfillment. West of Glacier, within my own fiction, truth revealed itself and I forgot I wanted to ever kill myself.

After we hugged that big bend, the lead-unit straightened us out and brought us over the Flathead River. Everything seemed so perfect for a stretch. And maybe it was…

The sun was bold and bright,
But was falling after 5 o'clock.
I sat high but sober between double stacks.

River at my front,
High cliffs on my back,
Camera interlaced to my arm,
Wires recklessly sparked in the wind as they
Overcame my veins…
Bleeding arteries soldered,
As I became a cyborg!

If I had tried to stop using the camera,
I'd have bled to death.

The 24P, became me!

In between the cars in the middle of the danger, I was right where I needed to be… life, history and endless space for as far as my mind could chase. And my cohorts Ruin and Sepher took it in just as I. We all shut up and watched!

Focused on eternity, my body vibrated on the racing train as I lost myself in the royal blue sky. When I reconnected with time, Ruin had her goggles on and her back to a container as I picked her up on video.

Sepher stood next to her with his still camera taking some shots between personal moments. I remember their long hair brushing their smiles on their crusty sunburned faces.

I felt at that moment just as I had years before on certain dance floors, like a beautiful person with beautiful people. Out there I surfaced again… happy, euphoric and dancing to the rhythm of the rails. And when I thought of the dance floor I was on… I wondered where my brother was and wished he were out there on this edge with me. It had been too long since we shared some outlier joys of any kind. …Later, I'd find out while I was out there on the trains trying to fail my way to the top, Richy was home burning through some of his hard earned, high-risk savings. What I didn't realize then was that he was on the same downward spiral I was years before. But I didn't see it because he was better at hiding his problems than I. And was better with money at one time than I'll ever be.

Yet far out there as we crossed Idaho and entered Washington State rushing on the rails, I wasn't depressed, jonesin' or ever hung over. I was in the world enjoying myself with two other people in the same pure, uncut moment. It was beautiful! Could my dreams be my new drug? Hardly. The drinking and the drugs trained my brain to get comfort in a matter of seconds. Perusing my dreams took much more time to materialize in life than that of the buzz from taking a bump. But I was very high in these moments I'm describing on these pages, just as I was playing basketball or tagging a brick wall when I was a kid. But like running ball and developing my graffiti hand as a youngster, storytelling as an adult took too much work and consistency that I was unaccustomed to after getting high on drugs for so long. It's safe to say I confused suffering with hard work over the years. For too long, the hardest part of my days was working off a hangover. And for me, I didn't find that the building blocks of an efficient day of writing, as those I'd admired reading sometimes. I let Bukowski's hangovers and Carol's horseplay mislead me! I always envied all those who could get high and function on some level. I thought by living like them, I could one day write like um'. But today I don't think my perception of them, was actually their reality. But during the years when I admired those writers and related so well to all their stories, I was creating my own. When I woke up on the rails from a lifetime of hangovers, I hopped a boxcar filled with a handful of my own stories. The challenge then, became revising them all. But the titles come easy.

As we continued our ride through Washington State, night fell as we crossed a few trestles into the cold night. Their one hundred dollar sleeping bits, cheap hammocks, and bedrolls helped Ruin & Seph sleep, while my hammock slept with the snakes in the tall grass many States behind me.

The next day, as I unzipped the sack from over my head in the morning, I was greeted with the fog of my breath when it hit the cold air. Then, I noticed the coastline!

"We made it!"

It was a beautiful but frigid morning when I felt the first sense of accomplishment I'd had in years. A gratification found at a finish line not in a deal or a purchase of any kind. But a joy felt from adventure and not just a rush from a risk. It was something very new to me.

As the train crust put another layer on my life experience, the changing landscapes out there had me forget about the scars of my dirty past that filled my journals. I stood there on the backside of a 48, coast to coast, feeling it all on life's terms, shooting my picture all the while. Within the many self-curing highs and crashing lows I'd come to know, organic good moments for a guy like me are rare. Before these train rides, every good time was coupled with substance abuse. But at the end of our ride and as we got closer to the heart of Seattle, it was obvious that I was on a better path than pursuing the compulsions of instant gratifications in the Philly Bad Lands.

As our ride began to slow and we tunneled through the city near the Space Needle, we cut through downtown. When Seph and Ruin finally woke up, my camera found them with the sun behind overcast skies in a white washed New Orleans Grey Ghost graffiti sky. Dreary days such as those are my comfort zone.

After shedding her big blue sleeping bag, Ruin put on her black leather coat, and Seph his grumpy morning face, before we began to gather our gear and hop off the now parking train. After we rolled from the downtown area and landed on the outskirts somewhere, the boxcar yogi Ruin was the first one off. She could climb off a train and roll a cigarette at the same time. Sepher was next to touch down and step from the steel ladder. Once he was off, I motioned over to him to take the rolling camera from my hand and get the coverage of me climbing off too. But as I handed the camera off to Seph, the parked train jerked backwards, nearly knocking the camera from our grip. It was back moving again! So I had to move quickly with my gear. The ladder was on the front side of the double stack behind me, so I had to walk to the other side before climbing off. Usually, the walk between cars is a breeze, but with my 80 pound pack and the steel camera case in hand, I took it slow as the train picked up speed. Once I made it across to the other car, I made my way down the ladder with the camera case in the other hand as the train rolled away from Sepher shooting me.

The touchdown was pleasant and peaceful when my feet came from the train and hit the ground. And with that, my escape from reality while on the rails, ended. At that moment I felt as if I were a kid again, walking from the Wildwood Boardwalk after a long night of rides with my little brother. It couldn't get any better than that!

As I made my way towards Sepher, he was shooting my departure from the moving train with a shaky hand on the camera during his walk towards me. It was as if he didn't want to shoot me hopping off at all! Or, maybe it was just another moment he wanted to keep as just ours, and not everyone else's. He's a humble guy who became a good friend and a strong partner along our journey across the country. Ruin was just as strong a component to the shoot as he, but she was always a little closer to him than I. Maybe it was my lack of personal hygiene on the rails; I never got used to that. I'd think of Green sniffing me when I smelled the worst, and responding…

"Aaahhhh… Home."

BOOK SAFE

…Like she did when traveler kids passed her bye in Philly when she was off the road, waiting tables, and getting clean. She was simply comforted by the harsh body odors of others. What can I say?

As Seph and Ruin caught a smoke on solid land again… I felt signs from centuries inside me as Stumps duh Clown sung from Troubles from somewhere with Huddie Ledbetter's guitar. Then I took out my journal and wrote over the background music in my head, that…

My heart punctures through my skin
As the lips of an Edison cylinder phonograph
Speaks to me
Through rough crackle of a field recording
Originating from a needle in my soul.
My vinyl heart wines like Sigor Ros
On grooves recorded in a derelict
Icelandic warehouse,
As flashes of time-lapse graffiti fill the
Space in my brain far from my
New age fulfillments in Philly
That spawned from watchin'
Deepak Chopra on Oprah!

Gregorian wind chimes from another time
Are sown together with dental floss
Hanging from the grey clouds.
And through some ancient static…
A presence from another dimension
Makes my heart beat on and creates wine with words
Till I'm way gone
At dawn
On this ordinary day…
Breathing
Breathing
Beathing

Everything common is bent, patched, troubled and layered inside me, and others such as Stumps singing…

I got troubles over here,
I still got troubles over there.
I got troubles over here,
I still got troubles over there.
I got troubles over here,
I still got troubles

And in no time at all, that old guitar and those wind chimes silenced. And I was in between thoughts once again, alone and at peace, with Sepher and Ruin.

In Seattle, I think we all felt a poetic sense of accomplishment after making it to the West Coast on The Highline creating The Art of Train Hopping; as well as having our fill of each other for a spell. It wasn't long after we hopped off the train our last train before Sepher parted ways with us for a week. He had some school business at Evergreen College where he was graduating that year, in part due to the work he was creating in the movie. Yes, the man found a way to hop trains to graduate! If it were possible for more people to get through school hopping trains, hobos could spare change people for book money and fly signs for tuition! Sara and I stayed in Seattle while Sepher took a bus to Olympia. Though Sara ditched me quick too.

Alone, I made the lay of the city and scouted locations to shoot the script that fell apart on the East Coast. I looked for graffiti that I could substitute for the environment in Philly. Seattle is a graffiti friendly city so finding a good spot didn't take long. After I nailed down the location, Sara and I met up for food at a supermarket. She spent very little of her daily fifteen dollar a day pay along the way, so we both had some cash in our pockets.

On our way out of a supermarket, Ruin introduced me to chocolate covered espresso beans for the first time. Then a sweet Young Crusty read our personas and called us out, asking…

"Housed up?"

"Nope."
I replied.

"I have a house just a few blocks away."
She mentioned,
"You're welcome there
if you contribute
some food or something
to the household."

I looked over at Sara, who then shrugged "why not."

"Cool! This is Ruin,
I'm Mes."

Then we followed her home. Just another example of good kindness and kismet I gathered.

Moments later the three of us walked through the neighborhood to her house on a very quiet street of single standing homes with nice well-trimmed lawns. And then we got to her house… condemned with a demolition notice posted to the boarded up front door. The place was as shanty as 1313 Mockingbird Lane, but without the charm.

"Entrance is on the down low
around back. Follow me,"
she said.

The place was in shambles, but she walked up to it like she owned it. It was definitely a squat, but it was hers. No doubt.

Once inside… it appeared as if it was turned over by a stubborn search warrant! Her Dude was there and woke up, still wasted, when we walked in. But he was just as friendly, and sketchy, as her. The Velvet Underground played from a tape cassette of a single speaker boom box in the corner. That's when I realized the place had electricity. They must have tapped it under the radar because these young folk didn't look like they were into paying bills… I guess, but I just don't know, as Lou Reed agreed from that little speaker in the corner.

Ruin and I talked for a while about our train travels to Seattle. Then Dude shared some of his story that led him to the squat. He was a working guy who had considered himself once a person who led a decadent lifestyle smoking pot, drinking wine and going to concerts and strip clubs all the time. He missed those days and wanted them back, but knew they were far in the past. I understood that, we both longed for old days. But unlike him, I was optimistic about the future. And once again I felt a little awkward carrying the passion of my project, as I befriended another assed out punk who had nothing but gloom to share. Many of the gutter-punks didn't seem to have better memories to look back on but this Dude, he really missed the life he left behind. He was stuck, but not me. I seemed to duck and weave in and out of this and that with more ease then others it seems; it's just a manic energy thing I guess.

I often heard a lot of train hoppers say they wanted to retire one day. But they didn't put it like that. But like this, acquired during interviews with a group of young travelers somewhere along the way…

"I don't want to be a career hobo."

…They all agreed on that!

"Give me a girlfriend,
dog, white picket fence
and I will get off the street
and BBQ every Friday night."

Most had an exit plans like that over beers. But had too many inhibitions to get anything without a drink.

Later that night after long patient talks with our squatter hosts, I slept with a screwdriver in my hand and rose to my feet every time I heard them walking around. I even rapped to myself through out the night so my new friends could hear I was on point in my sleep and ready get Kung Fu if I had too. Ruin slept right through it all.

The next morning, I hurried us out as the other two slept in. It was rude to run out on our hosts, I know, but I was paranoid. And though they didn't make a move on us, I couldn't deny the highly desperate impression the place gave me. We left ten dollars under the rest of the chocolate covered espresso beans.

When we walked from the squat, I took a close look at the demolition notice for their address stapled to a telephone pole a few houses away. My heart bled Jane's Addiction thinking of those two buddies waking to wrecking ball in… Three Days! Later that same morning, Ruin and I split up to explore the city and get some more alone time.

I went on to scout a safe place to crash that night. I ducked down alleyways and looked for a rooftop we could gain access to, to camp on. My search led me to the end of Broadway where I found a hip bowling alley with the look of a nightclub called The Garage. It looked swank! But then again maybe the bowling hall wasn't even that nice, and it just seemed so on the outside looking in.

"The longer you're on the street…"
I murmured,
"the farther things get
out of reach."

I realized that as a few pretty girls passed me bye exiting the place laughing about some outrageous bowling shoes they rented.

Next to the bowling lanes stood a two-story parking lot, the second story was an easy walk up a ramp off Broadway. From the street, this looked like easy access to the roof of the bowling alley. When I got up there, I immediately found what I was looking for… a perfect spot to crash with Ruin.

Then, after scouting a few more locations to pick up the script once we regrouped, I hit a coffee shop to journal and charge up my camera batteries. When I took a seat by a young couple with their head in their laptops, they moved away from me. I must have stunk that bad! I knew it. I walked out embarrassed. I just didn't notice how foul I smelled on the way in.

A couple blocks away I wash up in a park fountain to shake my stink as thoroughly as possible. I took off my clothes and jumped in, in my boxers! Wet but clean, I then meditated in the sun to recharge my spirit, before I napped under a tree to recharge my mind.

When I woke, I walked downtown to a designated meeting spot where I was to catch up with Ruin. I got there early to set up "shop" on the sidewalk and sell some of my graffiti watercolors. Across the street, I couldn't help but notice a pawnshop. As I hustled some pieces and made a few bucks, my inner consumer began to get hungry! So after I sold a handful of paintings, I walked across the street to take a look inside the pawnshop window, and I liked what I saw. Dressing the window was one of my jobs at the pawnshop I worked at in West Philly back in the day. I walked in. Once inside, I was drawn to the jewelry case to look at the watches.

"Can I help you?"
asked the pawnbroker.

I looked up, paused, then I smiled as I imagined him waiting for me to reach into my backpack for something to pawn. Or to place the big steel camera case I was holding in my hand on the counter and ask for a loan. Instead, I said…

"I'm in the market for
a timepiece."

"Well,
how much do you want to spend?"

"Do you take food stamps?"

"No.
But if you have collectable stamps
we can work something out."

"Let me see the Bulova there.
On the top shelf."

It probably retailed for around 400 dollars, far from a Rolex but a step up from a Mickey Mouse watch. He handed it over to me, with a good price…

"That's 100 dollars."

Putting it on made me feel good, like eating donuts at the bakery on Baltimore Pike when I was a kid. I began to feel slightly taller and get a buzz with the piece dangling from my wrist. I looked at it for a beat and then, at my reflection in the jewelry case. There I was, homeless but self-indulgent. And then, my lower self slammed my higher self once again! And I didn't mind it, not one bit. I knew I was shallow and had trite desires, but it was better then waking up with the taste of crack in my mouth! I stood there in a food stamp pimp stance with my timepiece danglin' like a chump on payday. Just looking at myself, thinking, aloud…

"That's my boy."

I had nothing, no roof overhead and, no money in the bank, no career with a title, nothing. Not a damn thing to my credit in life. But I had a couple hundred in my pocket!

"It's a nice watch
but I only have half that."

I thought he was going to halfway my halfway. And sure enough…

"Well,
meet me halfway today,
and it's yours."

Sure, I was tramping… but I was Mackin' in my mind like the love child of Iceberg Slim and Richard Pryor! Why people like Gandhi didn't come to mind at times like these, is a character flaw of mine.

"Do you take cash?"
I said sarcastically.

"Flat no tax."

"Thank you!
And may I ask…
can you please take one link out?
So it hangs proper like."

"…Done."

Ever since I hopped those trains, the luxuries of life had never been more apparent! I never wanted to give them up, I missed being fresh dressed like a million bucks with Bally shoes and some fly green socks. And that's one thing that set them apart from us.

The travelers on the cheap give up the luxuries you and I have, to have a freedom we don't! The nice cars and landscaped front yards we so work hard for, are traded off for a freedom we can only find on the weekends or on a vacation once a year. I don't see one life better than the other, but I wish everyone could experience both ends as I have.

As I looked down at my new watch, I contemplated the challenge ahead to acquire finances to rent a train for my grand finale in the movie and thought… what was another seventy-five dollars?

When Ruin returned to meet me at the spot, she was happier then a pig in mud!

"You got laid?"

"Nooo."
She laughed off.

Maybe I was wrong and it was just on my mind because I was so horny, I could hump a dumpster! But every home bum had dibs on one after Harmony Korine blew up the scene.

With Ruin, rested, I decided to shoot some script. But once again, she was way too smiley to convince anyone her boyfriend fell off the map. It was Chicago all over again! I scraped the shoot, again.

Later that night we went to that bowling alley roof. It was slightly illuminated by street lamps and pulsing disco strobes from the skylights of the rock & bowl lanes below; the kind of light that brought me back in time to the "Circus Town" all ages dance club of my childhood. When a can of paint and or Aqua Net was all we needed to express ourselves! All my old friends names, ducktails and hair-do's up-rocked in my mind, as Planet Rock played downstairs in the bowling alley! I laid out my sleeping bag and caught some winks as people partied below like Bambaataa at a block party. I was so jelly!

During the night I dreamed of Seru, Impact, Del, Game, the real Ruin, Issue, Mac, Rede, Deper and Kaos as we shared the risks of writing at an outlaw meeting together in my dream. The world stood still in my head, as we began to bomb it! Our passion was to write one word of our choosing, as many different ways as we could with style those… academics, could never learn. I never dreamed of making movies or writing books. But along the way I acquired bigger stories I wanted to share, so I was forced to write more than my word of choice… MES. When I woke up, I went straight to my journal…

The next morning,
Gear under my head as pillow,
Rooftops around me like urban lily pads in a
Gutter punk pond.
True blue sky overhead,
Blanketed inner city chill between my
Sleeping bit and bones.
Elements of a page from My Own Private Idaho,
Ruin my River and I as Gus
Far from the pinball machine that spawned this trip
in Center City after my last suicide
Forever ago… I woke again breathing.

I was living out the narrative I wrote and shooting Picture from the edge of my dreams. The power of desire, intention and writing were never so apparent to me as they were out there burning at both ends in such lowbrow bliss. Then, I looked at my new pawnshop find, with Schoolly D on my mind, and said to myself…

"It's about that time."

Then I looked over those lines I wrote in my journal before Ruin unzipped herself from her sleeping bag. She was really comfortable out there, much more than me. Though I found train traveling fulfilling, I was usually torn between where I was coming from and where I was going. But I slowly pasted it together with purpose in the movie.

The sun began to climb in Seattle and the office lights across the street began to wake, as did Ruin, slowly. I watched her gather her gear on the roof while others in the windows across the street came to position in their cubicles. If I completed my project and made the movie, sleeping on that roof could be considered work too.

I guess those rooftop moments are what I enjoy most, simple seconds that burn the hairs off my forearms. It happens to me when I'm observing something alone, and feel as though I'm the conduit between the past and future of my universe. I became passionate about making my experiences, my life's work; since my days on the Market Street rooftops of Philadelphia I suppose. By the time I was in Seattle, I was ready for this vocation and familiar with the workload. Duty called that morning for me to sneak off the roof and into the morning pink with Ruin. Sepher was still at Evergreen wrapping up his schoolwork so shooting his pages were on the back burner till he returned later in the day.

With some coffee in us, Ruin and I found our way to some steps I scouted out the day before. They were in front of an apartment building that had a long u-shape entrance. It felt slightly Drugstore Cowboy to me with mid 70's charm.

I had Ruin run her lines as I established the scene with the branding of passing taxis, buses and fire trucks of Seattle. And finally, things went smooth and we were done by noon and ready to shoot with Sepher! But he called us to say he was staying in Olympia a little longer. I was so angry! So she and I had to kill time. Easy on drugs, but without um' I was stirring with emotions.

I had to find more patience in times like these, when the tides of others brought me out far from every emotion I was sure I could deal with. To stay on top at that stage of my sobriety, I didn't fight the currents of others. Because when I lost it, I drowned in my anger, I just couldn't do that anymore. I needed help. And Matthew and Sara, despite all my complaints, were more help to me than they knew! Though Sepher wasn't rushing back to shoot script, The Art of Train Hopping was worth the growing pains; maybe I was too.

When Seph came back a couple days later, the three of us got to work and shot a scene in a graffiti drenched parking lot that I found while looking for a rooftop to sleep on days ago. This was the scene that we failed to get in Philly. We shot it a dozen times back East, but it never felt right. I wanted to shoot it in Chicago, but they had a heavy case of the giggles. Now on the West Coast, I had to make it work!

I found the angle I wanted and ran the lines a few times before we started shooting. It was a nice day with the sun behind the clouds as we took our time and ran the scene for hours. It felt great! I had my Mr. Mes swagger back and felt "Ruin" showed up in the story. But the fact is, she and I were rookies… what feels good doesn't always look good. So I stayed in the scene and ran it dozens of times. Seph shot the picture every take as described in the script. Finally, when we felt comfortable enough to stray from the script and pull off some improv, I knew we were flowing, and got it. And I assure you that my fear of "playback" was real. So I had to just hope Sepher picked it up. By then, between New York and Seattle, we all had our turns shooting each other.

After we wrapped that day, Seph dashed back to school to get more work done. He said he needed a few more days to himself before we could pick the script back up and shoot the last two scenes I had slated during this final leg of our journey. And Ruin decided to go to Olympia with him. But I chose to stay behind in Seattle and get a room in a hostel for a couple of days. My feet and toes where really mangled from carrying my pack across the country. When I got in the room I don't know what felt better… lying in a bed, or just taking off the hobo gear.

Hours later when I woke from a long nap, I took a shower and "bum-bathed" in some cheap cologne, got myself together, and walked from the room smelling like a born again gigolo. Walking the city streets in some clean threads, with no pack on my back, Cool Water on my face and a new watch on my wrist had me feeling like my old self; who often thought he was someone else altogether.

Overly confident, I walked into a bakery to buy an everything bagel, then asked the counter girl out to a movie. Later that evening, we went up and caught the movie Scanner Darkly. At the movie I remember thinking how much I wanted to see the movie I was making in a theater one day. And that maybe, my movie would play there in Seattle and Sub Pop would see it… and, I don't know. My mind races and wastes so much of my time!

Eventually I caught a bus out of Seattle to meet Seph and Ruin in Olympia to complete the remaining scenes. One set in the woods, and the other in a drugstore, both locations I'd yet to scout. The majority of the picture was doing what we could when we could, led by my little screenplay and if edited correctly, I hoped it would have people debating the existence of a script at all.

A couple hours later I got off the bus and they were waiting for me. And as soon as I got off it, I noticed a drugstore across the street that I thought would work to shoot the movie in. So I went inside over there and bought some mouthwash and two bottles of Gatorade. While making my purchase, I asked the Cashier if he wouldn't mind if my friends shot some video outside his store through his big window at me shopping inside.

"Sir, I need to drink one of these bottles
on camera for a school project at Evergreen State.
Is that OK?"

I found when you have no money people are more open to help with a school project than a no budget indie film. The cashier smiled and agreed to let us shoot. I locked it down as easy as always.

But outside, the real challenges of the location became apparent. With the bus station across the street, our sound would suffer. And it being very late afternoon, the sun created a glare on the window the camera couldn't shoot through to the aisle where I wanted to capture Mr. Mes. The Sun really screwed things up! Instead of finding me in the aisle shoplifting and drinking a bottle of mouthwash, all that could be seen was Sepher and Ruins' reflection. And as far as the sound, shooting between the passing buses would make it possible to record the dialogue. But that glare on the window looked like it would trash the shot. But we had to try.

BOOK SAFE

Before I went back inside, I dumped the mouthwash in the gutter and replaced it with Gatorade. Then I went in and played out the action as Ruin & Sepher rolled picture from outside. But to no surprise, when I came out after the first take, Seph wasn't happy…

"The glare just makes it impossible
to shoot through.
But I think I have a solution."

Despite my rule of no play back, Seph insisted we play back that first take. Under the circumstances, I agreed to it. In that first take, he found that some of the action inside was evident through Ruin's shadow on the glass. He then pointed it out to me, and said…

"That's our shot right there."

He decided to shoot me guzzling the mouthwash entirely through the shadow of Ruin who gazed in the store with disgust at my desperate act of pounding mouthwash just to ease my character's alcohol withdraw.

After the second take Sepher said it worked shooting through the shadow! So we did it again. Now on the third take, I was encouraged and really played it up by drinking the entire bottle of prop mouthwash. But after that take, the plug was pulled on my way out. The Cashier, who watched me drink three bottles of mouthwash in twenty minutes, said…

"That's it! I don't
want any more of this in my store."

But I had what I needed by then.

"I understand, thank you."

…Then, I left five dollars on the counter, and walked around the corner to vomit on the sidewalk right in front of Ruin. In true Mr. Mes arrogance, and recklessness… I laughed off the vomit, and took out a bottle of cough syrup to swig, asking Ruin to…

"Kiss me! My breath it
smells so good!"

She played it off well and Sepher got it all on video. Then we moved on to scout the next location in the Evergreen Campus woods.

Hours later and once on campus surrounded by the trees, we made our way down long winding paths through the shade of tall beautiful timbers. It was nearly silent out there and felt to me like a private place to get down and dirty in the last scene on my shot list from coast to coast. In this one, Sepher finds Mr. Mes with his pants down behind a tree, appearing to be masturbating, while watching Ruin do Yoga in the woods. I thought it would be a moment caught on camera within a situation found only in an unscripted story. To me, it was all about creating a movie that the audience would debate was a documentary or not. After three quick takes deep in those woods, we got it. And our shoot along the Highline was complete! And the next day I gave Seph and Ruin 100 dollars each and we all parted ways. She took a bus back East to Baltimore, he hopped a train to Mutant Fest, and I flew standby to New Orleans on an airline pass from my Mom.

EDITING AMATURES

Blurring the Line
Between truth & fiction at Times

I returned to NOLA and exited an airport shuttle on the edge of the French Quarter. As I pulled my bag from the back of the van, I noticed Stumps duh Clown walking across Esplanade Ave.

Stumps was living at the Clown House at the time with a gang of young gutter punks who paid the rent, I think; I du-know. But I do know he was too royal to pay rent at the time. He knew what I'd been doing all summer. And I was happy to see a big smile on his tattooed face!

"Coast to coast!" Stumps cheered, "To hell with
them people talking shit about you going
out there to make your movie."

"Yeah man!"

There were in fact a great deal of train riders in New Orleans who were lets say… unenthusiastic about our project. Fearing I'd blow up the scene.

"You had no idea what you were doing,"
Stumps continued,
"and you went out there and did it!"

We had a pretty good laugh about it, before it set in…

"Wait a minute…"
he wondered aloud,
"Did you just take a shuttle bus
from the train yard?"

Not long after I returned, Matt Sepher called me with some news while he was still on the road hopping boxcars with a couple of young ladies. In a phone conversation, he mentioned…

"I found a train to rent."

"Where?"
I asked surprised.

"In New Orleans!"

Turned out, an organization of retired engineers had an old steam engine they ran for various events and festivals in the New Orleans area. They rented it, and other train cars, to movie productions too. This was almost too good to be true! Having this resource at home in NOLA was another stroke of good luck along the way. Matthew forwarded me the contact and I rushed off the phone with him to call about that train. While dialing the number, I hypothesized on how much a train would cost to rent?

"Twenty grand, maybe?"
I murmured.

I really had no idea, but speculated…

"Tracks? Operators? Twenty-five grand maybe?"

I honestly didn't know what it would take to pull it off and had absolutely no money to even bargain with at that point, but I needed a train. And my mind doesn't stop racing.

When I got a man by the name of Bruce on the phone at the Louisiana Steam Train Association, he described all the cars they had available and boasted endlessly about the 1921 Southern Pacific Steam Train… Old Engine 745. The thought of using an old Steam Engine in my contemporary American Hobo movie didn't seem to fit at first, but after thinking up a quick twist in my script, it sounded even better then ever! It gave me the opportunity to create an ending for the story that could create more magic than using any of the trains we road on the Highline. Then, I asked.

"How much Bruce?"

"When do you need it?"

"I can't nail down a date, until
I raise the funds to rent the train."

At that point, he realized he wasn't speaking to a Hollywood producer and started to work with me on the price. He told me how the train works… about firing up the engine, letting it warm up for a day or two to reach a certain temperature to operate safely, and filling up the tank with $5,000 of recycled motor oil. Turns out this steam engine had been converted into an oil burning train.

"The train cost 25,000 dollars
a day to rent."

Though I had speculated that before I called, I was blunt at this point…

"It's impossible
for me to raise even
half that Bruce."

But he had an idea…

Well Braze,
if you can wait and trail
Brad Pitts production of
Benjamin Button's next year…
I'll let you use it for a day if
you fill the gas tank
back up when he's done."

"5K?"
I asked him to clarify.

"Yes."
He confirmed.

"It's a deal.
I can do that Bruce."

"Come out to the yard and check her out,"
Bruce suggested,
"any Saturday you like."

I thought the editing would take a year or so and the train was to be used in the finale scene, so waiting to shoot it was no big deal to me. I had a lot of work to do in the meantime. The next week, I went to their train yard in Jefferson Parish and created a shot list to be used when the time came. I made a list of 27 shots, to be shot along a half-mile of train tracks. And realized I needed to acquire some dolly tracks of my own, to place next to them. I also needed a crew, movie extra's and… and more money.

After regaining my strut with my new train connect at L.A.S.T.A. I rolled into Delgado Community College where my "skate video" friend Todd was the Assistant Director of the school TV & Film Studies department. I met Todd when I first got to town, before the storm, at a skateboard video screening of his at a bar on Decatur Street. He's a serious skater, and a good filmmaker! After our initial meeting back then, I began connecting with him at the club One Eyed Jacks. He was a resident DJ there every Thursday night spinning classic 80's dance music. It was a blast! He always invited me in the DJ booth and we'd talk music and movies in between the tracks he dropped. His energy was laid back and our conversations where good. He was the first friend I made in NOLA outside the traveler kid subculture.

When I got back to town after hopping trains, I didn't have a computer to digitize what I spent all summer shooting. So I went to Todd at Delgado for help.

"So… is it cool
I work on a computer here
at the school?"

"Yeah sure.
Whatever you need."

"Well… can I sleep in here too?"<br>"I don't have a place to crash right now."

He laughed at me, then asked
"Where'd ya sleep last night Scorsese?"

"I crashed in the laundry matte at
Check Point Charlie's."

"…Oh."

From there on, he let me work in the lab where I could log video and made notes of my coverage. Day after day I would sit alone working on my movie as the students across the room learned how to make one.

Occasionally Todd would use my story as motivation to get the kids to create something bigger than them selves! And when class was over, he'd let me catch a nap and rest in the empty classroom.

For weeks I brewed over the footage… naming chapters, making long hand notes and reconnecting disconnected files all the time because I had no idea what I was doing. I was so afraid of computers! I never knew what key I would press that would scramble my screen. But Todd was there for technical assistance. I'd often be looking at the monitor doing just fine, before it all went to shit!

"What? Ahhhh no!
Yooo Todd?"

He'd always come walking over with a smirk on his face, or laughing at me before he fixed whatever problem I had. People laughed at me a lot along the way, but it never really bothered me. I was always too distracted by my own emotions.

In the beginning of my edits, I saved all the files on the school hard drives. Then, I backed up the school hard drive files on an external drive that was the size of a cinder block! The sucker was so big it had a little fan in the back of it to keep it cool. I guarded that external drive as if it were a kilo wrapped in a Spanish newspaper from North Philly.

Finally, I got a real job in New Orleans at an art gallery on Royal Street. And soon, I rented a shotgun in The Marigny. At that point it was fall 2006, a little over a year and a half into the project. After Matthew took his time getting back to town, he approached me while I was assembling an early rough cut of The Art of Train Hoppin, and asked…

"I want to help edit the movie."

"You ever edit video Matt?"

"No,
but I can learn."

So I gave him one train montage to edit and suggested…

"Maybe you could put
Stumps duh Clowns song "Troubles" to it."

I spent the next week laying down some cuts and making a very short teaser for Saddle Creek Records in hopes to acquire a Bright Eye's song. And while doing so I found myself constantly looking for the best shots and making the cleanest cuts possible within the barrage of hand held coverage and bumpy train footage I captured during our run on the rails. With much of the shaky-ass footage cut out, I thought it was beginning to look pleasant enough to maybe not get seasick looking at it. Then, Matt showed me his cut.

"What do you got Seph?"
I asked not expecting much.

Then I sat quietly watching his work. At first I thought, how am I going to tell him to leave the editing to me Todd and his boy Eric who was assisting us with post. Then I looked at his cuts again. His were worlds apart from ours!

"Pretty much everything I would've cut out,
you put in Matt. But Daaaaaang!"
I said with country awe.

He had no smooth shots or even one graceful transition in the entire cut. His montage was very shaky, cuts quick, everything I thought I should avoid. But it occurred to me that… his cuts, were closer to the experience I remembered out there! Much more than the peaceful picture I was trying to paint.

And once I had that in mind, I warmed up as my heart raced with the memory of the rails I found in Matthew's cuts to the steel guitar of Stumps duh Clown.

"I just finished the book
In The Blink Of An Eye by Watler Murch.
It's really good!"
He said with certainty,
"Would you like to borrow it?"

"Yes!"

It was a struggle out there on the rails. And that's what Matt's cut painted and my cuts didn't! Mine looked good, but his felt good! From that point on, he took charge as the editor. I'd have been a fool otherwise.

"We have a lot of action,"
he continued,
"If we just cut on that,
we should be fine."

He soon was so motivated to keep editing, that he bought a new desktop Mac and we got to work in his house in the 7th Ward.

At that time, I was busy most days at my new art gallery job on Royal Street where I was supposed to be selling Michel Delacroix paintings, but I only did that half the time, at most. Art can be a slow sale and a bit of a courting process with prospects, so my movie was on my mind during down time. I had my own desk where I did more producing of The Art of Train Hoppin' than emailing prospects about fine art. It was the perfect job for me at the time! Not only did I have a lot of down time in the gallery to do what was needed to keep my movie rolling, but I was making pretty good money. During this time I really got to know my boss Joseph, and gained his personal support. He added some class and vocabulary to my pawnshop hustle that improved my salesmanship. He believed in me! And soon, I was selling 10-30K a month, as was asked of me.

"That's why I hired you Braze."
Joseph said,
"You're a hustler.
I knew you could sell."

"I didn't imagine hustlers would be
welcome in the fine arts."
I said foolishly.

He laughed!

"We're all hustling!"
He pointed out.

BRIGHTDAWN

Throughout the winter of 2007 and into the spring I continued to produce The Art of Train Hoppin from my desk at the gallery, as well as having the occasional hobo friend in for a glass of wine and discussions about the movie. Most of them where still concerned about what I was doing, and thought my picture might "blow up the scene" as they say. At the end of every conversation I would have to remind them that…

"I'm not making
a how to hop trains film.
Just relax."

As I began to polish my conversation skills in the art gallery world, I approached Fugazi to ask them for the song Blueprint. Though Saddle Creek had not got back to me yet, approaching them was easy for me. But Discord Records intimidated me! I thought so much of that company that I got tongue-tied with just the thought of approaching them with an email. But after watching an interview with Shane Smith, and him referencing Ian MacKaye, I just had to keep moving forward. I mean, what was I scared of? It's not that I thought they were unapproachable, but if in fact they would deal with a guy like me… a common criminal. If you know about Fugazi and their standards, you'd know why a common criminal like me, who looked up to them, may feel a little… foolish, approaching them. Yet once again, my feelings were overblown. Ian gave me the song "Gratis" along with his phone number (That I keep on my refrigerator.) if I have any questions. He just asked me to donate to a soup kitchen some day. Years later, I would do so, and keep doing so.

I think I began to grow more painlessly at this time. Most of my life I was tormented by sadness and teased by euphoria. But now, I was just too busy to hurt or get too happy. Combine that with the passion I had for my project, I made progress in every direction despite all the mistakes along the way. Such as when I emailed Saddle Creek Records, and wrote at the end of it that…

I eat edits for breakfast.
Yours truly,
Braze

Then hit send, before it occurred that I screwed up. Eating edits for breakfast only works in conversations at film school. Which is where I sent the e-mail from when I started the edits at Delgado College. Words like "Cordially" or "Best" are much better notes to close on rather than sounding like a Rocky Balboa. I was embarrassed when I realized what I did. But when I tried to tell myself to relax and that maybe I was wrong and it wasn't so bad. I asked Todd about it. He said…

"Ah… Yeah,
that's completely retarded Braze."

But eventually they got back to me with a positive response. And after mailing them the cut of my movie I'd been working on, they asked to see a little more to take my project into further consideration. My patience and determination may have been born on the rails, but it learned to walk in postproduction. I had things cooking on every burner it seemed!

Weeks later Saddle Creek e-mailed with a number of other attached e-mails along with one to Conner and others. They all liked the project and agreed to let me use the song *When The Calendar Hung Itself*.

Matt and I bunkered down for what would be a more epic project than we had imagined. Editing it was overwhelming! What the script said to me, and what it said to him, seemed miles apart sometimes. I was shocked at how he could have gone along with me that far in the project, without fully believing in the direction I wanted to go in the first place. If I didn't keep my cool during our arguments, my emotions during the editing process would have surely dissolved the relationship between us. During these conflicts both the experimental nature of the movie, and our friendship evolved through conversations during the editing. We would come up with an idea, or make some choices within the cuts and transitions, and he would ask me to leave him alone to make it happen. That's when our collaboration devolved into a relationship between that of Captain Picard, and a couch potato. He operated the controls, while I couch surf in the background.

Through the endless conversation in the months that followed, I learned how to articulate myself like never before. I think my personal growth was mammoth at this time. Until then, I was never big on conversation outside my own poetic abstractions about street culture. But in New Orleans, a passion surfaced in me that burned in many of my conversations. I found I could turn people on with my energy easily, but being really clear was still a challenge. And being patient was even more challenging! But the lack of it would be the end of my project. It was in long conversations during our breaks on Matt's front stoop on Marigny Street that I began to grow up and be the person I'm working on today. For the completion of the project I pushed myself in directions to go places I've never gone. Up and down the roads of patience and sobriety became the only way to find my way through the challenges of completing the picture. I'd follow the path and make many wrong turns, but something truly unbeknownst to me seemed to keep bringing me back on track. Or, maybe it was just my undying desire to get somewhere.

Matt was always there to help me sort through all my bad ideas and keep us moving forward. And the fact was that he and I didn't have much going for us yet. I don't think he really knew what he wanted to do, and I never thought of a career for myself. But together, we began relying on each other to get this movie done. He had the mind, and I had the drive. Neither one of us thought the movie could make us rich; we just did it because we wanted to. I think he just wanted to complete the project, but I wanted to complete a successful one. At that time, success to me meant film festivals, magazine interviews and making some money back.

For weeks at a time we would cut and brainstorm ideas and directions for the movie. Late night into early mornings we'd work with no schedules or deadlines. And that worked OK, the first year. But by year two… I think he wondered if we'd ever finish it. But not me, I just wondered if it would be any good. I could see the potential, but had some doubts that we would reach it. Though it was seldom that I actually engaged those doubts. I had no distractions of any kind while editing the Picture. I was completely focused on the project. Then, I met her…

BELLA BOMBED ME

The allure of this young Lady
Would eventually lead me to the Maybe

My obsession radar found a new twist when I met a barista named Bella at a Royal Street coffee shop. I never met someone who looked so pure and beautiful… milk for skin, sunshine for a smile, perfection for a body. After days of going back to the coffee shop and admiring her from afar, I finally spoke up…

"I'm making a movie.
You want to be in it?"
I asked like a jerk.

"No,"
she said with certainty.

"Oh?
Oh, yeah. I understand."
Realizing how stupid I sounded,
"But… you,
don't even know what it's about."

"I'm not comfortable in front of cameras."
She said with something else in mind,
"But if you need help behind it,
I'm open for that!"

"So…
you want to be a P.A.?"

"Sure!"
She said with confidence.
"I am in Film School y'know."

"Perfect!"
I celebrated, and continued,
"I've acquired a 1921 steam train for the last
scene in my train hopping movie."

"Interesting."
She pondered. Then asked,
"Is it about The Depression?"

"No, more about me
getting over depression.
And a contemporary look at
people riding the rails!"

I quickly wrote the train yard address down before she changed her mind and handed it to her.

"Are you open on July 3rd?"
I asked.

"Yes."

"We start at 3am."

She thought about it, and pondered it for a moment.

"Are you in?"
I asked.

Her response would someday come to haunt me. She said…

"Maybe."

When July 3rd came, she showed up and helped us with the shoot. I brought in dozens of people to help me pull off the final scene! The steam train shoot speaks for itself in the movie. I suggest you try and find a DVD of the movie and give it a watch; they're out there.

With the help of the L.A.S.T.A engineers, I organized a small team to acquire the shots needed around the Steam Engine. We ran the old train up and down a half-mile piece of track over 150 times to acquire the shots I needed in just 17 hours.

From before dawn till after dusk I ran an efficient show. And I must have made a good impression on Bella that day because later that week, she agreed to have dinner with me.

Our first date was at The Palace Café. Where during our long conversation before dinner I edited out the many reckless chapters of my life. She was so young and beautiful I was afraid too much too soon would just scare her away. Besides it's my personal history, not billboard material. I found it easier to just say…

"I'm allergic to alcohol."

"I don't drink either."
She said.

"NO?"

"I'm only twenty."

And so cute! So much so that I forgot about the The Art of Train Hoppin after I met Bella, it was no longer my obsession; she was. I really forgot about everything else. On the forefront of my mind was her after that night, the rest of the world was somewhere in the background.

Immediately at work that week in the art gallery, I began writing Bella a poem a day. I'd address and mail each one. Then, two poems a day! Soon, I began drawing her graffiti and mailing that too. And then I'd draw graffiti on the pages of poetry I'd mail her! By that time she would be getting up to three letters a day from me at her midtown home near Bayou St. John. I couldn't stop writing her! I totally love bombed her like a horny scientist! And lucky for me, she couldn't stop reading. But her stripper roommate Lorry had her concerns when she noticed all the mail at the house.

"Is this guy a stalker?"
Lorry asked.

"He's trying to make a film."
Bella told her.

"Film about what?"

"Basically about him
hopping trains across the country."

"Oh… he's a narcissist."
Lorry concluded.

"Maybe, but all of these
letters are poetry about me."

Maybe Lorry was right about me, but Bella didn't seem to think so. Nor did she realize how my insecurities were driving me to give her such an intense level of attention; she was too naive to notice. On the contrary, she loved the attention! It was as if I was the first boyfriend, she ever really liked. I got the impression she was just bothered by boys her age, till she met me. Although she wasn't a young teenager, it seemed in some ways she was. She was in fact very smart, clued in, conscious… but oddly inexperienced at the same time. She grew up on the bayou and had just moved to New Orleans for film school.

BOOK SAFE

As we got closer, I got even creepier! I began sneaking up her driveway late at night and climbing through Bella's window and into the bed with her every night after movie edits where done. We weren't making love, but her softness was more than enough for me.

Most mornings I would leave before her roommate Lorry woke up from her late nights as an "independent contractor" on Bourbon Street. Bella rented a room from her in a house filled with odd belongings. Lorry was evidently a yard sale fanatic! The house and walls were delicately filled with art and other scores from shopping on weekend mornings with hundreds of one-dollar bills in her pocket. Eventually, Lorry and I met over breakfast with Bella.

"So,
you're a filmmaker?"
Lorry asked

"I wouldn't call myself a filmmaker.
But I'm a writer."

"But Bella told me you were
trying to make a movie?"

"Well…
it's just a side effect
of my writing."

"Who do you like to read?"

I don't know what's more revealing about my character… the books I've never read, or the walls I did.

"Suroc, Espo, Mac"
I responded.

"I never heard of any of them."

"They're…
outlier writers of Philadelphia."

Soon after that conversation with Lorry, Bella asked me to take her graffiti writing. So I brought her down by some train tracks one day to show her some can-control. After just one day bombing with me, she set off on her own stencil campaign against Burger King who was exploiting tomato pickers in Florida at that time. She bombed twelve fast food restaurants in one night! Bella called what she did Conscious Graffiti. It spoke volumes to me, and Burger King.

Everyday, if I wasn't over Bella's house, I was getting coffee at her work. Eventually, I shared some of those deleted scenes of my life with her over soy lattes. After hearing a few of my war stories, she thought I could probably learn how to drink responsibly if I wanted to. But knowing better, I just smiled and blew that talk off.

It was at the coffee shop on Royal Street, when I met her father Harry sitting at the end of the bar after I walked in one day in my suit on a break from the Gallery down the street. Bella introduced us…

"Dad, this is Braze. Braze this
is my dad Harry."

"I knew that was you."
Harry said to me.

"Nice to meet you Harry,"
I said shaking his hand.
"How did you know it was me Harry?"

"By the way Bella looked at you
when you came in."

Harry and I got to know each other. I learned that he was a successful artist in The Quarter for a few decades and at heart, a hippie who admired communism and free love. Though I had a new suit on and told him I worked at a fine art gallery, he just wanted to believe I was a hobo hopping trains and nothing else.

"You're just like me Braze.
You're an outsider!"

"Well,
there's truth to that Harry."

If that's what my girlfriend's father wanted to think about me, I was happy with that. He was a nice guy, but seemed a little troubled; I'd yet to know why. But as far as first meetings go, I didn't think I could go wrong with someone who stood where he did… so far on the outside of basically everything. He was a true outsider.

Later that night after my initial meeting with her Dad, Bella and I sat on a stone bench in a cemetery at the top of Canal Street. In between kisses, she expressed her disappointment after I met her father.

"Now you're not mine anymore!"

"What?"
I asked stunned, and continued to kiss her!

"My whole family will be asking
about you now."

"So."

"So I liked you being my secret!"

I didn't get it, but also didn't care to ask why she felt that way. Bella came from a big family. When we first started dating her phone was always ringing and she answered calls from one guy after another. Later I found out that they were all her brothers calling her! As we continued making out in the cemetery that night, she shared more…

"I have something
to tell you Braze."

"Shoot."

She was really nervous now, so I stopped kissing her.

"I'm. I'm a… "

"…What is it Bell?"

"I'm a virgin."

"Whoaw. …What?"

She nodded yes. I was… shocked!

"That's…
a beautiful place to be in your life.
You're… twenty though?
Right?"

"Yup.
You still like me?"

Like her? For me, this was a dream!

"Yes!
Very much so."

But she was nearly in a panic about it, so I tried to calm her down…

"Listen, it's OK.
I'm not too confident
with sex myself."

"Why?"

I thought of all the bathhouses I had frequented, escorts I phoned, and Mexican back alley strips I searched for track stars, and responded by summing it up that…

"It's, complicated."

I never felt very dynamic in the sack, so when she said she was new to it, I felt more confident then ever. My passion burned for Bella as much as my desire to finally complete The Art of Train Hoppin! But a few weeks later, when she decided to sleep with me, it nearly smothered the flames I had for the movie. Sex with Bella was amazing, beautiful and precious! She was always so wet for me that she was nervous about it, even embarrassed. It was all so new to her! And as I got lost between her legs four or five times a day, she got more aggressive! I suppose it was the long wait she undertook before choosing her first love that in fact added to her newfound erotic energy. How a guy like me could get this lucky, is just not fair… for if things were, I would be dead or in jail I think.

Most anyone can hop trains, but not too many people can make love to a young woman as beautiful as Bella. Those days and nights are forever tattooed on my heart and engraved in my memory banks. We laughed, loved, and dreamed so big, how was I not to think we were anything but, soul mates. That term never crossed my mind, till I met Bella. I just gushed with goofiness, romance, and bad poetry around her.

Not long after meeting her father Dad, he started stopping by my galley job to chat me up. I thought it was great that my girlfriend's father liked me so much. But the more he talked endlessly about his radical points of views, the more I realized how far out he really was.

"I was told I have
a cult of personality."
he said with a hint of pride.

I smiled, a little bewildered, but he continued talking and telling me more and more about his background and experiences. But when Harry's visits became longer and even more frequent, things began to get a little uncomfortable with my boss Joseph around. Between producing my movie at work, and talking with Harry when he stopped in, my daily art sales were getting less and less attention. But then again, Joe didn't seem to mind when he'd catch me making out with Bella in the back storage room. He'd get a little giddy himself! She just carried that kind of beauty.

And then, there were a few weeks there where I was juggling both Bella and Harry at the art gallery. My conversations with Harry were as deep as I was getting in with Bella. It was really weird! And they both talked about each other to me, things just between two of us, and not the other. I couldn't tell either one that I'd just been with the other because I felt as though I was cheating on one of them! You know what I mean? Things just got too close for my comfort.

Bella would quickly pull her pants up when we saw my boss Joseph through the air vent on the storage room door as he returned to the gallery after his lunch break. Then, Bella and I would walk out from the storage room, smiling.

"Hi Bella."
Joseph would greet her with great delight.

"Hi Joe."

"Bye Bella."
he said, salivating.

After Bella left to walk back up the street to work at the coffee shop, Joe ran over to my desk…

"You lucky dog!"
he said and punched me in the arm, and continued,
"Did you show her the Joe-Diddly?"

He was very proud of this foreplay move he explained to me one time. It was in fact, a good move. He believed in it so much that he named it after himself.

Then, quite often, minutes after Bella left, Harry would pull up and park his van out front in a loading zone; only to collect parking tickets he didn't care about paying.

"Here comes epic conversation."
cracked Joseph.

"Damn. Do I smell
like Bell?"

I could always make Joseph laugh!

"You dirty hobo Braze!"

"Is there any other kind of hobo,
Joe-Diddly?"

And then for hours sometimes I'd talk with Harry about everything from hitchhiking to Noam Chomsky, and small business to organized religion.

"Filmmakers are demigods."
said Harry.

"That's a bold statement."
I remarked.

"I have million dollar
movie ideas Braze."

"Well… I think
they're only worth what someone
wants to pay for them Harry."
I rationalized.

"My problem is,"
he continued,
"I get the ideas while
I'm sitting on the toilet."

And, he was serious. I'd get frustrated sometimes that he wasn't aware I had to get to work and not sit around and talk such shit!

"I suppose the challenge in that case Harry,
would be to get that shit from your head,
on a piece toilet paper."

And often he would just ponder my sarcasm…

"Yeah,
I see what you mean Braze,"
he concurred,
"I should leave a pen in there."

Then, he'd continue on, and on and on. My conversations with Harry were much longer than the sex I could ever have with his daughter. Though he was around a lot, too much even, he was my girlfriend's dad… so I just rolled with it. I mean damn, I was happier then ever with her! And the more people I spoke to about Harry around the Quarter, the more admirers I found he had. His artistry had inspired many other artists along the way to venture out and focus on creative outlets they'd not otherwise been encouraged to pursue before meeting him. I didn't meet anyone who didn't like him. So I thought whatever problem I had with him, was that of my own. What I found uncomfortable with Harry, I blamed myself, for not being more open to his alternative lifestyle.

As my relationship evolved with Bella, my happiness seemed to be uncontainable at times! I would often wake up laughing from one of my dreams about her while I was on the "editing couch" at Matt's. Then I'd talk about her while he was cutting and pasting our Picture together. Eventually, he couldn't take my insensitivity…

"I'm really happy you're in
a good place Braze.
But I'm not right now!
Can we just focus on the movie?"

"Sure thing."
I responded, and curbed my gloating.

Matt was having big troubles getting sleep, and he was working at a Strip Club on Bourbon Street too. At the same club Lorry worked. She loved it there, but for him… working the afternoons there wasn't his life's dream by any means!

"In fact,"
he continued,
"maybe I can work at this on my own.
Just take off.
I'll show you what
I have tomorrow night."

"Sure man. Thanks"
I said, and hurried off to Bella's.

Having an editor work alone on your movie is not uncommon in the making of motion pictures when you're getting paid to edit. But that wasn't the case here. Matt did it because he wanted to, because he believed in the project and was up for all the challenges. And there were many working with me! My editing sessions with him started to be cut much earlier. But I was happy to jet and climb through Bella's back window anytime. I was going bananas over Bella's. Maybe hippies weren't so bad I began to think; I loved this one.

As Matthew and I moved forward with the movie, being amateurs at editing created many problems along the way that slowed us down. The flip side was, there was not one issue that Matt couldn't find the solution to. I certainly didn't have the head for it, or so I thought. Then he got real with me once again…

"You think I'm so smart.
But I just research the issues on the Internet.
You could do it!"
he pointed out.

"Ok then.
I'll sit there and edit."

"No!"
He yelled with certainty.

"Don't touch the computer…
Never,
touch my time lines!"

We were both frustrated quite often. He'd call it my movie, but it sure felt more like ours to me. He'd often say in heated discussions regarding the direction of the Picture…

"It's your movie,
I'll do what you want Braze.
But I think..."

And his thoughts always made a huge difference. The only way for a guy like me to get something done of any real artistic merit, was to partner with artists better than myself. I'd done it time and time again growing up in graffiti. Everything I am as an artist and collaborator was born back then. What I was trying to create in the movie was no different than any other piece I painted as a youth. And in this painting, "The Art of Train Hoppin", Matt was the man to shine with.

"The movie is being layered like
a wicked jawn, on a brick wall."
I said in Philly way.

"What? Jaws?"
he asked confused.

"No. Jawn!"
I clarified.

In my mind the script was our outline, the drama was our fill in, the interviews were our 3D, and our travels from coast to coast made the piece grand in scale. While the broken camera glitch we created in the transitions of our edits, made it gush with drips and primo paint splats! Thus, layered like a "jawn". As Matt and I continued with these punk rock style edits on multiple time lines, things were a little disorganized, but I could see the story clear as my love for Bella. She was always on my mind as the hobos were being assembled on the timeline.

I continued to share clips of our edits to many of my hobo friends on a laptop at my art gallery gig over glasses of wine. But none of them seemed too impressed. In fact, nobody seemed to dig what I was doing. Not even Matthew at times, but he kept moving forward by finding themes within the documentary end of the picture he was more enthusiastic about. He was much more confident with the doc, then the drama. The acting just turned him off. But I wasn't so critical of it. I just hoped people down the road would swallow the script better than him. He always wanted to cut pieces of the story I wrote out, which led to many long conversations between us. As he criticized the quality of our acting, I just took the hits and reminded him…

"If we cut Ruin and I
out of the film,
we don't have anything original.
We'd just have a doc."

"Maybe it's not to late for that."
he said seriously.

That burned me up!

"That's what you want?"
I barked.

"No, it is too late for that!"
he yelled.

That burned me up even more.

"You… granola-head."
I murmured softly.

I guess what I wrote meant more to me than I realized in the beginning. But he wanted to finish it with me despite all the discouraging moments we had editing the picture. At one point I was so discouraged I sent for a bottle of Ketamine to try and resurrect my spirits. Why junkies think tranquilizers will uplift anything is perplexing. I justified the purchase by writing "K" into the opening narration, which needed some "cook up" coverage.

A week later, when the bottle oh "K" made it's way to NOLA thanks to my boy Valle, I shot video of me cooking up the bottle as an insert for the opening narration of the movie. Then I bumped up and looked at the cuts on the timelines some more.

I had my legs crossed on the couch while the monitor ran the video as I began to levitate over the couch high on "K". Soon, I found myself just under the ceiling over Matthew. On good K, like that was, I turn into helium balloon! Up there, I was in full Yoda mode trying to execute a mind whammy on the cuts as I floated as gently as a feather, back down to the couch and into my body below once again.

When I woke from my "K-hole", I walked out to Matt's hammock in his back yard to try and reconnect the brain waves the ketamine had disconnected. Moments later, Matthew found me outside, swinging back and forth, dreaming. I shared my vision with him…

"In after effects…
could you create
a stray planet on the horizon?
And maybe have Saturn
dripping in the background?"

"Ahhhhh, no Braze."

"I see spaceships within a universe
of aerosol art above the trains."

"That's not,
what our movie's about Braze."

Matt just blew that off, but didn't get mad. Instead, with the utmost clarity, Matt stated precisely why spaceships could not be created in the frame. Why he even took the time to respond to such ludicrous talk of mine, I'm not sure. He's just a nice guy! And became the best friend I had in New Orleans. He had me find solutions to personal and creative conflicts through conversation because drugs where not a part of his equation.

Matthew encouraged me by pointing out the good I didn't see in myself. But Bella was getting closer and closer to bringing out my bad self more and more. And I always loved what duality in me did for my personality disorder! I was beginning to feel just like my old self again after bumping that bottle of K.

HOBOS OF DARKNESS

Hopping trains is strange and Hard
When shrooming in the train Yard

After looking at the edits for over a year, I decided to take Bella on a train hopping adventure to the West Coast. After seeing so many clips of the movie, she was jonezing to catch out too! So I looked at my old crew change, and found a train for us to ride out of the Avondale Yard in the West Bank of New Orleans. It was a hot shot to LA that pass through daily. To highlight the drastic difference in our backgrounds, let me share this… when I set out to hop trains for the first time, my mother wanted to disown me! But Bella's family, they threw her a going away party. Her Dad had always wanted to hop a train and her Mom thought it could make her daughter a stronger feminist, hippie, or both. Though her brothers had mixed opinions about me and who I was, filmmaker guy - graffiti writer dude - city punk, they were all excited for Bella to hop a train! And her little stepsister Kirka wanted to go with us so bad she packed a bag with her skateboard sticking out of it! I remember her crying when we said that she couldn't go.

Her lil sis Kirka wanted to get out of the bayou so bad she would often run away to Bella's forty miles away by "skitching" rides on her skateboard down Highway Old 90 to New Orleans. I had to admire Kirka's guts! And unlike all the academics in the family, Kirka couldn't care less about a schoolbook. There was a lot in that little girl that reminded me of myself.

Now… how my Mom always discouraged me from doing the wrong thing, and Bella's parents seem to celebrate it perplexed me. In that, I came out so bad, and she came out so damn good it seemed. Despite how cautious I was to not get too close to Bell's family, I was happy to be admired by them at times. But not very comfortable around them just yet; I can't explain why.

Bella & I had our bags packed extra light because it was the end of June. I figured we wouldn't need much to keep warm. But just in case, Bella brought something to warm us up. And this is where it gets trippy. At that time, Bella and roommate Lorry were sitting on a lot of magic mushrooms; pounds! Here's why…

Lorry met a guy she like named Justin while giving him a lap dances at The Rising Sun Strip Club. Later they started dating. And that's when he turned her on to… growing mushrooms, in the closets of her apartment. Bella got in on the project too! Together, the three of them successfully grew so much that it found its way from the ice tea in the refrigerator to the honey in the kitchen cabinets. Underneath every bed in the house were screens filled with fresh picked fat caps drying out. In many drawers and closet shelves, you could find oversized zip locks filled with pounds of shrooms! Now I sold a lot of drugs in my life, but never had I made so much at home. I was impressed! But also shocked that this guy let these two girls in on his thing? Now I liked this guy, Justin, who was schooling them in fungi. But here's the funny part! He was growing shrooms at his apartment too. And this guy, being a photographer, always took "film" photos of the entire process. He was a nut about the process of it all and dreamed of being a photographer one day. But he wasn't "professional" enough yet, to develop his own photographs. So he dropped them off at the drugstore to get developed. …Yup. Eventually, one of the drugstore employees developing the pictures noticed the smurf village Justin was growing… and the photo matte employee called the cops. Busted!

Justin got busted with a search warrant and the cops locked him up, while Bella and Lorry dodged the bullet. But by then the girls knew the growing process, and kept on keeping on. So, there were plenty of shrooms around to eat. And ohwww, did we! We shrooms dosed and screwed so much that we began coming spores on each other. I even began just putting them in my tea in the morning before I went to work. Eventually it wasn't as if I was tripping anymore, but on a permanent vacation. The drug was good, and I could never get enough of a good time. No one ever knew I was high. I could handle it.

In fact, we we're both having such good time on the shrooms, that Bella decided to share some caps with her Mom and Dad at her "train-hop going away party." I found that so far out man! There was a big part of me that thought her family was my kind of people. How could I go wrong here? They made me feel as though I had nothing to hide about myself. Their hippie boundaries seemed limitless; like me.

When we packed our bags the next morning, Bella brought a full jar of Blue Honey with her. I was certainly not rolling sober on the rails this time, and was really looking forward to it! The monster in me was back!

"You going to make love to me
tripping on a train?"
I asked sweetly.

"Maybe."

I was very excited at the prospect of a shroom rush while racing on the rails with my pants down at sunset as I took Bella from behind with her long hair brushing my face. I pined for it, her, my fantasies, all at once; just like everything else I ever overdosed! Copping crack on a corner can really suck. But tripping on a train and making love to a beautiful young hippie chic is much too epic for me not to partake in, and have any regrets what so ever.

That night, Matt dropped us off at the yard to hop out. We found the yard really active with workers. And soon after we found our way in the yard, some of those workers chased us out on quads as we tried to sneak towards the trains.

Defeated at our first attempt to hide in the yard, Bella and I had to camp in a cemetery next to it and sleep just a few feet above some dead dude to wait for our train the next day. And y'know… they can't bury them too deep in New Orleans. I had Poltergeist nightmares that night with that casket just under my head. Bella caressed my head back to sleep every time I woke up startled.

A little after dawn we woke up and had some water and trail mix for breakfast, as I started to day dreamed about the ride ahead while I watched Bella's lips wrap around the top of the water bottle and her throat opened up to take it all down. The thought of Bella and I having dirty hobo sex on a train made my legs rub together like a cricket! But I kept my composure, despite my uncontrollable thoughts. Back then my thoughts owned me. After breakfast we devised a plan to enter the yard more discretely this time; it was daylight now. To try and stay under the radar of workers on our way to the train, yet to arrive… we built a bridge to the yard over a sewage canal. Then, we found a huge tree to perch in and wait on our ride at noon. After our failed attempt to enter the yard the night before, the bridge was to help us enter it a little quicker, and more covertly. And sitting in the tree helped us scout the trains as they entered the yard, without actually being in it. With the parked trains lined up track after track on our side, hanging out up there was the only way to spot the trains coming in, without being in the yard where we could get ousted once again by the bulls. On the other side of the yard was the office, so it was this side, or nothing.

It was comfortable in the tree after we found some branches that we could actually lay down on. Relaxed, my imagination raced to monkey business in the tree, as Bella's long legs opened over paper shedding branches as I filled my journal with positions I had in mind. Her braless breasts hung out and moved gently with the branches under her dirty T-shirt. Then, she scooped out a spoon full of the good stuff from the magic jar, and fed me, then her, some honey.

We kissed for what felt like an hour in the tree as the leaves gave us shade and some privacy so that my mouth could suck on her nipples while she played me, vigorously. And eventually with a honey soaked brain and a belly sprayed with spores, I had to climb down from the tree to go to the bathroom, and clean myself off! When I got back to Bella up in the tree, she was sleeping pleasantly like a beautiful, wondrous birdy.

Totally tripping at this point, I unbutton my pants to relax and let my sneakers fall off my feet to the ground. I caught a trail from my falling pumas.

Goodness warmed my body and my hair started dancing in the breeze. Then I laid back and must have dozed off as well. The next thing I knew, Bell woke me up really excited!

"U.P. double stack!
Coming in!"

My eyes opened wide and clear, but my mind was still soaked in blue honey. I've woken up confused like this before, but tripping with my pants unbuttoned in a tree, with no shoes on, and a big bird next to me that could talk… was a first! My mouth was dry! My face was numb! I could barely breath in a wild attack of psilocybin rapture as I quickly rose from a dead sleep. Dazed…

"Oh, man, wow.
I gotta hop this train now, huh."

Then, as if the scene wasn't too much to wake to already… the feathers fell from the big bird next to me like petals from a flower. Then that wondrous birdy, morphed… into Bella, magically! Once I noticed it was Bell and not a big bird, I got more comfortable in my skin again. She was so excited, like a little girl with Christmas in her eyes! With the excitement of a child seeing Santa she seemed to look right through me though, and at our train rolling in to the yard. And then, when it truly dawned on me where I was, and what was going on… it dawned on me

"Damn!
We gotta hop this train, tripping face,
in broad daylight?"

But none of this, and nothing ever seemed to freak her out. She had a wall around her that nothing could get through… but me. She carried a thicker aura then I'd ever seen around anyone!

She climbed down the tree and snuck over towards the yard without hesitation. When I got down from the perch, I had to find my shoes before I could catch up with her as my head filled with the sounds of the trains in the yard. It was all very intimidating to me this time, unlike hoping out with Matt & Sara, sober.

Though we packed light, we had a four-day train ride ahead of us and we were carrying five gallons of water. When I caught up with her at the edge of the yard, we looked at each other and just took some deep breaths. Then, she leaned in to kiss me; mouth full of rose petals! I kissed her till the petals turned to rose water, opened my eyes, and noticed her looking not at me, but at the train yard.

"Do you smell that?"
she asked.

I sniffed, and smelled what I thought was her beautiful body, beating for me.

"I smell…
all that matters to me."

"I smell the train diesel."
She told me.

"Smell is matter."
I murmured.

"That's the smell of adventure,"
she added.

Obviously we were on different wavelengths; hers on the train, mine on her. Her sweet scent drove me so crazy I blurted out, for the first time…

"I love you."

I think she heard me. Orbs around her body seem to panic, then she vanished right in front of me! Leaving just a silhouette of her self after what appeared to be an emergency exit from this dimension! I stood there alone in a psilocybin honeycomb wondering if any of that… really just happened? It felt as though she made herself disappear in an emergency response to my feelings for her. Then, she popped back into my presence! And said…

"The hairs on my arm are standing up."
That's not exactly what I wanted to hear, but not exactly bad either. I believed…

"That's your body talking to
you Bella."

Then she slipped back out of the fabric of my reality once again! I couldn't tell if we were just not on the same cosmic waves, or my awareness had the effect of a broken TV! And then suddenly I was shaken by something rumbling in the air over the train yard! When I looked up, I noticed helicopters flying very low, and in slow motion just over our heads. I looked back down and found Bella there with me again gathering her backpack like a movie marine, before she double timed it to our make shift bridge, leaving those orbs in her path like a trail of animated bubbles. Within all the chaos, I began to find my comfort in the danger zone once again, and was once again in a state of oozing euphoria!

"Damn.
Damn good shrooms."

As I chased after her I had Jim Morrison in mind as her orbs swarmed around me and made me feel as special as a Rockstar. I gathered what I could of my marbles and put them in my backpack as I followed Bell. Like Ruin, Bella was a strong leading woman. As we slowed down and crawled on our bridge over the sewer water below us, I morph to a child with my grandpa!

In a flashback… I found myself with my Grandpa on a train trestle in my childhood; actually, below the trestle where he and I climbed on the crossbars over what I remember… was raging creek below! Falling wasn't an option, and it was impossible for that to happen with my Grandpa there. But I was independent!

"I got it Pop,
just let me walk!
I got it!"

My Grandpa would encourage me to climb anywhere I wanted to, as high as I could! But I wasn't with my Pop at this time, but Bella. Time and I have what I call, an open relationship.

"Look at me!
I'm doing it Pop."

"Pop?"
Bella asked,
"You OK Braze?"

I breathed, my Grandpa vanished, and I came back to whatever reality I was in with Bella…

"I'm good Bell,"
I tried to assure.

As we entered the yard on our hands and knees, it began to sun shower, beautifully, under a bright sun that had a big cartoon smile, dimples, and puffy, happy cheeks. I, it, was all, a perfect mess! In drenching tiny drops of wetness, and crystal daylight, we ducked and weaved; tripping over parked trains and across the yard to where the mainline was and our ride was parked, temporarily. It rained without a cloud in the sky and with Bella, felt nearly pornographic to me. As if it were manifested just for me to see her wet and sexy crawling in the dirt on her hands and knees with me and only me.

I looked up to the blissful sun above for reassurance that this was all somewhat… real. Only to find that big star sweating pure agent-orange juice from its sun flares! I opened my dry mouth and closed my eyes to wet my tongue with what I believed was magic, or just plain acid rain. And when I opened my eyelids… my head was in the clouds with a huge hawk wearing… a basketball jersey? Yup! As it got closer, I found myself in The Philadelphia Spectrum with Julius Erving soaring over my head to the basket making a tomahawk dunk! Military helicopters followed him and brought me back to the tour at hand where Kraftwerk layered the industrial beats in the train yard as I followed Bella forward.

I was comfortably confused, and slightly victim to all in the Giger Room at the upper most chapel of my Limelight mind where Keoki mind fucked me in the ear with candy flipped nonsense… obviously, tripping face indeed. My awareness often plays shoots and ladders with altered states beyond outer limits. How could I ever explain any of these thoughts to Bella in the beginning? So I didn't, as we set up underneath a boxcar next to the Union Pacific double stack we wanted to hop.

"Does that car look good?"
she asked.

"Nope,"
because I noticed,
"it has no bottom Bella."

As the rain fell and gathered next to us in a small drainage ditch, I felt as young as ever, on another outlaw adventure! I breathed it in…

"Out here,
I'm fifteen forever."
I murmured.

By this time in our relationship, my murmurs often went unnoticed, or maybe just ignored by Bella; like a person with a chronic cough or something. But she was stoned too! I could see it in the way her lips gently brushed her teeth and her eyeballs vibrated with electrical voltage oscillations of the third kind. On the shrooms, everything in the yard pulsed with energy from elsewhere and stain glassed my vision with tainted religions. The honey throbbed in euphoric streams from my eyebrows, passed my cock, to my toes.

"Bella,
I'm going to find us a bottom."

…Any train hoppers goal, every junkie's nightmare!

But that didn't come to mind at the time. I was just looking for a double-stack bucket with a floor. And after walking just a few yards to scout a double-stack with a bottom, the train began to roll back! I double-timed it over to Bella and watched the cars roll by us, back into the yard.

"Is it leaving?"
she asked.

"No,
they're building the train Bell."

While on the ground hiding and chewing dirt, we could see clearly underneath each car passing us. So I kept my eyes open for the "bottom" I was looking for because as much as I've wanted to die at times, I only wanted to stop the suffering. Riding suicide (on the crossbars of a double-stack bucket without a bottom) sounds more like suffering than a solution. And suffering was something I never wanted to introduce to Bella. Soon enough, a car with a bottom went by which wiped the thought of suicide from my mind.

"That's our car Bella!"

She was on the ground next to me, wet, super sexy, breathing heavy like a dirty extra in a Motley Crue video. She was too cute to look like a train hopper, but hot enough to look like a model posing as one! So much younger than I, she was probably too young to fall in love with. But, I already did…

"I love you."
I said again, softly.

"What?"
she whispered.
Unable to hear me by the moving train.

"I love you Bella!"

She glowed through the grime as the rain steamed off of her. I knew she heard what I said. Her eyes exploded wide, reducing her to just a little girl as trains on both sides of us moved and created a sound garden around us. She looked so young and eager that if we got caught at that moment in the yard, I felt they'd put me in cuffs till the Amber Alert checked out. Maybe it was the mushrooms, but the gravity of her youth began to pressure me. Then, before I could retreat, she crawled out of her pickle pack, grabbed my face and made out with me between the trains. A few months ago she was a teenager, now she was hopping trains with an older man, and with her families blessing. In retrospect, I needed to know she loved me, more than I wanted to tell her that I loved her. I was very insecure, moments in my life often weighed on how much I was liked by someone, if not everyone.

"That was the first time
a guy ever said that to me."

"I said it earlier,

but you seem to run away Bell."

"I didn't run away.
I went to my place."

"Your place?"
I asked.

"Where I go when I'm scared."

"Why were you scared?"

"Because…"
she paused,
"I know you're the one."

She looked at me with utmost trust, as if she'd follow me anywhere. But she would never follow anyone. It was I in fact who was following her around. I knew that, and so did she. She wouldn't have it any other way! Bella didn't give guys attention, nor would she accept any from them. But finally, she welcomed me in her life. My wicked letters and fauvist poetry broke the lynx!

"Were you ever in love before?"
I asked.

"No.
But a boy
kind of said he loved me before."

Bella still thought in terms of boys, and I had the emotional maturity of one, so, I went with it.

"He kinda said it?"
I asked in a way so she would clarify.

"He carved my name
into his chest."

"What happened to him?"
I asked concerned.

"He enlisted senior year.
They all wanted to be heroes,
if they couldn't

play college football."

Our train finally stopped rolling backwards when it locked onto the cars it was picking up in the yard. Then, it began to roll forward again. Soon after it did, I spotted that car with the bottom.

"It's time Bella."

"You la mi?"
she asked very happy.

I spoke her slang by this time.

"I luv ya,"
I assured her.

With our spring love and deviant courage, we rose to our feet and ran along the train to catch up with the steel ladder on the side of the double-stack car. It was going slow. I hopped on first to show her how it's done. With three gallons of water in my hands, I climbed up the ladder and hoisted my backpack over my head and into the bucket; it was easy. But when my body followed with some shroomy acrobats, the water bottle in my teeth snapped in my face. Then my ass hit the bottom side of the bucket with the other two water jugs in each hand as they hit the floor and blew up!

"How the… what the?"
bewildered by my stupidity.

I made it on, but all my water was gone! I stood up and looked over the steel wall of the bucket I was standing in and found Bella right there in step with the train.

"You go girl!"
I cheered.

I was a little nervous for her, but her mind was made up. Then, as she ran with the train, it started going a little faster. On the shrooms… I caught trails off her, dash towards me! My imagination began to remix reality once again and go horror show. DJ Swamp set fire to the grooves in my mind! The strong young woman I admired hopping the train, began to morph into a little girl chasing a school bus! Her backpack became a school bag! Her plastic containers of water in each hand… became a textbook and a lunch box!

"This looks twisted,"
I murmured.

Guilt flooded my cells! I instantly felt responsible for bringing this girl to a dangerous place like a train yard. But lust blinded me. That's no excuse!

"You're older and
should of known better!"
I told myself.

In this nightmare of mine, I felt she was chasing me, not just the train! As she ran for the freight car to catch up with me, lunchbox and books in hand… the shrooms morphed the train I was on… into a tan van this girl running after it to get inside as if it were full of candy. I could take watching this! I wanted off the train, and the trip to be over immediately! But I couldn't seem to form the words to communicate with Bella. My… No please wait, thought; came out…

"Mo primus wonka!"

Which reduced the creep show to lower emotional depths for me. School bells rang, police sirens roared, the little girl kept coming towards my kind of danger. And then my mom cried in my mind, as always…

"Why Braze?
Why!"

Hopping a train never felt wrong until the moment I felt like a man luring a schoolgirl to his kind of excitement. As Lil Bella risked her life with a smile, the fear I felt at that moment was real. I violently shook my head to shake the snaps that came to me from mushroom caps! And when my head cleared of that girly nonsense, I wondered… where'd that come from?

I consider myself a seer of sorts at this point. One who can see where he's coming from, and where he's going, in his dreams. But that was new territory. What did that hallucination say about us? I felt there was more to come from that direction and wasn't looking forward to it.

As I regained my composure, the train raced out of her reach. But at least I saw Bella as the adult she was once again, though she couldn't catch up and hop the train after all. I was still overwhelmed by the shrooms, but relieved all this chaos was coming to an end when I began to climb off the train and abort the ride and maybe try again some other time. But Bella didn't seem to think it was over.

"I'm coming Braze!"
she screamed.

I loved it when she said that. But not that time!

"NO!
Bella stop!"
I urged.

She tried to throw her water jugs onto the train, but they smashed against the container and broke. She picked up her stride and gained on the train! Her hands reached forward and her fingers inched out for the ladder. When she caught hold of a bar on the ladder with one hand, there are only two ways to go at that point… with it, or under it! I climbed back aboard to get out of her way! And just as I did, her other hand found it's way to the ladder and with the grace of a beautiful ballerina, she hopped her first train… and made it look easy.

"You go girl!
You did it!"

But just at that moment, as she began to pull herself up to the top of the bucket, we approached the yard office where the bulls were sitting in their parked truck. When I noticed them, I looked back to Bella and found her first leg up and over the side of the train.

"Bulls!"
I cautioned.

And then she ducked her head down.

"NO!
No, get in Bell!"

With one leg over the top of the bucket, and one leg on the ladder on the outside, she froze and straddled the side of the train. In my life, I rarely thought… don't do it. But rather, don't get caught doing it! Bella was on the same page by hopping trains, growing mushrooms and writing graffiti.

As the train made its way out of the yard, and far away from the yard office, Bella made it inside the bucket with me. Her eyes told me the shrooms continued to have their effect. How she held it together on them, I'll never know. Her blue veins pulsed against her pale skin while her overheated body thunderstruck me like Morgan O'Kane playing his banjo on a subway platform in New York City. She was everything I could physically want in a person at that time. And her mind and ways aroused me even more so. While the train rolled West and the rain continued to fall gently, she took off her clothes and decided to shower in it. Then she laid out across the trestle between two trains as if she was poolside at the Bi-Water Country Club. Together we trained out of New Orleans, dirty naked and liberated.

Later that day after a few more spoons full of psilocybin honey, the sun fell on our burning skin. As the trip raced at high speed, the rain finally stopped after rinsing us thoroughly. And the wind polished us dry with train exhaust, like heaters for the homeless found on the sidewalk above a subway. Though on blue-honey everything intoxicated me. What a day! Yet later, in the middle of the night… we woke very, very cold in those winds of travel.

"Why didn't we pack warm clothes?"
she yelled through the wind.

"I thought it would be
a hot ride in June!"

She looked at me with the sarcastic anger of a WWF wrestler. But hell…

"I was mistaken!"
I admitted.

"Gravely!"

Turned out Miss Bayou Bella was just a thin-blooded person; she couldn't take the cold! So I wrapped her in every piece of clothing we packed to keep her warm that first night. Still cold, I jogged in place with her till the sun came up.

Much later that day we found ourselves at the other side of the weather spectrum as the sun came back with a burning need for fluids, other than honey. But the day before, we broke all our bottles of water! Getting off the train to get more would be hard, but necessary to make the trip to LA.

"We need to jump off and get water."

"We can catch another train…
right Braze?"

I nodded yes. But I wasn't enthusiastic to scout another yard. I wanted to stay on that hotshot to The Coast. So, like always, I kept my eyes peeled for options.

And as the train got closer to the city of Houston, it began to stop and go again, and again, as they often do entering big cities. Like airliners circle before landing, trains inch there way into the cities sometimes. While doing this crawl into Houston, we started to hug a highway. And when the train came to another complete stop, I noticed a gas station just across the road. So I decided to make a fast break for it without a second thought!

"Be right back Bell!"

Then I jumped off the freight car and darted back and forth across the highway like a desperate video game frog to that gas station! Once I got there, I ran inside the mini mart, grabbed two gallons of water, butted to the front of the line at the register, then I dropped a fiver…

"I gotta run peoples!"

I ran out of the mini mart from the bewilderment of everyone inside and raced my way back across the highway to the chorus of honking horns and a few cheers from the gas station! As if Spike Jonze choreographed me to stand in for a Beastie Boy.

And without a slip or fall, I got back inside the bucket of our double stack with no problem, easy! It was a love story, and I was the gentleman who then leaned over to kiss the dame I retrieved water for. But she slapped me!

"You jerk!"
she screamed in my face.
"Next time you make a big decision like that,
I want in on it!"

"What?
Why are you so pissed?"

"We are hopping these trains together!
So we make the decisions together!
Are we clear!"

"Ah… Yes?"
I answered nearly speechless.

"Promise me,
you won't do that again!"

"I, promise Bell."

Then she swigged from one of the water bottles like it were a handle of whiskey, and then made her way to the other side of the bucket really pissed off, just eight feet away from me. That's as far as she could get.

All I know is what pop culture and back alleys taught me, neither of which defined a strong independent person such as Bella. I was learning everyday how well she carried herself, stood her ground, and made all her own decisions. I gave her space the rest of that day. Then when night fell, we shared the same hammock.

When our ride hugged Mexico, we entered the hottest yard of all my travels. On the U.S. border in EL PASO, it seemed we entered the Alcatraz of train yards! It's protected against riders at the border with tall watchtowers, rows of barbwire fences and camera's that detect the heat from your body some say. As we rolled into it, we stayed low and under a grey sheet I brought with us. I couldn't hide the heat from my body, but I could blend us in with the floor while passing the towers. We made it in no problem. But then, it made a very, very long stop inside the yard. After being parked in it for hours, I noticed a break in the fence under a highway overpass. I couldn't understand how this yard with such security had a breach in the fence. But now that the shrooms wore off and I was sobered up again, I was filled with love and guts. And not afraid to challenge myself further! So I pointed out the opening to Bell, without saying a word. She read my mind…

"I want sugar."
she said.

"Caffeine too!"
I craved.

And before we snuck over to the break in the fence, we made that decision together this time.

Once out of the yard (and not knowing exactly where we were going) we hoped to find a gas station just a block or two away to score some snacks. To double down on our bet that we could get away with doing this, and to move quicker, we left our bags on the train before we went on our quest for instant gratification! We ran straight up the middle of a dark quite street together… under street lamps, holding hands, and laughing like an after school special just before it goes horribly wrong! We looked for the mini-mart we had in mind like a scientist looking for a planet just beyond Neptune. And I kept checking behind us to see if our train got back on the move. If that train left without us, our gear would be gone. And then we'd be really desperate drifters!

After running three blocks from the yard, the Etnos gas station manifested! Inside, we were an excited couple on a one-minute shopping spree filling our hands with Cokes and Twizzlers before leaving more cash than was needed on the counter by the cashier.

"Thank you!"
as I rushed out.

"We have a train to catch!"
Bella informed the cashier.

And ran out together! What a blast! At this time I was well beyond my teenage years, but acting every bit like one, with a beautiful girl who just left her teens behind. I knew that what I was experiencing at that time, may be the last time I ever get a chance to live like that again.

As I ran in the dark with a lust for life in every kick, love on the tips of my fingers entangled with hers… no movie to shoot, no camp to motivate, no batteries to charge or interviews to acquire with Bella… my life took on feelings of success racing across America on a steady diet of fungi that I'd thought were long behind me! I knew where I was, and what I was doing. I was high again!

"A lil love and drugs
will do it ever-time,"
I murmured.

And why not enjoy it? Because out there on the edge of edges once again I realized that jail or death could be right down the road! I felt the carefree energy that pulsed through the bones of all the train hoppers bodies I'd met researching my project for the first time, when I hobo'd carefree with Bella.

And maybe… that's what "On The Road" is for most people. Not about writing a book, as I think of it, but living one out! I've been doing it the whole time, maybe we all are. But I didn't realize it till I was there on the rails with Bell. I was so project and caper oriented my whole life, enjoying the ride was only found in altered states, not in the present one. Being with Bella brought me to an appreciation of life I never felt before. Loving her was worlds apart from being left alone on this planet with everything I couldn't forget. As we laughed and raced down the street to our train like children at play, it was clear that I couldn't have real times like those on the best pages of my journals.

We found our way back in the yard and under the bull towers to our "bucket" where our bags and journals sat waiting for our return. Just twenty minutes later, while fucking like dirty rabbits, the train pulled out bound for LA into another cold night. So as we rolled from El Paso, Bella bundled herself up to catch some winks as I came upon a headlight that burned itself into my fabric. Just as some only can when you're alone with them. I looked down at Bella sleeping, then ahead at that special moment of mine... when the unit of our train was a mile or so ahead as it snaked around the side of a cliff. That single headlamp on the lead unit created another intimate moment for me. One more within all the other untamed shows on the rails! With that headlamp stabbing into blackness, cliff side of the Earth, on the edge of the globe, held together by science knows what, I Was There! On that train, far from the industrial aftermath of our history to come, closing in on my own extinction, on metal burning fuel that stars birthed long before I was born to race off this big Blue Island and create spiritual tourism for all! It was out there in the greater expanses of land and space that I felt as close to the universe as an astronaut. Overwhelmed by what, and where I was within it... lost, and found, in words that did more harm than good. And if not for the rides that anchored me in The Art of Train Hoppin, I would have drifted into the abyss of all my fears and lost myself to the drugs that nearly killed me before I hopped out of Philly from them. My lifetime of mistakes flashed before me out there. Thoughts of suicide surfaced again from nowhere, but I held myself back from jumping off the train I was on with the woman I loved. Exit by suicide is a door that some can't seem to ever close; like me. If belief in a higher power can save you, then the trains were my saviors when I was in need at that chapter of my life. I finally saw the light that night, on a Union Pacific hot shot!

More brisk air swirled through our bucket as we full throttled through the desert when Bella woke up shivering as I jogged in place singing "Eye Of The Tiger". She swung out of the hammock, took it down and used it as a windbreaker and jogged with me, but she didn't know the words to the song.

The next day, we burned up in the sun and rationed what was left of our water. The spectrum of extremes is dire out there, like that of my own uncontrollable emotions at times. And at last, as if reaching an oasis, we went through the pleasant windmill farms and orange groves of California before hopping off just outside LA. Where we bussed downtown to the city, took a subway to West Hollywood, and back to old stomping grounds of mine when I was trafficking ketamine. Under the radar, Bella and I camped in Runyon Canyon Park at night and attended the free yoga classes there every morning. Some might say hobo-glamping.

"Someday, I want to study yoga,"
she mentioned.

During the brighter day, we sat at the bench at the top of that big hill in the park and meditated over the infinity pools, read paperbacks, made notes. And at night, we walked The Sunset Strip to lie on a mattress at the Sky Bar, stopped at Canters Deli on Fairfax afterward, and wrote graffiti on the boulevard of bought stars. And a day later after dining at Musso & Frank Grill and having Roscoe's Chicken & Waffles for desert, we copped some French dip sandwiches at Philippe's and caught an AMTRAK train home where we discretely squatted in a sleeper car. My grandfather reminded me more than once growing up that…

"I got class,
it's just last class."

FINAL CUT

CURE for the CRASH
The Art of Train Hoppin

Back in New Orleans with a fresh train in my veins, my attention was recommitted to the movie as we neared the final cut. With just a few scenes to be polished, the end was in sight, at least to me. But Matt wondered if the story would actually come together and make sense once all the work from the multiple timelines was married. Besides the tough crowds in my hobo circle, and Bella, no one else had seen the Picture. Out of mushrooms, but yearning to escape from my racing mind, the hairs on my arms led me to a house to score in the 7th Ward. An old lady named Auntie became my good friend there; it was after all, her crack house.

Occasionally, I'd stop by there to blow off steam. I'd be buzzing with euphoria, shaking in mania with outrageous ideas for stories to come with strippers, Jesus, shopping karts, Buddha, infinity, Muhammad, and scitzoprenia… that hitting on some crack, actually brought me down. I could hit on shit and get a fix quick; I had no time for drinks! And when I'd stop over her house, you'd think by Auntie's reaction, I was one of her grandchildren stopping by, not some dude copping rock. She'd spring from the couch every time I walked in the door and start straitening the place up and apologizing for the mess. The house had no electricity, there were crack-heads always looking around on the floor for dropped rocks (as if) and the place had little to no furniture. But not Auntie, she was just turned on and filled with life when I came in! Maybe it was the conversations I had with her, the ice tea I brought over, or the fact that I was the only person who walked in with a smile. Perhaps I just brightened her day, I du-know. But once I got "grounded" again, and the mania subsided with the help of jogging and not listening to any music for a while, it saddened me… yet I said goodbye to Auntie, and turned away from that escape from the war.

During that time Matt & I continued to spend early mornings after long nights at the Mac, cutting and pasting our experiment together. It was a Mary Shelley of a project that we hoped to give life to. In fact, I felt the movie and I may be on the same path and showed signs of life together. After all, we were both monsters. All the energy I put forth on the Philly streets most of my life, was channeled into completing that movie in New Orleans. And once we had each Act completed on the multiple timelines, it all fell together like bones and parts in the game Operation! Finally, in 2010'ish, we completed a full cut on one timeline.

"Do you think anyone will like it?"
I asked Matt

He shrugged his shoulders. He didn't know. But I kept thinking of all the punk music and early hip-hop productions I drew ideas from and thought this movie was my wicked interpretation of those influences. And I was happy with that! From the start, I was wise enough to know I couldn't make a good movie by having the best camera. But I could produce something worthy of note with anything, as long as I had a good story.

"We did our best,"
Matt concluded,
"It's something original."

When we got that good rough cut of the picture completed, I felt better than ever! I think that energy led Bella and I to become even closer, as if we weren't nearly glued together already. When you're happy and positive, like we were, you're magnets for each other. So, I asked…

"Do you want to move in together?"

"…Maybe."

She always used that word, but I don't mind a maybe. Maybe's are nothing but a speed bump to me when I want something. I could always flip a maybe. And did so days later.

But rather than one move into the others apartment, we decided to find a place of "our" own. I was living in the Marigny Triangle and she was in Mid-Town Bayou St. John. After looking Uptown and in the Bi-Water, we found "our" spot in Old Algiers. It was a big enough change for us to get really excited about. The ferry ride over there from The Quarter made it feel to me as if I was moving to an island. And… the apartment sat a few blocks from the old house of Bill Burroughs! We talked about that on a ferry ride over…

"Some find a writer on the road at their door, "
I contemplated,
"While others,
find a naked clown on a bicycle."

"What's that suppose to mean?"
Bella asked.

"Stumps is my Karoac"

"Stumps is no Jack Karouac,"
she laughed.

Then, she read my mind.

"You're no William Burroughs."
she laughed.

"I have some books in me."
I said in defense.

"Then do it.
Writers write!"

She's right about that.

Once Bell and I moved across the Mississippi River, Matt & I relocated our "editing bay" to my place where we continued to tweak and re-shuffle the scenarios. Now let me remind you, that Matthew had absolutely no experience with editing or its software when we started. But as we neared the final cut of our Movie, two years after we started editing it, he quit the Bourbon Street club life, for the tech life, and took a job with a local production house. He was becoming a self-taught expert in areas I had no experience in. I mean, the only areas I considered myself experienced in were the tricks of the shade… like sneaking around, hopping trains, selling stuff. But I began to realize that maybe that wasn't all I knew, but rather that was just my comfort zone, one that needed changing.

Through the years of producing The Art of Train Hoppin' I spoke to 100's of people about the project and many of them would check back with me again and again and ask about its progress. Or when and where they could see it. The title The Art of Train Hoppin' said different things to different people. It gained the interest from intellects, the envy of dreamers, and some jeers from crusties. It seemed for years I was saying to everyone…

"It will be done in a couple months."

I said it so many times people began to laugh at me. So much so that The Art of Train Hoppin' became the title of an unfinished movie, rather than a movie coming soon.

Realizing this, I had to reinvent the project before I screened it. So Matt and I brainstormed some new titles. We narrowed it down to two… A Boxcar Named Ruin or CURE for the CRASH. Matt was leaning towards A Boxcar Named Ruin and even designed a web page for it that looked quite fresh and complete. But he's a font snob and was never happy with it. Yet at the end of the day, producing the project in New Orleans couldn't justify a Tennessee Williams mash up for a title. So CURE for the CRASH won.

I think the new title spoke as much for the movie we shot, as it did for my own story. With all my struggles and growing pains along the way, perhaps the rails in many ways did become my rehab, and the movie my program. I obviously didn't work a perfect program, but I worked at it. CURE for the CRASH… the Art of Train Hoppin' came to be in 2010, five years after the ideas conception. I entered the rough cut into a few festivals. Then I began looking at sound and polishing the opening narration of the picture with a local sound engineer from the WWII Museum. A couple months later, we got accepted to our first film festival, The Seattle Truly Indie Film Fest.

FLIPPING ROLES

I became the award-winning Criminal
What happened to him I never thought Possible

Rent poor, Bella and I didn't have an extra dime. While I finished the movie narration, the art gallery I worked at closed after making a bad move to another location. In the months that followed, Bella and I collaborated on touristy "graffiti-folk" paintings to sell in Pirates Alley for extra cash. And though our hearts were not in it, it fed us and paid the rent, but not enough to get us to the Film Fest on Seattle. So I had to call home for help. My Mom & Richy were always there for me. My dad was too, but I seldom spoke to him at this time. He was busy leading the good life in New Jersey with a new family, work, etc. Once Bella and I paid the bills, we jetted up to Seattle on two of my Moms airline employee benefit passes and got there a week before the screening to promote the movie.

When we made it up there and to downtown Seattle from the airport, we immediately hid our backpacks behind a dumpster to attend the Film Fests opening party. A few hundred people were there for a concert the Festival threw… a good time! And to save money up there, we decided to sleep on the bowling ally rooftop Ruin and I camped out on. So later that night after we partied with some other filmmakers, we gathered our backpacks from behind the dumpster, and went to the roof to crash.

Just as I rolled out my sleeping bag on the roof, Richy called to see how I was doing. When I told him I was crashing on a roof, he laughed.

"Rooftops!
You're forever a graffiti writer
sacrificing for your art!"

By this time in life, he knew how comfortable I was on the streets, though I'd rather sleep in lofts by now like him. And I could hear him in his place getting comfortable… scraping a plate of fresh cooked ketamine. I could hear it being done in the background of our conversation. I envisioned Rich standing in his kitchen by the microwave, chopping up a plate of K with a spatula. I could hear it happening! Or maybe, that's just what I wanted… to hear. I duhno.

"I admire you Bee.
But when I get there,
I'm not sleeping on a roof."

In the days that followed, Bella & I handed out flyers and hung up posters around town. And at night we'd attend the screenings to some of the movies at the Fest for free with our "Filmmaker" badges. And afterwards, with no one at the festival knowing, we snuck back on the bowling alley rooftop. It was great! Every morning we'd eat some breakfast at the supermarket across the street. Sharing that pseudo struggle with Bella was one of the best times of my life! And once again… I knew these times would end one day. So I noted what I could in my journal in hopes one day I could draw from them.

When Richy got to Seattle, he put us up at The Hotel Max; elaborate grunge rock themed lodging. I was ecstatic to see him, but felt a little embarrassed that the movie was still not 100%. When I met him in the lobby, I felt the need to clear the air immediately, by joking…

"Yo bro,
you came a long way to see
an unfinished movie."

"It isn't done yet?"
he asked surprised.

"I have a good rough cut done."
I said with an uncertain smile.

"They'll let you show that?"

"Well…"
I laughed,
"I'm not sure they know."

Richy just stood there with his mouth open. I could see on his face he couldn't believe that after all those years, the movie still wasn't done! So I decided to change the subject quickly. And do what I should have done in the first place…

"Richy, this is Bella."

"Pleasure to meet you Bella.
Are you a train hopper too?"

"I hopped one with Braze!"

"Please,
tell me about it Bella."

We forgot about my movie that was being screened that night, and traded stories all day. It's in the story that Richy and I lived out, that gave me the courage to hop the trains in the first place. I was always fronting and telling stories, but Richy was very humble, he didn't have to front, he was a pure player.

Now, it's common for Festivals to accept a movie from what they found in a rough-cut submission, but screen one? I du-know. Despite the incomplete state of the movie, it was curtain time. And despite all the promo Bella and I did that week, a crowd of maybe… forty people showed up. A biblical number, but…

"I came this far,
to show… so few, my movie?"
I murmured.

I just should have been happy that my brother made his way across the country. But once again, I felt more embarrassed than anything else. The lights drew down, the picture came to focus, I sunk in my chair, my brother rose to the edge of his as the movie began. A minute later… the camera broke on screen in the movie. The audience sighed.

"Hmm… maybe I got um,"
I murmured.

"You really break that camera?"
Richy whispered.

He looked puzzled, and I hoped everyone else did too. Moments later, when I dropped some cocky Mes swagger on the side of a train, Richy started to get into it.

"Ha ha haaa Braze!
You asshole!"
he cheered.

People in the theater even laughed at Mr. Mes, it was a relief! It really was nice to share a moment like that with Richy, and not be high. Whenever good times were in our lives, we were usually high, but not this time. We just had some food and ice teas during the screening. And 90 minutes later when the credits rolled, Rich turned to me.

"Yo bro,
your movie is like, like…"
he searched,
"…like a stream of consciousness."

After the lights came on, I was asked to come on stage and do a Q&A. When I got in front of the small audience, I crossed my legs and tried to get comfortable. I could see Richy from there with a smile on his face the size of a football as I leaned back on my hands and felt even more comfortable with him and Bella there as the questions came in…

"What gave you this idea?"
asked a student.

"Did you hop trains before the movie?"
asked a hipster.

"Did you ever see Emperor of the North?"
asked an old man

"What's Ruin doing now?"
a Mom wanted to know.

"Did you really drink the mouthwash?"
wondered a stoner.

It was my show! I knew all the answers without any double talk, not once. I thought about this project everyday for over five years. I found nothing anyone asked, or pointed out, could throw me. You could tell me it was great, or I was a loser, I knew there was truth in both. The story I wrote and played out was not just close to home, it was a homogenized glorification of my recklessness. Where my addictions, insecurities, imperfect poetry, and passions where structured to create a comfortable space for me to not be ashamed of any longer. I just titled, branded, and put it all in an artistic light that I was comfortable talking about. Many issues of mine were merely departmentalized in the project to start conversation. That night after the tiny screening in Seattle during the filmmaker Q&A, conversations grew into the cross talk of my addiction recovery.

I found that I began to be truly honest with my self and others by sharing CURE for The CRASH in all its flaws and character defects. The story may not be about me, but it feels like it at times. My story of recklessness is not much different than the other war stories I've heard over the years.

The next day Richy jetted back to Philly where he had a lot of balls in the air. He just cashed out of his landscaping business and completed building two houses from the ground up. But he was having a lot of trouble selling the properties when the real estate market crashed. If those houses didn't sell soon, he'd lose everything he worked for from the time he was sixteen. A half a million dollars was at stake. That's very big money on our block.

BOOK SAFE

In Seattle, there were a few more nights of screenings and, an awards party still to come. Now that our screening was over, Bella and I could relax every afternoon instead of passing out CURE for the CRASH flyers. During that time, I spoke to other filmmakers and learned a little bit about the distro process. I was told a film rep had to deal with a distributor for me.

"Cut them out."

"You can't."
responded a filmmaker.

"Why not?"
Bella asked.

"Distributors won't deal with you."

Then I immediately thought of all the musicians in my movie who were busking on the streets at the time. And who sold their own CD's to make money! Then I thought of ravers promoting events who made a lot of doe at outlaws parties. Even punk shows I'd gone to that were thrown in vacant spaces to make rent money. And so many more examples of DIY businesses I'd been apart of over the years sped through my mind like a dealer shuffling cards faster than light. A moment later, I interrupted the filmmakers in conversation while I was in a trance brought on by those flashbacks…

"Maybe you don't need them to get
your movie out there."

"Who? The film reps, or the media distributors?"
one asked me.

"Both."
I responded.

"The world will never see your film!"
they concluded.

"Who cares?
I'm more concerned
about making money."

"I've made five films."
one of them went on to say,
"I break even most of the time."

"Then… what's the point?"
I asked.

"Did you hop trains to make money?"
he questioned.

"No."
I stated,
"But I made a movie to make some."

"This is your first film?"

"Yes."

"First things first,"
he broke down,
"you just have to get it out there.
Maybe next time
you can make some money."

"If I don't make money this time,
there will be no next time."

We left it at that. They were nice guys just sharing their experiences. I had to hear it, because it wouldn't be the last time.

At the end of it all in Seattle Film Fest was an Awards Night Party held in the same theater I screened CURE for the CRASH. But this time, the place was packed, hundreds showed up! Bella and I were living it up at the festival screenings so much, we actually fell asleep on each other at the Awards Party in the back of the theater. Going from the Max Hotel back to the bowling alley rooftop made things a little less comfortable up there. We didn't sleep as much at night after Richy left, and ended up dozing off in our comfortable seats at the theater during the shindig. And then, Bella woke me up…

"Braze,
I think you just won."

"Won what?"

"I think your movie just
won an award.
I heard them say Cure for the Crash,
and I woke up."

"Get outta here.
Really?"

The thought of winning something there never crossed my mind. But people where clapping and looking back at us. But… maybe I was just paranoid. Or they were all looking at someone behind us. I turned around to see, but we in fact were in the last row.

"Everyone is looking at you,"
she whispered,
"You better go up there."

"Are you sure Bella?"

"I'm sure."
She said with a bright confident smile.

I took a deep breath, wiped the sleep from my eyes and brushed my fingers through my hair, got up, and walked on stage. Up there, sure enough, I was handed an award and then gestured to the microphone. I looked at the trophy, and found myself a little confused by it. It was a glass…

"Dildo, Wow!"

I was speechless and forgot where I was for a second. I was so confused by the sex toy award and the unfinished state of my movie, that I mumbled into the microphone…

"It was just a rough cut.
And this is a glass dildo."

"It's a work of art!"
someone yelled out laughing.

Not sure if he was referring to my movie, or the blown glass dildo, I went with the latter and held it over my head!

"This award speaks to
my inner hobosexual.
I do like it dirty!
Thanks!"

It was in fact a dirty, nasty lil award, for a crusty, movie no less. CURE for the CRASH had in fact won Best Picture! And later I would find out that the awarded trophies are locally made Seattle Truly Independent Film Festival or… S.T.I.F.F.Y awards! I knew my brother would do anything not to see me in an emergency room again, so it crossed my mind that night, that he paid someone off to encourage my efforts with an award. But Bella squashed that…

"I knew you could win.
Everyone did!"

The next morning we filled our water bottles, gathering our things, and commuted back to the airport. But as soon as we entered the terminal, I got busted going through security. The security screener took a second look at the contents of my bag through x-ray. Then they took it off the belt to search it.

"Oh damn.
I know what they found."
I said to Bell.

"What did you do?"

Then another security guard spoke up…

"Will the owner of this
bag step forward."

I did so, with my head down. As the guard walked over to a stainless steel table and placed my bag down. Then, he put on rubber gloves.

"Stand behind the yellow line please."

"OK."
I agreed.

"May I have permission
to search your bag."

"Maybe."

"Sir?"
"Just promise when you find it,
You'll be discreet."
I said softly.

He began to radiate excitement! He knew he was going to make a find and could hardly wait, so I gave him what he wanted.

"Go ahead my buddy,
I want you to find it,
I need help,"
I told him quietly.

Then I let my chest sink in, and made my shoulders nearly touch my ears while he looked through my pickle pack filled with dirty laundry. With my head down, I looked up towards Bella who was standing a few yards away from me. Her eyes were wide and her mouth was wide open not knowing what to expect! Then I spoke to the guard and decided to explain that…

"Listen, I'm in town for a film festival.
My movie won Best Feature Film."

And then, just at that moment… JACKPOT! From the very bottom of my bag the guard pulled out the Glass Dildo! And took a real close look at it! I don't think he knew what it was at first. I mean after all, it was a piece of art! Then I winked at Bella, who nearly laughed her head off when she realized I was just playing around! An old woman passing in a wheel chair looked at the dildo and dropped her jaw with astonishment. The geezer pushing her stopped and started to choke. A crowd of other onlookers whispered and snickered to each other. The guard stood holding the dildo like a judges gavel, looking at me for an explanation of some sort. So, I told him…

"I'm a filmmaker."

"Of what kind of movies?"

"An American hobo movie."

"American Homo's?"

"Well, yeah.
Some are."

I shook my head, laughed, and then I gave up screwing with him. The piece of blown glass he held so firmly a moment ago when he was trying to figure it out was then placed back in my bag with the delicate pinch of his thumb and index finger as if it was contagious! This security guard gave me the strong impression he was homophobic. But then again, maybe he just didn't like sex toys. Out of everything I ever trafficked, getting busted with that was a most memorable way to retire as a smuggler.

After our commute home to New Orleans and once back in the Algiers editing bay, I felt more determined then ever to get the final cut done! After winning an award with a rough cut, I felt more awards were possible if we worked a little harder on it. But Matt had something unexpected to share upon my return.

"I got a good job.
Editing for a production company
in Texas."

He must have seen how shocked I was, because he then began reassuring me we would finish the movie!

"We can continue working together
through screen sharing.
Don't worry!"

But continuing the collaboration with him on the movie was only half my worry. I felt my life would be a little less solid without the rock he had become in it. I could always count on him… his calming voice, generous nature, sharp intellect, cast of colorful friends and his address in the 7th ward where we ducked a house fire, gunfire, and emotional infernos of our own. Now, he was no longer to be a local anchor to all my outrageous ideas in New Orleans. Some of my best investments of time where spent editing the movie with Matt.

When he moved on, all I had in town was Bella. I was in love with her, but how long was she actually going to put up with me? There was still no roof on my enthusiasm and no bottom to my lows. Who want's to live with that? Not even me. Though I was playing the fence better than ever, I could fall at anytime. I even tried calling my brother about my concerns, but he was harder to reach these days. Pressures from his new investment properties mounted when the houses continued to sit on the market with hundreds of others in the neighborhood not selling.

I wouldn't say that he or I are very smart, but pretty very determined. As I taught myself to make a movie… Richy taught himself to build a home from the ground up, deal with city building permits, swing bank loans, manage labor and other challenges. If his houses sold when they were completed months ago, he would have been in better shape at this time. Things were tough all around, and we were too far apart to be of any real service to each other. So we dealt with things on our own.

Sick of living on the cheap in New Orleans, I took work and spotlights wherever I could find it. Such as graffiti painting coffee shop bathrooms for pay, and doing magazine cover commissions, as well as putting up Royal Street shows to play the "Street Artists" roll with Barry "Sole" Veda. We were good artists in a small city. I just had the skills to make things happen where other more talented artists from the street couldn't it seemed. Lowbrow/Street Art was slow to be embraced in New Orleans. What happened in the 90's everywhere else… came to NOLA ten years later. It's no fault to any artist down here, but to the galleries who wouldn't embrace them yet. It seemed everything I ever did wrong in Philly; I made art out of in New Orleans! The jobs, projects, interviews and awards to come from my work in New Orleans… followed the jobless years, unobtainable dreams, and unarticulated stories of crimes I tried to leave behind in Philly. I was a world from everything I thought I knew, but my new surroundings had me feeling comfortable in my skin like never before.

And soon, I found another gig at an art gallery across the street from Pirates Ally where I was selling my graffiti canvases daily on the fence. I had to "double dip" if I was going to get ahead make more money to travel to other festivals. So with our "graffiti folk fusion" canvases on the fence across the street from the new gallery gig… I hustled both ends and "worked a program" as we say back home. But to make it happen, I had to spread myself pretty thin on Royal Street. You see… instead of just sitting at my desk in the gallery, I'd stand in the middle of Royal Street going wherever the prospect traffic went. If they walked into the gallery, I'd follow them in there and introduce them to the fine art inside. When I found people on the street admiring my work on the fence in Pirates Ally, I'd be the only artist over there talking his work up with a suit on, and a big old credit card machine with an antenna in one hand. I'd run back and forth across the street like a racquetball player in a game of cut throat while Loose Marbles busked old timey music on the corner commanding everyone's attention. I've always been quite opportunistic.

By the end of the summer I got word from the New Orleans Film Festival that CURE for the CRASH was accepted and I was a nominee for the Louisiana Film Maker of the Year. Enthusiastic about that, I stopped by the Film Fest Office in the Contemporary Arts Center where I found a couple of people brooding over a large piece of construction board creating the schedule for The Festival, as they talked about which movies screened elsewhere. I introduced myself, and my movie…

"I'm Brian Paul,
I made Cure for the Crash."

But they did not give me the impression that they ever even heard of the movie. Nor did they care too much for me it seemed. They were busy I guess.

Nonetheless, Matt was excited about the screening and made plans to fly back to town looking forward to finally showing a good cut to everyone, in NOLA! The venues were first rate at The Prytania Theater & The Canal Place. But the closer it got to show time, the more I felt unwelcomed by the festival.

At the first screening an Usher came to the front of the theater and welcomed everyone to the New Orleans Film Festival. Then, he asked the audience to consider buying a membership to the New Orleans Film Society because…

"It's the New Orleans Film Society,
who make films like
CURE for the CRASH possible."

I looked over at Bella, and asked…

"What'd they do to make my movie?"

In all, that festival was far less enjoyable then my first screening in Seattle. The program coordinators were busy in New Orleans trying to look like a big festival. And filmmakers wasted time bumping into each other with wine glasses looking for distributors that weren't there. The Hollywood South thing made dreamers out of everyone from City Hall to Bourbon Street.

A month later, and after years of working, I felt nothing coming my way. So I decided to go out there and get some. And with only thirty-five dollars in my pocket, I felt I had no choice. So I burned six DVD's. Put them in small brown paper bags. Cut the top of the bag so the DVD's fit snug and folded the top over to make a lip. Then I tagged CURE for the CRASH on them with a sharpie marker. I knew what to do. I'd been bagging and branding since I was sixteen or so. Then, Bella and I took the ferry across the river to The Quarter. We stood on Decatur Street near Cafe Du Mode' and approached tourists with simple pitches.

"I got an Award Winning Film
I made on The Art of Train Hoppin.
Eight dollars!"
I announced on the sidewalk.

Bella was on the other side of the street…

"Want to buy an award winning film
about the American Hobo?"
She asked pedestrians.

In two hours we sold four movies. Just some burned DVD's in brown paper bags. But the next day I sold more in Pirates Alley. I sold them off the back of my Vespa from Bella's old Samsonite suitcase with a little poster I recycled from the film fest screenings. I sold a dozen movies that afternoon! After selling those DVD's I don't think I could stop. I was hooked. I quit my gallery job and started pushing CURE for the CRASH on the street full time as if I were a hustler on 8th and Butler. I was beginning to feel like my old self again. And we all know that's not good.

I spent day after day pushing DVDs to pedestrians on Royal Street, Pirates Alley and Decatur Street. And every night I'd burn more into the AM, one by one on my Mac… the brown bags, my coin bags, the Mac, my microwave, CURE for the CRASH, my color, Tuff Crew, boomed with bass from the Bose on the desk top. I was back in business!

Couple weeks later after selling a few hundred on the street, I was on my way to see Bella at her coffee shop gig, when I passed the French Market on my Vespa… and it dawned on me. I instinctively circled The Market like a shark. Before I pulled over and went to the office window…

"Hi, I'm Braze.
I'd like to apply to be a vendor."

She instantly handed me a list of products that were prohibited.

"Is your merchandise listed?"

"I sell a hobo movie."

"No porn!"

"HO-BO, movie."
I clarified.

Two weeks later, I found myself in front of the French Market Board of Directors with my laptop as I showed them the trailer of CURE for the CRASH.

"It's a contemporary look
at the American hobo.
An award-winning movie
made here in New Orleans."

The board made the unanimous decision to allow me to sell in The Market. I began immediately!

The next day when I went to The Market for the first time, I loaded up my Vespa with a six foot folding table and the old Stetson suitcase. Then I took the Algiers Ferry while sitting on the table as I drove through The Quarter.

With the DVD's at a Fugazi eight bucks, I moved some units the first day in the French Market and became a D.I.Y. Distributor not because I had a lot of first hand experience in the early punk culture, but because I found "do it yourself" no different from any other street marketing I've done.

After hustling in the markets for a couple months, CURE for the CRASH got accepted to the Indie Grits Film Festival in Columbia South Carolina. By that time I sold… many, many more DVD's. I thought the world of what I was doing to get my movie out there and raise money to continue on the festival route. It was a steady climb forward, as was the evolution of my marketing.

I went from selling the movie from my laptop, to using a DVD player and flat screen TV. I chaptered the movie to moments I found that could sell the DVD better and, so I could skip to them easily with the remote. These were also moments I was more comfortable showing to the general public, because there are moments in the movie it's even hard for me to swallow in the company of others. Some scenes that I felt spoke clearly for the character Mes in the movie, didn't speak for me in my life. The blunt, arrogant, desperate nature that MES carried throughout the story was made up of many of the character defects I came to address in my own life. And though I may be a confessional writer, my honesty embarrassed me in public at times. I found myself torn between creating the work with passion, and then sharing the work with less confidence. Yes the material in my life makes up some of the drama I write about, but it's also the activity I hid from others before I sobered up. I suppose chaptering the movie helped me continue to hide a little longer.

To get to Indie Grits Bella and I packed the saddlebags on my 1500cc Victory Motorcycle. The Stetson suitcase was bungeed to the back end of the bike with our sleeping bags. Even though I struggled at times, I still knew how to get around in some style!

I drove the bike for half a day to South Carolina, before a cylinder started giving me some real trouble; my bike began to putter as I gave it gas. But after a minute or so, the weak cylinder would kick in and bring us back to full throttle. It went back and forth like that a few times, but nothing could bring me down, I was too happy with who I'd become and with the movie I made. I knew nothing at the festival could change that.

The gas I burned along the way was bought with the money I made from my movie. Screening at this point was to collect award laurels to help sell more DVD's. So while I didn't have money to get a hotel room, Bella and I didn't need one. As in Seattle, we planned to camp in our sleeping bags, somewhere. We did what we had to do, and enjoyed it. I realized then what I had to do and what I wanted to do became the same thing since the rails. I could see the road paved clearly.

We checked in with the Indie Grits Festival Coordinators and got our filmmaker passes, event schedule and other swag. Then we parked my bike in the alley behind The Old Nick Theater before we walked around town to scout a location to camp at after the long ride. We found a tall concrete tower that looked pretty good. I think it was an old fire tower right in the middle of town just a few blocks away from the Festival. It became our campsite.

After attending a slow food festival that first night… the cold breeze became a brisk blanket on that tall tower as music from bars across the street kept the college crowd going. Just after dawn hit the dew on our sleeping bags, we woke up.

"I'm so cold Braze."

I unzipped my bag and stuck my head out.

"You wanna make love to me."

"You want to get… a hotel room?"
Bella asked

"How about… a kiss
and a cup of coffee instead?"

She zipped her bag over her head and went back to sleep, I suppose I just liked how unhappy she could be at times, and still put up with me.

A little later that morning, we climbed five stories down before hanging from a fire escape to fall to the ground. Up there in that tower was a real good place to camp in the city. The spot was hard enough to get to that other people had to make great efforts to stumble upon us. Home bums and college kids alike! Some of the cheaper views where becoming as good as first class to me.

It went smooth and cheap at the Indie Grits, just gas and food. Each morning we walked back to the motorcycle that was parked in the alleyway behind The Nick Theater and rummaged through the saddle bags for clothes before coming round the corner to the coffee shop to bath in the bathroom sink there. We camped out every night on the fire tower till my brother got to town. Then, we checked into his downtown hotel.

When Richy arrived, I thought he was acting really weird; he didn't have much to say. When I looked at him, random thoughts of The Hunger distracted me because… he looked much older, overnight! He was dressed well but looked a bit haggard and nearly elderly looking. He stopped dying his hair. Richy had a touch of grey since he was nineteen, but he always dyed or bleached his hair. Now in his 30's, my lil bro was starting to look like my older brother. I found him a shadow of the presence I knew just a few months prior in Seattle. Like a starved Vampire, it looked to me that his aging happened overnight. Rich was always pretty quiet, but now, he was more… speechless. As if he was a survivor of a plane crash and not sure why he was still alive or something. Though it was hard, I blew my racing mind off and just tried to enjoy his company. But I found him somewhere between spooked and confused from one moment to the next. Not only was it hard seeing him like that, but why? What happened? Was this flip in personality a result of stress and drugs? Or was there more to it? I tried to overpower the atmosphere with positive energy. But his sense of humor and big laughs had been replaced with anger and forced smiles with a front crown weathered grey. His slim build and bleach blonde hair, gone big belly and grey on top? He was four years younger, but looked ten years older. And it all happened in a few short months. He did not look like this in Seattle! While he was quiet and somewhat paranoid in my presence in South Carolina, I thought back to the things Richy said to me in private while in Seattle. Things like…

"Braze, these contractors keep
talking about me. They are laughing and
calling me a crack head!"

AND

"People keep following me Braze,
trying to rob me everywhere I go!"

AND

"My neighbors are trying to
sabotage and booby-trap my work sight B!"

I blew these odd remarks off in Seattle thinking he had just had some stress issues. But when obvious paranoia was evident on his face in South Carolina, I was really worried. And to make things more complicated during this time at The Indie Grits Film Fest, he was dusted a lot. You would think that would explain everything, but not so when you come from where we come from with the drug diet of Jerry Garcia.

I mean if you were using, you had to be on something. Dust was our chill out drug at one time; what we came down with after a long nights rolling at raves. And then I noticed him roll out of bed and crush pills in the morning, before Bella woke up.

"Yo… what are you crushin' Rich?"

"Oxys.
I can't get out of bed
without um' B."

"Rich, are you sure these are
working for you.
You seem, troubled, since you arrived.?"

"I can't function with out
these pills bro."

"You have to slow your roll down bro."

"I know.
Everything is just so hard
for me now without them.
So Hard!"

He felt he had no choice but to keep on, keepin' on. Richy was good on his oxys till noon, then he hit the angel dust on the balcony when Bella showered after yoga. I'll say this about Richy, even at a low like this he was still honest with me, and himself. That's rare.

On the third day in S.C., it was raining outside, so he smoked a blunt in the room while Bella got some lunch for us downstairs. Up there with him, I got a nice contact high from the dust. And it felt good! So I took a nice, deep, long hit of the wet blunt for myself. When I blew out, I felt like sweet, slick, and sloppy seventeen year old again. Man, I wanted to ball Bella immediately! My dick went straight to attention! It was then, I noticed for the first time, the room had a late 60's feel. Or did it? I wasn't sure, because then Richy started to morph and look six feet tall, with his hair going back to the blonde I remembered him having years prior. Then, things got really weird! His casual Armani attire, cross-faded to a country stitch! And his paranoid jargon sounded more like the beginning of a Harry Nilsson's hit…

"Everybody's talking about me Braze.
Everybody is talkin."

I wasn't sure if he was making me paranoid too, or my mind just went Midnight Cowboy for a spell; I was spaced! Whatever the reality was, or wasn't at that moment. It was out there flying on chemical spaceships that my brother and I had circled the Earth together time and time again. And Richy just took me for another ride that day. All day! Later that afternoon, we glided from the room baked like Freddie Jay Rubin in the back of the bus, Bella too! We were really on a roll. And of all days to get spaced, this was the day my movie screened. I came late and left early so I didn't have to do a Q&A. My movie was one of the last to screen at the festival.

Later that night was the award ceremony, but I was so spaced out and racing with visions, I really couldn't care less. I just wanted to keep dreaming! Once we finally made it to the theater for the ceremony, Richy got us dusted again in the alley behind the Nick Theater where my motorcycle had been parked for a week. I had to keep smoking! It was better than coming down at that time! Trust me when I say I'm better high, than hung over.

And just as we finished that dust session, I thought about all the times Richy and I got high like this. The things I really connected with Richy on were music, money, and drugs. Back in the day I woke up in the dandiest places from my highs with those three things in mind with Richy. Such as after hour joints, Asian wishy washes, hotel theme rooms, Pocono Caves, inside the Brooklyn Bridge, Atlantic City suites full of friends and No2 balloons… and now, as I floated in South Carolina at The Nick Theater. Where CURE for the CRASH won Best Feature Film, once again. I was awarded a 8mm camera trophy and a check. And though I should have been happy and excited, I just felt awkward in my dusted head around those nice people. Then I glanced at the check, and made a fool of myself. Blurting out after reading the amount on it…

"Indie Grits doesn't talk trash,
Indie grits talks cash!

Then, with everyone smiling, I proceeded to high step back to my seat like I was on the moon, holding my trophy in one hand and the check in the other, as the Indie Grit folk laughed and applauded. Dust is dangerous.

Through the process of making the movie and screening it, I occasionally mirrored the lack of composure that I played out in the movie. But I was still liked by people. And that was the scary part! When new friends and others didn't seem to mind my slips from sobriety, I began to think I could get high again and no one would care less. But then, I remembered when I didn't care what anyone thought. And where that got me before. Because it really doesn't matter who cares, if you don't.

The more I befriended those who seemed to give up or just let themselves go, the more it made me want not to. My movie constantly reminded me not to let myself loose my composure again. Because I met people from coast to coast, flying signs and spanging who didn't seem to care enough about a higher quality of life to even think of elevating themselves from the lifestyle, when in fact some could! You can be forced to be homeless, but nobody forces you on a freight train. People on the rails often lower their standards to live the dream. But when the drinking and drugging turns the dream into a nightmare, the pink cloud rains on you. I can tell you that chronic homelessness and physical dependencies are much different than my tours through "poorism" and getting high. Though I put myself through it all, I always had the mind and energy to do better when I wanted to. Some just don't have that. And I never felt unbearable withdrawals from any drugs I ever did. Though my actions had nearly killed me time and time again, I was always fortunate enough to bounce back. Many… just don't have the energy I have. The same intense energy that nearly killed me is the same that saves me and creates what it does.

Before we left Indie Grits, I found my name and movie in the conversations of other filmmakers at an organized event regarding what the city and festival can do for filmmakers in the future. My name came up not because I hopped trains across the country, but because I had some success selling my movie on the street. Most of them got very excited to hear about my sales in New Orleans. While others thought it was foolish of me to sell it like I was because they thought that distributors don't like it when you sell your own movie. I just didn't share those concerns. I was the distributor. Most of the filmmakers holding on to dreams of distro deals where the one's who wanted to be Sundance Winners someday. My response to them as I stood in front of a crowd of dreamy filmmakers who expressed all this to me was…

"I'm happy for those who screen and
win at Sundance.
But what do the rest of us do?"

It went silent in the room.

"This is what I do.
I make a living
moving physical media myself."

Later that day, after a long talk with Richy, I hugged him goodbye. Optimistic he was going to bounce back once his properties sold in Philly and relieved him of the stress he was under. Then, I bungee corded my new trophy to the front of my motorcycle before easy riding home on 1500cc's like Thompson from The Angels.

A day later, as we crossed the Mississippi River on the Algiers Ferry after an epic long ride home, I parked my bike to stretch out. Then Bella hugged me, put her head on my shoulder, and looked to me and said…

"You're my hero."

For whatever reason, she was impressed I could drive the bike like I did. Behind my motorcycle, as she stood in my arms, my hand discreetly found my way down her underwear.

"Ahhhhh…
I love it
when you touch me dangerous
out doors."

I knew that, that's why I did it! She liked it on the trains, in the gallery, on the roofs, anywhere and everywhere it seemed. It's a three to five minute ride across the river and at that time in the spring of our love, I could work a program with her in two! She got so hot when I touched her that I always knew I was with the right girl. Never before could I please someone so effortlessly.

The next day I hit the French Market, but I couldn't stop thinking about Richy. His whole life he knew what he wanted and went out there and got it! I liked that about us. But by now, it appeared he stopped making moves, and was just trying to make it through the day. Although I knew where he'd been and how he got into that shape, I couldn't imagine him not being able to make a comeback! I believed he could make it back to start, because I did.

Sales in The Market increased with the help of another Best Picture Award. And as I kept slinging media in my boogie down production way in NOLA, I got a message from a guy named Larry in New York. He produced Sling Blade and many other movies and was then in the launching stage of a new company. Larry's first message he simply stated…

"Congratulations on your
award-winning picture and your success
on the streets of New Orleans.
Maybe I can help
you sell some more movies."

I was happy that someone with some recognizable credits was approaching me! So we scheduled a phone call. A few days later I took that call while hustling in The Market. The beginning of the conversation was encouraging. And he seemed really impressed with my efforts on the streets…

"You sold that many copies
off the back of a god damn Vespa?!"

He wanted to launch a marketing campaign grounded in my efforts on the street and talked about a small theatrical release in his Tri-State area, NETFLIX, Wal-Mart and other outlets as well as putting me on tour in different cities to distribute my movie elsewhere, just like I was in New Orleans. But this was nothing I hadn't thought of on my own. I created my own small business and I strongly believe Netflix would kill a great portion of that. Like Wal-Mart kills culture, NETFLIX exploits most small Indie Filmmakers. But I think some filmmakers like getting screwed because at least someone is showing them some attention. Personally, I find saving money last longer than quick sex. Because there are no stars in my dreams, there is some paper in my pocket it seems. But Larry didn't know that about me, yet. At the end of the conversation I simply asked him to e-mail me the power points of his plan, including the numbers we talked.

"I don't share my business plan
with people I'm not doing business with yet.
I'll need to put you under
contract first."

"How long will the contract be for?"

"It's a standard ten-year contract."

"Will the contract
have these numbers and plans
we're talking about in it?"

"Braze,
I've produced over 40 films.
If that doesn't speak for itself,
then we can't do business."

"Thank you very much Larry."

And that was the end of our correspondence. I love New York, but it's full of people Born To Steal. I'd hear that I should get my movie to Netflix for years to come. But some things like my movie and me are only found in New Orleans.

The movie then found its way to a Festival back home in Philadelphia. When it got accepted there, I was going bananas with distribution in New Orleans. But I was very excited to tell my Mom CURE for the CRASH was playing at the Franklin Institute IMAX Theater. A museum my grandfather would take our whole family to growing up!

"Oh that's wonderful!"
Mom screamed,
"I'm very happy for you Braze.
But,
have you spoke to Richy lately?"

"No Mom. Why?"

"He's not doing too good Braze.
They foreclosed on his houses."

"Both investment properties?"

"All three of them,"
she said with her heart in her throat,
"his home too."

"What?!"

"He's moving in with me,"
she continued to say,
"he's packing up a U-Haul now with
everything he owns."

When I hopped a train out of New Orleans, Richy had over a quarter million in cash, a nice home in New Jersey, a landscaping business, and two investment properties. Now, he was bankrupt? I had to get off the phone with her and call him at once. When he answered, I had no doubt that he was high…

"Yyy-yo Bee."

"Hey Man.
You making a move
to Mommy's right now?"

"Shh-Yeeaaah."

"Alright. Bro,
are you fucked up?"

"Lil bit.
I been smokin' some wet."

"Rich,
you're moving into mommy's today…
on PCP?"

"Kinda.
Yeah, I guess"

"When were you gonna tell me things
got this messed up?
You could have called me.
We could have worked on a solution together."

"Nothing you could do Bee.
I built my houses,
but they didn't sell in time.
The whole goddamn housing market
crashed Braze!"

He was angry, broke and lost. I'd been there.

"I know what it feels like Rich.
But you gettin' high over it,
all the time,
doesn't help you bounce back man."

"It's automatic now man.
These oxys really got me Bee.
You ever withdrawal off this shit!"

"No man.
No."

I tried to talk him down from his rage, but he was way too fried on everything. In fact, he never made it to our Mom's. Instead, he drove to an emergency room totally bugging out. There, I'm told he walked in suicidal and paranoid.

"People are after me!
I'm going to kill myself before they do!"

It was there at that hospital, he was later diagnosed a paranoid schizophrenic. And admitted to the psychiatric ward for treatment.

But he was just high, not mentally ill; I knew that! My brother always kept himself together. He's the neatest, well-dressed, together person ever. So when my Mom told me about the paranoid schizophrenic diagnosis, I dispute it. And got real with her…

"He's not crazy,"
I said frankly,
"He's dusted Mom."

"What!"

"He's high on PCP."

"How could he be high?
He's been in the hospital!"

"He was high when he got there.
And sometimes,
it takes a couple days for
your wires to reconnect."

"The only thing he's on now,
are prescriptions for the schizophrenia
and high anxiety."

"Is there a number I can
reach him at there?"

She gave me a number to a pay phone on his floor. I got off the phone with her, and called him immediately…

"Richy Scanlan please."

As the receiver was placed down I could hear people call out his name and arguing whether he was in a group session or not. Then the debating of his where-a-bouts stopped, and conversations continued on in the distance about other people's medications, doctors and upcoming court dates. It set in, that Richy was in a very serious situation just before he finally answered…

"Hello?"

His voice was low, in real heavy whisper of sorts.

"Yo, Richy?
It's me Braze".

"Hey Bee."
he said as if he were drunk,
"How are you doin'?"

"I'm… good Rich.
Are you OK?"

"I don't know B.
Things are bad, real bad.
I don't know if I'm
gonna make it."

I could hardly recognize his voice. It was as if he were trying not to be heard by anyone around him. Something was really, off about him.

"It's OK Richy,
Maybe… maybe you just need the rest.
Are you getting sleep?"

"Yeah,
but they all talk about me here.
They say I'm a crack-head
and laugh at me
behind my back."

"Don't listen to that shit Richy."

"There is a cat in here too.
It keeps walkin' on me in my sleep."

"Some dude is walkin' on you Richy"?

"No a cat,"
he said in a low whisper,
"a fuckin' pussycat."

I had to digest that, and take a deep breath.

"That's just bad dreams Richy man.
I have them too.
I've always been afraid of getting
crushed by snakes in my sleep."

"Why would you do that?"
he asked.

"Do what?"

"You know what I'm
talkin' about Braze."

His voice changed, he didn't sound sad or scared, but angry now. It was like he just changed the channel of his thoughts. And he stayed on this angry channel cursing and saying more…

"Yeah! You fuckin' know.
You fuckin' set me up.
You knew they were coming!
You had to know."

But in reality, I really didn't know what to say. And I didn't let him hear me start to cry on my end. I had to assume whatever they had him on in there, was worse than our drugs on the outside. Fore sure! I never heard him talk like this before! And how could this happen over night? I didn't know if he was in the right place or the wrong place, but I realized at that point that my brother expressed similar paranoid thoughts that I had most of my adult life. But he couldn't contain them at this point, like I could most of the time. Or, even question if they were real or not as I'd been able to do. I could see this happening to me some day, but not him. I was shocked! Up until the last year or so prior to this, he was one of the most together people I knew. Head to toe, kitchen to closet; his house was always in order!

I'd been haunted with cocaine psychosis for years before I rolled to New Orleans. My sleepless weeks led to paranoid delusions of snakes coiling around my body, cops staking out houses I was held up in, robbers casing my place while I tried to hide behind one closed eye. But all that and more was only in my paranoid mind, nowhere else. But I knew that it was the drug playing tricks on me as my body convulsed when my Mom cried out in my mind during those times…

"Why?
Why Braze? Why?"

…As warrants were issued to the address in my head! So when Richy said cats where walking on him in his sleep, I understood that no problem. Cocaine brought it on me, where the prescription meds responsible for this delusional state with him? Being a drug dealer, you're paranoid by nature. But neither one of us were crazy, I thought.

All these memories came crashing back after my conversation with Rich. I got off the phone with him when I couldn't hold back my tears any longer. I was in no better shape than him at one time. But somehow I didn't end up in the psychiatric ward because there was a reset button that sleep pushed in my head that seemed to be broken inside my brother. I prayed that in time his wires would just untangle, as mine always did.

As soon as I got to Philly for the Film Fest, I connected with Richy. Bella stayed behind in New Orleans to be with her father who was constantly troubled with his step daughter Kirka and her mom Carol; fights and accusations were always in the air over there. They drank too much; or at least she did. And Kirka was isolating more and more it seemed. But the rest of Bella's big family (That her father left for the other woman in his life; Carol.) were all doing just fine and moving from the Bayou to different universities around the county. And Bella's Mom found a big new boyfriend who grew up eating road kill in Mississippi. Her family's an interesting but far out bunch.

To my surprise Richy was out of the hospital, on meds, and was feeling better! So I took him to the Melrose Diner for lunch just as he had always done for me to lift my spirits over the years. But once we got there, I found the diner horribly remodeled! Which broke my spirit! Instead of the antique booths that were cut in half and often shared by two parties, new booths were installed. And the tile floors that screamed diner were now carpeted?

"What's up with this place Richy?"

"It changed hands or something."

Then I looked at the "new" menu, which was totally different than the one I grew up with! But I found my dish…

"They still have MP1 though!"

Richy laughed at me. That dish must have been everyone's favorite for the place to keep it on the new menu by the old "code" name; MP1.

"Have you ever had anything else here?"
he asked me.

"Once."

"Just once? Why?"

"They were out of MP1."

"What you get? MP2,"
he asked me sarcastically.

I shook my head yes,
"I had too man!"

At that point we were laughing as the waitress came up. When I looked up to her bitter sweet and wished it were my old friend Green waiting our table…

"You guys know
what you're having?"

And just like that Richy stopped laughing, pushed the waitress out of the way, and ran out of the diner and down the street! Scared of God knows what! I didn't.

A block later I was still chasing him as he darted down the middle of Broad Street towards Center City! The chase continued for blocks in rush hour traffic. As I ran after him, other images flashed in my head… Me running out of my shoes and clothes till I was naked and screaming down a street tripping face dusted out back when I was a paranoid teenager on LSD after that Jerry Show. But I shook those thoughts from my mind and continued chasing my brother! I was so afraid he was going to get hit by a car, go through a windshield or jump through someone's row home window. He was petrified! Only that kind of fear could out run me, screaming…

"Richy stop!
RICHY! STOP!"

When I finally caught up with him, dozens of blocks later, I grabbed him in the middle of Washington Avenue when a car cut him off. He tried to fight me! Car horns honked, people yelled!

"Stop fighting me Richy!
It's me man, Braze. It's me!"

I hugged him and tried to shake some sense into him!

"What the fucks going on Braze?"
he asked me terrified,
"What the fuck do you want?
Fuck you!
They are after me Braze!
Why! Why BRAZE!
WHY ME!"

He stood there raging, crying, confused and completely paranoid, but… present. It was all very real to him.

"It's not your fault Richy.
This is where life led us man!"

"I don't want to die Braze!"

"I know Richy. I know."

Together, but broken on Broad Street, I could see no one else to blame, but me. I told him to take the fifty bucks to buy a keg and sell cups when we were kids; he never looked back. He kept selling, doing and thinking that was doing your best, because it's what his older brother did.

"Why'd I fuck
my brain up Braze?"

"It can heal man. Mine is."

Car horns continued, and some drivers yelled out of their windows at us in South Philly…

"You smacked asses!"

"Get out the street you smucks!"

We stood there on the edge of Richy's sanity, together. Not hustlers, but rather helpless.

"Come on man.
We'll get through this.
I got you.
You're my guy."

He was in pieces and I could see the brain damage all over his face. I hugged him, and assured him that…

"You're my guy Richy."

He was defeated. And so was I, but I had his back. And I knew from that point on my brother was going to need more help, more help now than I'd ever been to him in the past. As I hugged him, I noticed four beautiful angels in pastel war paint standing in an open apartment window across the street. The passing traffic silenced, but it kept moving. The white sheer drapes from the apartment, smeared with colors from the fresh face paint, blew outside the window where those angels were standing. The war painted angels looked through me, and focused on Richy. At that point I knew the other side had its eye on my brother. I could feel it as sure as Billie Holiday felt her blues. It was then time to protect him just as I had on the subway platforms long, long ago.

The half scripted story I produced, CURE for the CRASH, won Best Documentary at the Philadelphia Independent Film Festival. Whoever gave it that honor, has a different understanding of a documentary then I. While I just wanted to blur the truth and fiction in my narrative, my hometown didn't think I was acting evidently. Even my close friends at home couldn't tell the truth from the fiction, but nor could my brother and I in our own lives at times, so nothing made sense. Through writing, I've been able to cope with my madness, when I don't sedate it. Rich never had that creative outlet. I never wanted to be a filmmaker growing up. I just wanted to be a basketball player and a graffiti writer. That's it! Recently, being a player in the flea market and a writer on the rails defines my creative life thus far. When it was necessary to share more of my new creative life with my brother, I just wasn't sure how too. I wanted to bring him in on my new thing in New Orleans, but I thought his head needed more healing first. I decided I would send for him when I thought he could handle it.

A month later, the movie screened at a festival in Florida where it was nominated for Best Screenplay. But I was just too busy hustling DVDs in New Orleans to attend. So my Mom volunteered to go on my behalf. She brought Richy with her because she was bringing him with her everywhere at that time… when he wasn't in hospitals getting treatment. I was ecstatic that my Mom could go and happy Richy didn't mind going with her. And it turned out the CURE for the CRASH did indeed win Best Screenplay!

At the convention center where the awards banquet was held, they called out my name and CURE for the CRASH to receive the Treasure Coast Best Screenplay Award. To my mothers' utter surprise, Richy stood up…

"I got this mom."
he said to her like his old confident self!

Then he walked on stage in a huge convention center and thanked the crowd on my behalf. Mom was shocked! Though Richy was struggling on different medications after being hospitalized, that night, for whatever reason surfaced the cool, confident, caring brother we all admired over the years before his breakdown. He was showing signs of life again! My Mom was so, so happy!

With a few Awards to my credit now, I decided to just "look around" for a "Film Rep" to see if a good deal was actually out there somewhere. After interviewing a bunch of them, I chose Circus Road in LA for assistance. There I connected with a rep named Christian who seemed on the level and straight forward…

"It will be no problem
finding distribution for your film Braze,"
Christian said calmly,
"but unlikely you'll make much money."

I couldn't understand why? I was making money off my movie for months now and I was just one guy on the street. After a few more conversations with Circus Road in the weeks that followed, they advised me not to look for distro after I, reluctantly, shared my numbers with them. He was in disbelief!

"If that's true,
just keep doing whatever
it is your doing!
I don't think anyone
can do any better for you Braze.
I certainly can't."

And this was a guy whose job it is to get clients like me to spend $5,000 plus for his assistance. But they didn't take a dime from me.

"I can find you a bigger audience,
but good God! Not more money than that."

"I appreciate your honesty.
Thanks man."

And then I hung up and got back to business.

Up to that point I was burning DVDs one at a time from my IMAC. The computer was still under warranty during this time, which made the start of my DIY business possible. During the first nine months of distribution, I went through five optical drives. Each time one went on me, I would strap the computer to the back of my motorcycle and bring it to the Apple Store where the Geniuses there don't fix a thing, but send everything out for replacements.

"That works for me, Genius."

Everything they find wrong with your computer seems to be a symptom of a bigger problem. They give out new hard drives like frequent flyer miles.

On the cusps of a successful small business in The French Market, I finally bought some DVD burn towers to keep up with demand, and found myself a legit street entrepreneur. Everyday more people caught on to this new thing I was doing in the flea market. Though it came natural to me, being a salesman wasn't my dream job. It was rough out there five or six days a week doing Q&A's with hundreds and sometimes a thousand or more of people a week. I kept my cool in The Market most of the time while things with Richy had me on edge. But every once in a while… I'd have to deal with a smart looking guy. But I find most smart "looking" people, not so smart. Such as this guy…

"Your presentation is superb."

"Thank you.
It's evolving"

The small crowds around my table would often listen to what I said as I gave presentations and spoke to those closer to me…

"You're a very good salesmen,"
he continued.

"Thanks man.
Do you want to take a movie home with you?"

"You've worked in sales before?"
he asked.

"Well, yes. Royal Street art director recently.
And in a pawnshop when I was a kid."

"Pawnbroker!"
He nearly yelled,
"I knew it.
You were born to sell."

"Maybe, but I don't
really like that about me."
I admitted.

BOOK SAFE

"Why not?
Everyone is a salesman.
If you're not selling something,
you're selling yourself."

Years ago, when I was a kid in the pawnshop, if this came from one of the big dogs cashing checks behind the bullet proof glass, I would think encouragement like this was great! But now, after all my emergency rooms, murmurs, hauntings and worries of my own and now for my brother… I was very disenchanted with others enthusiasm for my hustle.

"You think I'm born to sell?"

"I know so."
he assured me.

Then I took a breath, I had too.

"You're a college grad?"
I asked.

"Wharton alumnus."

"You have good job?"

"I'm an entrepreneur.
I see opportunity everywhere."
he boasted.

He had an arrogance and air of self-entitlement that burned me up! And I let it get to me.

"You're an entrepreneur too,"
he added,
"You just have
to get out of retail."

When I realized I wanted to attack him, it was obvious I was carrying way too much anger around. I soon went for therapy at Family Services in New Orleans to address my boiling emotions rather than go back to see Auntie at the crack house.

A week later, in therapy, I was reminded of the evolution of my progress. As I said before, the title

CURE for the CRASH hit so close to home, it probably says more about me than anyone else I interviewed in the movie. This project was in fact not just about my recovery, but depended on it! If I stopped working on the picture before I got the final cut done, who knows where I'd be today. In therapy I connected many of the dots to my personal recovery. With the help of my therapist Ruth, I could see it all as if it were on a Final Cut timeline in the edits with Matthew.

And yeah, as I've described, I relapsed since my days out there on the rails. But I'm forever changed by the profound experience I found on the trains and the relationships in my life born because of the movie I created. Being sober is the only way I can keep working at all this. The aftermath of the rails gave me a much richer life than I've ever had before them. I didn't have the money I used to blow back in Philly for good times. But now I have a future! One I dreamed up, and didn't want to screw that up! Before, when I was at my best, all I had was a good hustle. Now… I have a taste of something else, something new. I could see me making my livings in the future, by just living it seemed. Yes I'd have to create more projects to write about, but that didn't seem like work, just what had to be done. Then while things were manageable and moving forward, Mom called…

"Braze,
I know how busy you are,
but has Richy called you today?"

"No, why?"

She started to cry.

"Because Richy is missing Braze."

I tried to calm her down and told her he's probably just out with a girl he met online or something. Or worst case scenario, out getting high somewhere. I assured her he'd come home. But she was really worried because he left both his phone and his medication behind…

"I called the jails, and
emergency rooms…
but found nothing!"

"That's good news,"
I assured her,
"he's not locked up or in the ER
because he's ok."

I was 1,000 miles away and couldn't do anything at that moment to help at home. We spoke on the phone until she calmed down…

"Ok.
I just needed to
call you Braze."

"Sit tight Mom.
He'll come home a lil later."

But the next day she called with more news…

"Richy made a phone call to a cab company
and got a ride to a shopping mall parking lot."

"Ok."
…That's weird I thought.

"He paid for the ride in cash.
Then walked towards the mall."

That parking lot and the surrounding neighborhood became the starting point for the search for my brother.

"I know it's Jazz Fest Braze,
and you're working it day and night.
So I will just call you tomorrow.
My friends are here
and the police are on it."

"Mom,
I can come home now."

"No, stay there!
Keep working.
Just look out for my phone calls, please."

"OK Mom.
Love you."

"Love you too Braze."

Then, when I hung up the phone, I immediately found myself in a conversation with a Lady about the movie at my stand in the French Market…

"So you made this movie!
My daughter did this for years.
She traveled with her dog!
And her grandfather..."

In mid sentence I walked away from her and rode my motorcycle straight to Philly.

DEATH BY SUICIDE

It's not a Crime
To loose your Mind

When I got to my hometown the next day, I arrived in the middle of the afternoon and joined in with a dozen of my Moms friends to canvas the neighborhood where Richy was last seen walking from a taxi towards a mall.

Knowing how depressed he'd been, I thought he might possibly be hiding out like a home bum under a highway overpass or in the wooded area near the mall; no camera's captured him walking inside. While searching along some train tracks with my mind racing in every direction, I was torn between finding my brother strung out and depressed, or finding his body. By the end of that day, I think I felt more hopeless than ever.

When we got back to Mom's house, I closed my eyes on the couch and began to think the search for my brother may never lead to him. Then, the phone rang. The police called and relayed a tip given by someone who works at a homeless shelter downtown.

"Someone identified Richy!
He's ok."

So Mom and I raced Downtown to follow the lead. The day before, Mom and her posse posted hundreds of missing person posters on telephone poles, bus stops, windshields and homeless shelters. One of those posters paid off! When we got there to the shelter Mom said…

"You go in and
look for him Braze."

She wanted to wait in the car.

At the entrance, a guard led me inside the shelter where hundreds of homeless men crashed on cots and bedrolls on a gymnasium floor. But we couldn't find Rich at first. I was bending over men who were sleeping and resting to get a better look… waking some, disturbing others. I felt like I was looking for a puppy in a pound, but these were grown folk! It was sad. The guard assured me…

"I'm certain he's here.
I had his photo on my desk
when he arrived tonight."

The guard led me through the gymnasium with the poster in his hand trying to find him as I canvased the mass of homeless men.

"Why would he come here?"
I murmured.

At one point the guard was so sure he found him that he physically turned over a man who was out cold sleeping on the floor, but it wasn't Richy. I thought then, this guy may have only thought he noticed Rich…

"You sure it was him man?"

"Yes.
He signed in with his name too.
Rich Scanlan"

Once I heard that I looked around with more urgency! And was just hoping he didn't leave already. Then, in the middle of that sad, crowded, stinky place, I found Richy crashing on his side upon a bedroll similar to the one I slept on riding the rails. When I gently woke him up, I gave him the best smile I had.

"Hey bro.
What are you doing here Rich?"

"Braze… you came all
the way from New Orleans?"

I nodded yes.

"You're my guy!
Come on Richy,
lets get out of here."

As we left the shelter I didn't let him out of my sight! Just like I didn't when he was a kid on the edge of that subway platform. I was not going to let him run away from me if he got spooked again.

When we got back to Mom's house, I had him pack a few things and leave the meds behind. I decided to bring him back to New Orleans with me. I didn't see why I couldn't get him up on his feet again. I found my new business invigorating and thought he would too. It was now or never I thought because at Mom's, he felt like a burden. And it turned out, that's why he went to stay at a shelter.

"That's in his head Braze.
He's always welcome here!"

"I know that Mom.
But he's a hard working dude.
I don't think laying around here
is his style."

I believed my success in New Orleans would rub off on him because his success in Philly had rubbed off on me long ago. I thought if he saw me in The French Market, it might impress him. Besides, business was growing and I wanted Rich in on it. He was once Midas with money. So with him by my side, I thought we could get better, together.

When we made it back to NOLA, I had him take it slow so I could monitor his paranoia and schizophrenia. Mom believed it would surface because I insisted we take him off the meds. But I believed they were doing more harm than good. Nervous about it all, she phoned often…

"Hi Mom."

"…How is he?"

"He's fine.
We're both fine"

"Do you's need anything?"

"No. Just…
let me have a go at it."

"He needs something
for his brain.
Get him back on his meds."

"I'm introducing him to
a new lifestyle Mom."

"But he's so sad all the time Braze.
I can hear it in his voice."

"I have him on fish oil,
Niacin and 5-HTP.
It's worked for me."

"If anything happens to him,
I'm not going to be able
to deal with it Braze.
I just won't!"

"Nothing will happen Mom.
He's safe with me.
He tells me he's feeling better every day."

"If he wants to come home,
I can send a plane ticket."

"OK.
Love you Mom."

But none of his demons seem to come to light under my roof when he first moved in. In fact, he was completely optimistic about creating a life in New Orleans. He explored the city, started going to NA meetings, seeing my therapist, and posted pictures of himself on Facebook in the new city he called home. He did seem a little bored sometimes, but that's better than being sad all the time. He did sleep a lot the first few weeks, but I was fine with that. I thought he needed the rest. I made it as comfortable as I could for him and gave him a job at home creating the merchandise I sold in The Market. It gave him some pocket money and something to do at his own pace. He burned the CURE for the CRASH DVD's; stamped all the brown boxes, and matted the entire collection of photo's I gave away with certain purchases. I was impressed at how superb a job he was doing…

"Yo Richy, the boxes never
looked so good!"

He smiled and kept working. He was still after all, a meticulous clean freak! All the stamps on the boxes where perfect! Then, I found some boxes in the trash half stamped…

"Yo bro,
what's up with these?"

"I messed them up."
He said sheepishly.

"But they look fine to me Rich."

"The stamps are a little off."
He pointed out.

"No bro,
we don't throw things away like that.
If the branding is a little off,
it gives it the human touch.
Imperfection is our charm in this movie!"

He laughed at me and kept working. Richy was so systematic by nature that he even figured out how many DVDs and boxes he could burn and stamp per hour so he could schedule what had to be done every week. He did math that never occurred to me! He budgeted all the costs of doing business and profit margins became topics of conversation for us. Before he moved to town, I was just pocketing cash, paying rent and making more merchandise. But Richy didn't think like that. Money was his higher power and he treated it with that respect. When I counted the cash when I got home, he insisted all the heads were up before I put the paper in the safe. The boy was serious about them dead Presidents.

I knew down the road we could take on media distribution together with the passion that drove us as inner city youths pushin' pills. But despite me holding on to my adolescent enthusiasm, Richy didn't see enough potential in media distro…

"I just don't feel it man,"
he admitted to me.

I guess the money wasn't coming in quick enough for him, but I could see it down the road. Since making the movie, my goals took years to meet. Fulfilling this kind of potential didn't come in as quickly as customers to a hot drug.

"Well, This here's
the South Richy.
Money is on a different pace buddy."

He'd laugh and give me five whenever I started talking trash. It was fun joking and talking trash while I discussed plans for the future with him and Bella. I never was much for family life, but the three of us felt real good to me.

A few weeks later, when he was finally feeling up to it, I brought Richy out to work with me in the French Market. I was often open 6 days a week and would stay on my feet all day as I greeted those who passed my table with the enthusiasm of a doorman in Tijuana. Often after sales, I'd pose for photos with customers and sign autographs with my graffiti style because all I ever wanted to be was Suroc anyway.

"You look like you've been giving
autographs for a while,"
a customer remarked.

"I grew up a graffiti writer.
My mom hated seeing
my signature around town."

"But you're so passionate and driven!
What could she do about it?"

"Well,
she cut off my ducktail once
when I wasn't looking."

"She must be so proud now!"

"Hope so!
And to think she thought graffiti
would get me nowhere?"

It was easy to get a laugh out there. I poured it on even heavier with everyone while Rich was there…

"Graffiti made me rich!"
I boasted sarcastically.

And then more laughs from the customers trumpeted around my stand…

"I'm an award-winning criminal!"
I howled.

…It was an easy crowd.

And then, when I was serious to other customers out there, I'd get responses like this sometimes…

"Oh,
you give me goose bumps."

"That's your body talking to you."
I'd point out.

It was all a basic transfer of energy between them, and I. As I physically altered the energy in them to the point their bodies made them more aware of it. Once I realized what I was doing, I could almost do it whenever I wanted to. It didn't matter, male or female, I didn't discriminate. And then there were the times it would cause friction in couples when I was able to put the zap on one, and not the other! I'd just shrug my shoulders and try and make more eye contact with the one who was left out.

Out there in the Market, in my own little spotlight, I've laughed, conversed, hugged, signed autographs and shook hands with cops, moms, judges, social workers, teachers, elderly women, priests, nuns, lawyers, you name it. Many of these people who would not have given me a second look before I made this movie, now wanted their picture taken with the guy who made The Art of Train Hopping. They all admired my efforts. And I tried to share my energy, and theirs, with Richy… but it wasn't rubbing off.

I thought all this encouragement I was getting would help him get out of his shell. But in fact, it may have pushed him further in it. His laughs went from happy and amused, to once again being forced. And then, it wasn't long before his laughs were reduced to a smile and a short exhale. I saw him drifting away.

And then, he began to get confused trying to assist me with simple tasks around the table in The French Market. He wanted to help so much, but he just couldn't do, what I did. He was too caught up in his own head! When I asked him about it, he said…

"Braze,
what you have… is a gift.
I can't talk to these people
Like you can."

When he said that to me, I never felt so bad! He couldn't departmentalize his suffering at the time or channel the bad energy into something creative like me, OK. But to not feel as though he had what I had? That was preposterous!

"Bro, what I got,
I in part learned from you."

But he couldn't see that through his sadness. Years before the rails became my redemption, Richy had a conversation with me about all the different people he did business with. He pointed out to me, that people in the game come from all walks and that you may not talk to some, like you talk to others. He knew well how to communicate back then! But today…

"I don't know what happened to you
out there on the rails."
he said bewildered.
"But you brought something back with you man!
It changed you."

I thought about that for a moment. Then responded…

"I think once you find your
life's purpose…

…you'll find that what goes wrong in life,
can be for something good you're
not aware of yet."

I could see all that troubled him, surface on his face at that moment. So I tried to take the pressure off…

"Life can get easier,
once you stop thinking it's so difficult."

"Sometimes…
I just don't know what you're
talking about Braze."

Then I just shut the hell up. What did I know? I knew the isolation of sadness and the trapped feelings of depression and thought nothing I could say would trigger the epiphany I hoped for. So I gave him space in hopes he could find his own ways and means in New Orleans. I believed he could, and would, come around, eventually.

But as time went on he began talking to himself more and more. I believed that talking to yourself doesn't mean you're necessarily crazy, but that you're just in your head way too much; thus all my own murmurs. So I suggested…

"Maybe it's time to get a job Richy?
Getting out of the house,
might get you out of your head a little."

"Yeah.
I think your right Bee."

Later that week he bought himself an old pick-up truck, got a full time job landscaping, and continued working the NA program and going to see my therapist Ruth. I continued with my own alternative recovery program that included good foods, plenty of exercise, and keeping my passions burning.

Festivals continued to accept CURE for the CRASH and it went on to win 5 Best Picture Awards before I decided to stop submitting to Fests all together. I became more interested in doing my own thing in New Orleans rather then taking on the expense of traveling to film festivals and losing revenue while being absent from the flea market. Soon after I stopped screening at festivals, I was featured in Filmmaker Magazine & National Geographic after I met journalists for these publications in the French Market. For me… that was the frosting on the success!

And while things were moving forward for me, Richy was working a new gig cutting lawns at the end of the summer. But it wasn't long before his hours were cut when the seasons changed in the fall. Then, by the winter, he was laid off. He got really bummed again when he was out of full time work. He loved working hard!

Even Bella was in between jobs at that time because the ferry over to The Quarter was so unreliable that she couldn't open the coffee shop on time to keep that gig. The ferry was breaking down every other day! So both Richy and Bella stayed home and were doing what they could for me in the distro department.

While Richy was hitting a lot of meetings and looking for more work, Bella was spending more and more time with her father who wasn't doing too good either. Harry officially split up with Bella's mom soon after we met. And seemed to need more attention than ever because his new partner Carol… was basically a drunk if you ask me. Her aside, there was something rather eldritch about Harry that concerned me. His boundless thoughts that the family admired so much seemed more like a lack of decent boundaries to me. He really put the zap on his family! It seemed to me that they believed every longwinded double talking explanation he gave to his family to justify his own needs. One time he told one of his sons at a gas station…

"You see all these assholes here son,
how many woman have they been with in the
last twenty years? A dozen or more!
I've been with two."

…And his son took pride in that enough to share it with me. The whole family appeared to take pride in such matters; just kids not wise enough to know better. If the old man had only been with two women, they were both living under the same roof, at the same time? And the fact is, he had at least sex with one other woman, in an alley off Magazine Street a decade prior to all this. He told me so! Told his whole family. Evidently that woman moved to Portland after that encounter to have their baby, alone. So it appeared to me that he was more of a cheating polygamist, but he gave me the impression he was a pedophile since we first met. The old man's eyes would creep on young girl that walked by. Though he talked about his sex life openly, I could care less. I only hoped no kids where involved, because I noticed him gawk at his step daughter Kirka's breast one time in the kitchen, with family all around! And then he looked over at me to see if I saw what he did. He alarmed me from the start! Why not everyone else? Eventually the love gang split up. And Harry, Kirka and Carol moved out to New Orleans and left Bella her brothers and their Mom in the bayou. He told his whole family (Wife and 5 kids) that Carol was the love of his life. Well then… what was Bella's Mom to him? When I met Bella's parents, they were both in relationships with other people. I found that disturbing, but the whole family took it in stride. In Bella's family, as long as everyone was open with each other, it seemed anything was acceptable. But when her Dad finally did leave her Mom for the other women Carol, things went down hill for him after that! He was often sleeping in his car, or on my couch when things got bad for what ever reason at their place. It seemed to me that Carol was often jealous. But of what, I'm not sure. During all those hard times her father was having, Bella was always there for him. I respected that about her, and helped out every time, despite how I felt about what got Harry into this whole… sex mess of his.

When the landscaping season came to an end, Richy looked for more work everywhere! He put applications in restaurants, casinos, parking lots, and more. But no one hired him. Then he landed a job at a parking lot, but that only lasted a couple weeks; they stopped scheduling him. Evidently the manager just didn't like him. Part time, he was still stamping CURE for the

CRASH boxes and burning media. But other than that, he just laid in his bed. His struggle was painful to watch. He even talked about getting back on some meds for his anxiety and depression, but I kept the focus on helping him create a new life and not medicating the old one. I mean… It worked for me, why wasn't it working for him! And reluctantly, he kept trying it my way. But he began sleeping more and more of his days away. It brought back memories of my own when I hid under the sheets till they were soaked with sweat.

After a couple weeks of letting him sleep in day after day, I was forced to get more aggressive with him. I finally insisted that he please, lace up his sneakers, to go for a jog with me, everyday! Then, I bought us a family membership to the YMCA a few blocks away. A week later when I still found him hiding out in his room when I wasn't coaching him otherwise, I got even more aggressive…

"Richy, bro…
If you don't start coming
out of your room,
I'm going to take the door off the hinges."

But he didn't seem to be moved by my threat in the least! He was almost beyond emotions at this point. His anxiety, sadness and frustrations seemed to vanish and his presence was more ghost like, than a breathing mammal. I scared myself when William Burroughs description of his meeting with Kurt Cobain came to mind. And when I got emotional with him at this point, it didn't stir him. Not one bit…

"I don't want you in this bed
with the door closed all day man.
It's no good for you!"

I was frustrated, even angry, and he knew it. But my emotional state just didn't move him. His grey complexion made me think the worst, as if… the war paint angels were closing in on him. I knew he needed more reason to leave his room other than to just hand stamp DVD boxes. But even at the YMCA and on our jogs he was still lost somewhere far behind his eyes in my presence. So before I took him to a hospital or treatment center, I encouraged him again to go out in the world and make something happen!

BOOK SAFE

"Richy,
I know your a hard workin' dude
and just bummed to be out of work."

"If I could find work,
I'd do it.
I'd do anything."
He said in all honesty.

"Well,
I do know a few places
that are always looking for help."

"Yeah B.?"
he said with a spark.

"Go to Bourbon Street,"
I suggested,
"The strip clubs are always hiring.
My boy Sepher
used to work at one.
Apply for a job in hospitality."

"You think they'll hire me Bee?"

"For sure.
But it will test your sobriety.
You up for that Rich?"

"I think I am.
I really need a job Braze."

"I know.
Go for it man.
But you'll have to double up
on your meetings."

"Will do brother."
He said with the first smile
I'd seen in weeks!

He put on a nice suit that morning and left the house optimistic at noon. It was great to see that! But not long after he left, I sat there alone, and couldn't believe I sent him off to look for work in a sleazy strip club! But I couldn't think of any other place he could walk into and start working immediately. I wanted to talk to Bella about it, but she was out, so I called her. But I couldn't reach her. She was probably in another big, epic, dire conversation with her father somewhere I thought.

So after ruminating over him going to work in that shady environment, I finally gave him a call to stop him from taking a job on that shady street. But he didn't answer either! My mind was restless and racing now! I tried him a couple more times, but had to settle for leaving a message…

"Yo Richy,
come home man.
Put the brakes on that idea.
Lets talk it out some more."

I walked around the apartment stewing, punching walls and cursing myself out in the mirror. I tried Bella again, but she was still out of reach too! Then, he finally called me back.

"Richy!"

"Yo Bee.
I got some news for you bro."

"Wa-sup Rich?"

"It isn't good news man."
He said in a somber tone.

I instantly felt bad, but relieved because he didn't find a job! But at least he got out of the house again on his own. I felt a very, very strong sense of relief nonetheless. But I kept my relief to myself…

"What happen buddy?
No positions open?"

"No,
I got a job,"
he said bluntly.

"What?"

"Yeah but when I was in there filling out the
new hire paper work at the bar,"
he continued,
"I noticed Bella in there."

That puzzled me. Why would Bell be on Bourbon Street?

"What?"

"I don't know what to
tell ya Bee."

Then I got hyped up. What was he implying?

"Motha-fucka what'd ya see!"
I screamed into the phone.

"Well bro,
she was walking around the club
with the manager who hired me."

"Did she have her clothes on?"

"Yeah.
So I played dumb and asked the bartender…
who's the girl the manager was escorting?"

"What'd duh-bartender-say!"

"He said, he was giving
a new entertainer the tour."

"She see you Richy!
She see you man?"

"No bro.
I just walked out after that.
I never even finished my
new hire paperwork."

"Where are you at now?"

"Across the street front the place.
I can't work here."

I took some deep breaths, and tried to gather my composure, but it was way too gone!

"Just come home Richy man."

"OK B.
I'm a catch the next ferry.
Sorry bro."

"Yo Richy."

"Yeah man?"

"What's the name of the place?"

"The Rising Sun."

And with that, I hung up and chased my racing mind! Anger, insecurity, and lap dances and men's hands all over Bella converged in the traffic within my head! My teeth grinded, my stomach turned, and my fists clenched in a visceral response to my emotions!

"Why? How dare she?
Who the hell is this woman?
How could she?"
questioned the square I didn't know I was
until that moment!

My intellect abandoned me and left me a bewildered fool who let his emotions manage him, as they had most of my life. I thought I had a handle on them, but not now when I needed a grip! When I noticed her laptop on my desk, I threw it out the second story window and across the street! And watched it break into pieces with instant regret for doing so. But more anger quickly overflowed on any, and all remorse! Why her laptop? Why not! I screamed a roar out of the window at the broken computer!

"I'm done playing house with you!
I'm done!
You hear me!"

If she were there, I'd have… I don't know. Spit on her! But she wasn't there, so I spit out the window! Then, well, I think I noticed her dad Harry parked in his van across the street. But I'm not sure. He was living in it half the time and often parked in the neighborhood. That was weird, but he was a weird dude who wasn't on the forefront of my mind since my brother got to town. And, well, I don't remember much after that. Call it… a rage void! Something I didn't think was possible since I stopped abusing steroids long ago.

By the time I came out of that emotional black hole… I turned most of the apartment, upside down. There were several pieces of art smashed over lamps and chairs, every glass and dish was broken in the kitchen and I threw the metal frame for a futon through a wall. All the progress I thought I made curbing my old ways, disappeared with one phone call about my girl stripping on Bourbon Street.

Every time I pulled back the energy from arguing with Sepher and Ruin and did not act out violently since I reached New Orleans, exploded the moment I hung up the phone with Richy. And once I was down from the rage, I started picking up the pieces. And filled some trash bags up with them. When I took the trash out, I went over and picked up the laptop that skidded across the street and into the gutter where I thought her old man's van was parked, but it wasn't there any longer. And with her broken laptop in hand, Richy walked up. Neither one of us knew what to say. I think we just felt bad for one another. They say everyone reaches their bottom when they stop digging. That day, my anger dug me in once again. And Richy knew it.

"What can I do man?"
asked Richy

"I don't know.
But I'm glad that you're here."

"Can I do anything?"

"Just forgive me Richy. I made a
big mess upstairs."

About an hour later, Richy was in his room and I was crashing on the couch after we cleaned the entire place up together. So when Bella got home, other than the hole in the wall from the futon and some missing lamps, I didn't think you could see what I had done to the place, but she noticed immediately…

"What happened there?"
she asked pointing at the hole in the wall.

"I… I lost it."

When I'm in my right mind, I have respect for people. And I still of course had some for her. So I kept a cool head.

"Are you OK?"
she asked.

…I nodded yes. Then she looked at me skeptically.

"Is… Richy, OK?"

I nodded yes, and tried to give her a smile. I guess she thought we got into a fistfight. It was work, but I did keep my cool despite all the questions piled in my mind. I just knew I had to stay cool! Because if for no other reason that my brother was in the next room. And I didn't want him to see me lose my wig.

"I know where you were."
I said accusingly.

"What's that supposed to mean?"

"You gonna dry fuck guys
for forty bucks now!"

"What!"

"You know what I'm talking about."

She eyeballed me hard. Then gave me an arrogant smirk.

"Yeah,
I think I do."

"When were you going to tell me?"

"Tell you what?"

…I probably stared at her with the eyes of a madman.

"Listen Braze.
You're in the wrong here!"

"So,
you're NOT stripping?"

"Nope."

I took a moment, consumed it, and would have been quite happy, if I'd have not already reacted to my assumptions.

"You're not?"

…And then I laughed at myself.

"No. I'm not."

"Oh… well ah,"
I laughed, a little.

"But what if I wanted to?"

Then, I stopped laughing.

"Wanted to be a stripper?"

"Yes."

"On Bourbon Street?"

"Anywhere."

"I'm confused,
what are you saying Bell?"

"I did tour a club today,
And I thought about it.
But no.
I didn't take the job."

I kicked the legs from underneath the spring water dispenser and watched the five-gallon container bounce on the floor and pour out like my guts. I foolishly took her bait. Now she wanted to fuck with me?

"Why tour the Rising Sun?
If you didn't want a job!"

"I went there with Lorry after lunch.
She quit her job there today!
…Wait. How'd you know I was there."

I took a deep breath and remembered my brother was in the next room, so I calmed down again.

"My brother saw you.
Please, don't ask right now,"
I begged her, and took a deep breath…
"What happened over there Bell?"

"While Lorry was cleaning
out her locker,
her boss tried to schmooze me and asked me to
accompany him around the club.
He's a show off.
Like you!"

"Hmm, I see."

"Yes,
he gave me a tour.
Yes,
he offered me a job.
No,
I didn't take it.
Yet!"

I took another deep breath. Yeah I was still pissed, but mostly because I could see how wrong I was. Bella was one of the smartest people I had in my life. And I was one of the most emotional. I found myself once again, assed out at another crisis crossroad… make it better, or make it worse?

"Stay calm."
I murmured.

Bella looked around, floor covered with water, and laughed!
"It's too late for that."

The lower me wanted to protect his ego, but my higher self… surrendered.
"You're not working there.
That's all that matters.

So please, forgive me
for making an ass of myself."

"No!
That's not the point now."

"Well,
what is?"

"What if I wanted too?"

"What if you wanted to Strip?"

"You hopped trains.
You sold drugs.
Are you a bad person?
If so,
why am I living with you!"

And with that, she easily made her point.

"Maybe I'm square…
But I'm just surprised
you'd be OK with strangers
touching you like that."

"Who said I would let them touch me?"

"Have you ever hung out
at a strip club!"

Then she laughed in my face, again.

"Well it sounds like you have!
So it's ok for you to get a lap dance,
but not OK for me to give one?"

"Bella,
you were a virgin
just a few months ago.
Now,
you're open to give lap dances and grin on the
penises of many different
guys on any given night…
for a buck?"
"Well,
what if I wanted to do so?"

"I'm obviously uncomfortable with this.
And I don't know why you're not!
But regardless of your sudden openness
to the sleazy side on New Orleans.
Knowing how uncomfortable I am with this,
you would still work there?"

"What about what I want?"

And then I got it, and stopped taking the bait; this was what her father taught her best. The point she made was that taking her clothes off on stage would be her choice, not mine. And I carried so much of my own guilt… who was I to judge that or anything else? No I didn't want to sell drugs or hop trains again, but I did when I was her age.

Instead of debating it any further, I folded. After all, she didn't take the job at The Rising Sun, she was just arguing a point after I trashed the apartment. I loved her and had already done enough damage for one day by sending my brother to Bourbon Street to look for work. I was sober, but a real dope that day. So I just hugged her after realizing all that. And I was very relieved she accepted my hug. I whispered in her ear…

"I'm only really at peace,
when I'm in your arms.
My mind is at war with my emotions too often.
I'm sorry Bell."

Deep down, I knew she would never strip. And maybe that's why the thought of it affected me like it did. I could never even imagine her working in a strip club. She carried much too strong a mind, to be anyone's boy toy!

Later on I tried to sleep fetal positioned next to Bella that night. But I felt the weight of all my character defects I'd yet to address, which kept me awake. I twitched violently at times as I crashed there mumbling to myself through night. The only way out of it… was a fresh start the next morning!

BOOK SAFE

When the sun broke through the drapes I got up to go for my jog. Still sleepy from a restless night, I remembered it was a Sunday and that I could run through the train yard because…

"The yard's closed."
I murmured. Then I realized…
"The train yard is closed!"

I dashed from my room and woke Richy up immediately!

"Come on bro… get up!
We're sober not saints.
I need your help!"

Not sure what I meant, and not caring to ask, he humored me and got dressed. It had been a long time since he and I worked an illegal program of any kind! Here's what I had in mind…

A few weeks prior to this I painted some straight letters, with an old friend Seru visiting from Philly, on a dented up grainer in a train yard down the street from our place in Algiers. The car had obviously been in an accident and looked to me like the perfect car to paint CURE for the CRASH on!

But soon after I finished this piece above, they blow torched the entire grainer car we painted into pieces and dragged it away to a dumpster down the tracks. Evidently it wasn't track worthy any longer. I watched them amputate the steel dinosaur from both ends. I told Richy this whole story on the way to the yard and insisted that…

"I need a piece of that train Rich!

He still had the old pick up from working the lawns so we went in that to "salvage" a piece of the grainer from the dumpster. We just rolled from our place to the train yard right down the street. The yard is under the Twin Span Bridge off Mardi Gras Boulevard; it's a two-minute drive from where we lived.

I had him park the truck under the bridge while I found the piece I wanted. On Sundays this yard was closed for business and no workers were ever there. I knew the schedule because I jogged by the yard often. It was the best day to get in, and out! When I got to the dumpster and found what I wanted, Richy backed up the truck and we took the piece with the letter E painted on it, and drove off. It was easy! On the way home I was feeling much better than the night before. But not Richy, he looked beat.

"How you feeling Rich?
Get much sleep?"

"I don't even know Bee.
I just don't know."

When we got back home, he went to his room and closed the door. With his door shut, I was worried and disappointed once again. I knew it was time to take the door off the hinges or get him to a hospital soon. In the meantime, I'd let him sleep it off. My brother was alive, but the hustler in him was dead. It was over, and I finally realized it. He just didn't have the energy I had to come back with any gusto. The manic energy and racing mind that nearly killed me would come to save me. Richy just wasn't born with my wiring.

Bella and I went out and did some food shopping as we usually did on Sundays with Richy. But that day I decided to leave him behind to spend more time with her alone after my violent eruption the day before.

When Bella and I got back from Whole Foods, Richy's bedroom door was still closed. He really had me bummed out! I knew I had to do something drastic, but absolutely dreaded having to put my foot down with him. So when we put the groceries away, I just took a nap with Bella on the couch to cool down before I approached Richy and suggest that he see a doctor because I was failing him. When I was sad, I still crashed and hid under the sheets sometimes. A little later… in the background of my nap, I heard Rich get up and move around a little bit. Then he opened the front door to go out, which finally woke me up.

"You going out Rich?"

He nonchalantly turned back to me where I was laying on the chase and answered…

"Yeah Braze."

"That's great man."

"I'll see you Bee,"
as he closed the door.

He sounded sad, but at least he was getting out of the house to do something about it!

"Ok, see ya man."
I said to the closed door.

I could hear him walking down the hallway steps as I fell back to sleep with Bella.

Hours later, the sky opened up and rain smacked on the glass next to my head as water dripped through the old windowsills when I woke up much later that afternoon. A leak becomes a lake on hardwood floors in old apartments, so I got up to stuff the crack with a towel and mopped up the water. As I did so, I noticed Richy was still out. I assumed he was across the river in the casino watching a ball game. He liked to hang out there and watch sports on the big screens occasionally. But when the sun fell as the storm passed, I decided to give him a call. Then, I heard his cellphone vibrating in his room, and found it on his dresser…

"Damn,"
I said concerned immediately.

I instantly felt something happening. I felt… very empty. Then it started to pour again outside! Bella gave me some space, not knowing what I was going to do. I, as you know, trashed the place yesterday due to emotional problems. So she was, lets say, being cautious around me when I started bugging out around the windows that overlooked the river, wondering, if I'd be looking for him the rest of my life.

I was thinking the worst! Was he on the run, in the river? I didn't know. But I felt that he was gone. Yet then I thought of the day before, and what jumping to conclusions did to me then. And that awareness kept me in my skin, but standing there in the window, frozen, as the rain continued to fall enough to keep the streets filling up with an oily shine on top. Bella knew how upset I was, I told her so. But she just hoped my premonitions were wrong. There was tenseness between us and in the air that I'd never quite felt before. My hair was standing on my body as if I were volunteered for animal testing. I guess I was just going crazy with anxiety!

It was 8 o'clock that night, maybe 5 or 6 hours since I last saw him. I was just standing there in the window because leaving the apartment would be closer to me over reacting. And I was still shaken by my behavior from the day before. Once again, I just didn't trust myself! Although I was frozen there, my mind raced through countless scenarios of how this could all play out. I was petrified to physically chase one of those thoughts! So I just kept reminding myself that my emotions aren't my friend right now. But breathing is. Bella left the downstairs door unlocked for him as I waited in my office by that window, alone.

A deep bass line began to reverberate throughout my body and ring in my ears! An echoing note… deep within an endless apocalyptic subway tunnel of some sort inside me. A familiar tone I've experienced before in the isolated corners of my mind. Then, helicopters began circle over the neighborhood. I thought I knew why. Then I debated it.

"Maybe there are no helicopters?"
I said to myself,
"Maybe they're just in your head."

But they kept hovering in the background. I feared they were looking for him, somewhere, in the river maybe. Maybe I should go look I thought! But I feared finding him too much. I was open to everything I ever feared at that point! And when that happens, my Mom's voice echoes in the upper chapel of my mind like Gregorian Chants…

"Why, why, why, why, why Braze?
Whyyyyyyy?
Whyyyyy Braze?
Whyyyyy!"

I did my best to wipe those thoughts away and keep my composure by that window so I didn't punch or jump through it! But the choppers kept circling, and my Mom kept chanting inside my head! And that deep bass line in me kept shaking my bones and rattling my vision, shaking tears from my eyes! I felt Richy and I were moments away from getting busted, but how, and with what? I thought to myself… don't worry like that Richy.

"We're clean.
We're good now bro,"
I murmured.

Yet, I felt a moment approaching that was maybe long overdue. A direct consequence of not showing my brother right from wrong when we were little because… I only showed him how not to get caught! Now, I felt karma coming with her margin call. It wasn't helicopters after all, but angels coming down from the clouds with war paint on their faces…

"Here they come Richy"
I murmured regretfully.

Rain continued to fall, as our life together flashed in a reflection on the window…

Playing wiffle ball together in a back yard. Walking to catholic grade school together. Laughing at Pops house over a Sunday dinner. Dancing amongst hundreds of others at a Rave. Cutting lawns, walking the boardwalk, finding him in the homeless shelter, lining friends up at my front door to meet my newborn brother, my only brother! I wish… I wished I were a much better brother to him!

"I'm so sorry my brother.
So sorry!"

I wanted to break something! Break anything! Punch the window! But then my own reflection in that window… bore his likeness; facing me! I took some deep breaths, but I couldn't gain sanity or blow out my fears!

"We made it this far for what?
For what Richy?"
I cried.

Yet his reflection didn't respond. But faded away before I had a chance to even think to kiss him goodbye. I would have, had I thought of it.

All our roads led to this, in New Orleans? There was no sense of destiny or God in my heart. Everything felt fake and worthless! And everything I ever believed in, other than karmic debts, made me feel like a fool at that moment! I thought I could save him with a new diet? What was I thinking! He was gone forever. I was alone there with MY reflection. My own angry reflection! Richy was gone, I knew it.

Then, the door opened down stairs! I felt the cops enter. I ducked warrants, busts, and hard time my whole life. But I never imagined this kind of justice coming. If anyone was a bad example for Richy, and introduced him to the wrong road, it's me.

"Ohhhh Richy, I'm, so sorry.
I'm so sorry man."

But that didn't matter now. The bass line rolled through my body and caught a snare drum from the approaching news when the steps beneath the shoes worn by the law climbed the stairs. When I turned around, I found a tall cop peeking in my open office door like a reaper…

"Is this apartment A or B?"
he asked me.

"This is B officer. Next-door is A.
That's my residence. This is my office.
Where's Richy officer?"

"Who are you?"

"I'm his brother."

"Can I see some ID please?"

He didn't want to share what he had to say with the wrong person, I knew that instantly. I had to get it from my apartment across the hall. When I came back with it, there were five more cops waiting in my office. They looked almost angry. I knew Richy was dead. But by the looks on those cops, it crossed my mind he may have taken one of them with him. As I handed the cop my ID, I started to feel faint so I sat down.

"Sir, your brother's truck was found
on the shoulder of the Crescent City Connection
bridge by two officers.
When the officers approached his vehicle,
your brother for whatever reason… "

I cut him off and said,
"I don't need to hear it officer."

It didn't matter to me exactly what went down, and I couldn't take all the words that would describe his final act, at that moment. Yet that cop felt the need to fill me in, and tell me…

"Sir,
your brother committed suicide."

That just didn't sound right to me! I stood up, and faced the cop…

"What did you say officer?"

He then repeated that,
"Richy committed suicide."

"Officer, it's not a crime,
to loose your mind."

"No,
of course not sir."

"So lets be clear here…
My brother did not, commit, suicide.
He died, by suicide."

But these cops just didn't get it. Trying suicide myself in the past, I'd given the language those use to describe the act a lot of thought! My mind goes crazy trying to get it right sometimes! Then, that racing mind tried to defend itself with that horrible bass line reverberating in my bones, before another thought distracted it. I thought of the conversation I had with my brother at a diner as I took him back to New Orleans with me from Philly. When we did in fact talk about that damn bridge. I was concerned because on bad days of my own, my mind would still take me over the edge of it. I knew Richy's mind could take him there too. But after discussing it, depression, and coping, I said to him…

"I won't jump Rich,
if you don't."

"I don't have the guts to kill
myself Braze."

And well… that sounded good to me. I believed him. But I still had some doubts, because I doubted myself.

"If you decide to take off Richy,
don't you leave me
without saying good-bye.
You must say goodbye to me."

"OK Braze."

Then, I remembered Richy walking out of the apartment earlier that day as I napped on the couch with Bella, when I asked him…

"You going out Rich?"

And he sure did turn back to me just before closing the door to leave me, and said…

"Yeah Braze."

"That's great man."
I said.

"I'll see you Bee."

So… I guess maybe, he did keep his promise. He said goodbye. And that's what I asked. But remembering him saying goodbye to me… was not anywhere near the comfort I thought it could be when I asked it of him months ago.

Then, awareness came back to me in my office with the cops standing around me, who were explaining to me how I could acquire his body. I was too numb and in shock to really process anything at that point I think. They found his body under the bridge, on the street next to the tracks just off Mardi-Gras Boulevard. Not far from where we both ventured out to much earlier that day. I try not to think if it in fact occurred to him to jump earlier in the day, while he was with me below the bridge as I tended to my own desire.

When the cops were done filling me in, I walked them down the stairs. As they exited my home, I was handed a business card and a brochure reminding me where I could "retrieve" his body after they were done their investigations. Holding the brochure in my hand, I watched them walk to their cruisers, as if they were houseguests leaving after… something, I don't know. Because they gave me the impression they were just coming from a game or something. I suppose they didn't know I was still standing in the doorway while they walked away just talking to each other, and laughing. It was all so surreal to me, and business as usual to them. But then again, I guess it is.

I went back up stairs and found Bella in Richy's room on her knees by his bed, crying. When I went to her side, she grabbed me around the waist, and held on to me! Everything in me kept vibrating with that ongoing, ominous, bass line from somewhere deep inside me! My eyes watered up and the fluids vibrated over my pupils with that dreadful note from somewhere unknown.

"We made a run for it.
But we couldn't out run it."
I said with a cryptic tone.

"What Braze?"
Bella cried.

"I led my brother,
on a long road to his grave."

I introduced him to the road that dead-ended. When we were kids, I thought hustling on the street was what ambitious people did. I'm responsible for NOT showing my little brother early on in life, brighter sides of life.

"I never showed him right
from wrong Bella.
I just showed him how
not to get caught."

I am by no means attempting to make his death about me. Yet I do regretfully take responsibility for the influence I had on the trajectory of his short life.

Up until that night, we got away with a lot in life. Karmic debt, or a judging God, appeared to finally catch us, serve a bill, and collect! But I can't say for sure that "God" or "karma" was directly responsible. But I know I was. I encouraged his hustle from the start in East Lansdowne. A hustle that would bring things into his life that would later drive him crazy. I always thought the worst thing for us would be going to jail. But losing him to it all? I never imagined that! It completely devastates me far beyond my worst nightmares. And that ominous, horrible bass line note that was reverberating inside me… I think it's the sound of everything that you think matters to you most in life, dematerializing as it enters a black hole in an uncharted dimension in your brain.

When I finally looked at the time again, it was only 9:30. I knew my Mom was awake and that I had to call her and tell her, but I didn't. I decided to let her have one more good nights sleep. Because I knew it would be her last for some time to come. All I could do for her that night was let her have one more night's rest, with Rich alive in her life.

As Bella slept on the chaise and I dozed off in an armchair, a dream catcher in the room connected Richy and I later that night as…

Richy was naked, racing down a cold river within a steep canyon! It seemed like it was winter to me, but the temperature and elements didn't seem to bother him. The raft was nearly out of control, water splashed up and snow lined the edge of the waterway! Scared, but safe, I could hear him ask himself within all the chaos…

"Why aren't I freezing right now?"

With my birds eye view of him below, I could see a waterfall ahead! I yelled down to him and tried to warn him, but it was too late.

A moment later I found him in a… dimly lit emergency room, of some sort. Where others seemed to go about their business and didn't take notice of him. At this time he was very scared and crying softly, no more than a lonely whimper though. I wanted to comfort him, have someone there help him, be there for him… but I just couldn't reach him! His back and bones were broken; he knew it. He took very, very small steps forward because he thought he had to. And softly kept asking for…

"Help? Help me? Help me?
Help me please?"

But no one there seemed to hear him. He was in critical condition, but in no physical pain. As he walked like this, I could feel his bewilderment in that he could still walk despite all the damage to his body. He then found his way into a room where I lost track of him. All of this seemed quit real and not as an imagined dream. But rather a glimpse into anther dimension that was translated to me in Earthly scenarios, and communicated to me during REM sleep. But this very well might not be the case.

When I woke up, I thought that would be in fact the last time I'd ever see my brother. It was like loosing him twice! I stayed up the rest of that night, before I made the most dreadful phone call of my life the next morning…

"Hello Braze, good morning!"

"…Good morning Mom."

I wish I could forget the tone her screams reached in that phone conversation with me! But that's impossible. The decibels of her wailing reached such intensity that I can only imagine that the afterglow of creation itself is more ongoing than the loss Mom felt since that morning.

COMPLICATED GREIF

A mental health Consequence
While going through anger lacking Consciousness

For days leading up to, and after my brother's cremation, he tried to drop me lines. Fishing lines in my sleep! He'd cast the line from just above the Earth and dropped it in the shallow pond of our atmosphere. But just like a tragic comedy, the line kept falling from his reel, and through the rod, to where the atmosphere of the Earth, meets outer space. It was science fiction, but quite easy to understand. There, the fishing line floated on the atmosphere, like an ordinary string on calm water. The Earth never looked so much like an island oasis at sea, as it did for me from that perspective in those dreams. No words were passed between us, yet. But the impression of him trying to make a connection with me is undeniable! Though I can't say for sure if it was my imagination at work, or something else, the picture was quite clear nonetheless.

When I'm awake I often think about what I see in my sleep. I've gone through periods of intense activity while at rest like this before. I can't deny the impressions dreams and nightmares have had on me. Not long ago I thought that spirits haunted me. Then I thought I was getting glimpses of the future in my sleep. Today, I just think I'm troubled, or highly creative at best. But it wasn't long after Rich died, that my nightmares became unbearable! But I'm sure I brought the nightmares on myself this time when I started obsessively watching a particularly horrible Internet video unrelated to his death, but that of the deaths of so many other souls. Why...? I wanted to know what Richy might have looked like on his way to the Earth, from the bridge. So, I obsessively viewed a video, countless times… that showed people falling to their deaths from the World Trade Centers. Finally, weeks later, I managed to stop watching the video. But the damage was done to my subconscious. For nearly a year while revising these pages, I had nightmares set in New York City, as a result of watching those video clips of the Twin Towers burn during the morning of 9/11. In my nightmare, the buildings are smoking and people are falling to their horrible deaths. But in my head while sleeping, I got up close to the tragedy! Much closer than that the actual videos documented, and found my own brother on the edge of a building that burned below him.

In my head… he was on top of one of those burning buildings, crying, panicking; not knowing what to do! He didn't want to jump, but he felt as though he had no other choice. Up there he debated how he wanted to die… stay and burn up, or jump and hope God would indeed have mercy on his troubled soul. I had this same dream countless times! …And every time, the moment would come when he was on the edge of it all, that death it seemed was better then suffering. So he'd jumped from the building. To what I could only hope, was some relief? Once it started I could never turn off this nightmare, or the outcome. Waking wasn't an option. And to make it worse, it became lucid to me after having this dream hundreds of times. I could get closer to the building, and even speak to Richy on the edge of the roof in my sleep! Though nothing I could ever say would change the dire situation in my mind. He'd always jump. There would always come a time it seemed, when it was his time to die. And it was then that I realized that his step from the bridge was his to make. That last act of his life was not my fault. But what was going on and repeating in my head during these nightmares, was my creation, not his. So, them being somewhat lucid dreams at this point… I began trying to take greater control! It was after all, my dream. The nights to come would have dreams unfold that only I could imagine!

I put out the flames below him the first night! I did the same second night, and I cleared the smoke from the air as well. On the third night, I had the building stabilized with just he and I on the edge of the roof with the sky a clear blue above us, without the chaos of the inferno below us. Up there on top of the world with my brother, it was peaceful. By the fourth night, the dreamscape was all mine! With that kind of peace, I thought I could talk him down, and I started to do so… we laughed about old times, bad times, successes, regrets, the 76ers, Mommy, Daddy, and more in our personal history together. But just as all the other dreams ended, I could not stop him from saying at some point…

"I'll see ya Braze."

Then spontaneously just out of my visions reach, he jumped!

"Wait! Why! No Stop!
Don't Richy!"

I woke up screaming, crying, waking Bella…

"Why does he keep jumping in my head?"
I asked her,
"It's my head!"

"It's ok Braze.
It's ok.
Come here,
I'll rub your head."

Bella's touch is indeed that of the only person on Earth that could ever melt me back to sleep.

Afraid to sleep and being so unsuccessful in my mind, even when I did get some rest, I still got much angrier at this time in my life! And then, once again, that dreadful bass guitar note began to feed back on my bones louder than bombs, every day when I wasn't completely engrossed in something. It was killing me. In fact, I thought about death all the time! His death, and my survival! Why him and not me? I was so confused and angry. I even started to show up angry, in the dreams with him. When that began to happen, it made Richy feel really bad for me. Which made me even worse off when I woke up and went on with my days.

My grief connected to the loss of my brother began long before his death. In that I was in denial my brother could ever loose his mind! I bargained I would! And depression for me has been as frequent as the common cold; so that was nothing new when he died. So when I began looking for help when I wasn't in the self-destructive soup, my search altered between conscious efforts to heal, and many acts lacking consciousness. I tried more therapy sessions for anger management. I got more tattoos because I was unhappy with myself. I got on my knees and prayed for relief. Then, to no surprise, I tried to drink my anger away in The Quarter. After a bender I'd wake up and run off my hangover like old times. I found some painkillers on the street to manage the grief and lighten my dark moods around Bella. Because I was so angry sometimes, I wanted to hurt somebody! God knows… I was hurting. So I drank and got high because I was unable to go through the grief naturally. And when I wasn't buzzed, I was short with everyone if I didn't go so far as to just ignore them all! But eventually, after rereading my journal entries at this time, I realized I was just hurting myself with all this anger towards the world. A world that just kept floating in space with a sun appearing to rise over my angry existence. I tried to remedy this when I absolutely had to by often repeating, aloud…

"I'm not angry.
I'm not angry.
I'm not angry"

I began chanting it again and again, as much as necessary! To remind myself not to hurt myself, or anyone else! At the end of the day before I would lay down to sleep at night, I'd pray, softly…

"I'm not angry.
I'm not angry.
I'm not angry"

And woke chanting over morning tea, in a whisper over the steaming cup…

"I'm not angry.
I'm not angry.
I'm not angry."

At lunch at my stand in the flea market was more of the same…

"I'm not angry.
I'm not angry.
I'm not angry."

BOOK SAFE

On my jogs after work by the Mississippi River, in stride with every kick…

"I'm, not, an-gry.
I'm, not, an-gry.
I'm, not, an-gry."

And I continued with the same, every night by fold my hands, and getting on my knees, praying…

"I'm not angry. I'm not angry.
I'm not angry. I'm not angry.
I'm not angry. I'm not angry.
I'm not angry. I'm not angry."

The madness of such repetitive behavior only made things worse of course. My anger continued to surface absolutely everywhere, even when I was drunk and high. You can't get over a problem by reaffirming it all day. Though, I wasn't of sound mind at the time for that to register immediately. Before I knew it, every waking moment, the chant, looped in my head and came out in nearly constant murmuring…

"I'm not angry. I'm not angry. I'm not angry.
I'm not angry. I'm not angry. I'm not angry.
I'm not angry. I'm not angry. I'm not angry.
I'm not angry. I'm not angry. I'm not angry.
I'm not angry. I'm not angry. I'm not angry.
I'm not angry. I'm not angry. I'm not angry."

But in my every thought, I was indeed, angry! Eventually I woke up in the mornings after those dreams with Richy and found those three words bounced off everything in the room…

"I'm not angry. I'm not angry. I'm not angry.
I'm not angry. I'm not angry. I'm not angry.
I'm not angry. I'm not angry. I'm not angry.
I'm not angry. I'm not angry. I'm not angry."

I was going completely mad! And I knew it! And, it was getting really weird too when on pills and alcohol I would look at porn and masturbate while I yelled at the screen, screaming…

"I'm not angry!
I'm not angry!
I'm not angry!"

As if multiple distractions such as pills, porn and pilsner would some how comfort me? Not this time. Those words were concrete in my consciousness!

Bella was keeping her distance from me at this time because I was in my own world with only… three words. After writing hundreds of thousands of words in the past! It was as if I'd forgotten my history and had no future. The writing of this book ceased when those three words continue to type in ultra flat black on the meat of my brain and the seat of my soul. The last time things were that out of control for me was just before I came to New Orleans. When I couldn't die in Philly! Those three words bombed me to a purgatory of some sort. My head was a padded room with wheat pasted wallpaper reading…

"I'm not angry. I'm not angry. I'm not angry. I'm not angry. I'm not angry. I'm not angry. I'm not angry… I'm not angry. I'm not angry. I'm not angry. I'm not angry. I'm not angry. I'm not angry. I'm not angry… I'm not angry. I'm not angry. I'm not angry. I'm not angry. I'm not angry. I'm not angry. I'm not angry… I'm not angry. I'm not angry. I'm not angry. I'm not angry. I'm not angry. I'm not angry. I'm not angry. I'm not angry. I'm not angry. I'm not angry. I'm not angry. I'm not angry. I'm not angry… I'm not angry. I'm not angry. I'm not angry. I'm not angry. I'm not angry. I'm not angry. I'm not angry… I'm not angry. I'm not angry. I'm not angry. I'm not angry. I'm not angry. I'm not angry. I'm not angry… I'm not angry. I'm not angry. I'm not angry. I'm not angry. I'm not angry. I'm not angry. I'm not angry. I'm not angry. I'm not angry. I'm not angry. I'm not angry. I'm not angry. I'm not angry… I'm not angry. I'm not angry. I'm not angry. I'm not angry. I'm not angry. I'm not angry. I'm not angry… I'm not angry. I'm not angry. I'm not angry. I'm not angry. I'm not angry. I'm not angry. I'm not angry… I'm not angry. I'm not angry. I'm not angry. I'm not angry. I'm not angry. I'm not angry."

And not just visually in mind, but echoing in my head in the background of everything I tried to do! I thought the line was sent to drive me mad so I'd jump off the bridge myself. That's it! That's why! That's what I believed. All the pain was there to remind me I didn't die, he did. There was no escaping that. I became a self made man of anger who would spontaneously scream at people while I walked down the street…

"I'm not angry!"

Did they know why I was so angry? Or saying I wasn't? Neither did I! I'd even throw change at young spangers who asked me for a little help, and of course let them know…

"I'm not angry!"

They'd duck the coins I threw at their heads… then chase the change rolling on the sidewalk. I'd even scream at my dear Bella, randomly, and often, without warning.

I found a bottom I'd not thought possible. I knew what I had to do to stop the intense war I was in with myself. But first, I thought I'd try and read what I couldn't finish here on these pages, before I took my own life. And it was in reading, not writing the first draft of this story that I began to find a few moments of relief. It made me feel at ease when I realized how creative I'd been in life, while on this troubled road. Despite how hard things got at times, I kept writing through them.

Within all the personal links to guilt I have with my brother's suicide expressed here in black and white, I began to take responsibility on the page better than I could in the world. Just as I realized I did in the movie. I made art from confessions and turned tragedies into triumphs. Could I create a better ending for him? I had to. Reality was killing me!

It's one thing to write about mistakes and guilt, but sadly another to keep making them and feeling it! So maybe, just maybe I could get it right in this book, and possibly departmentalize it in such a way, that one day I could relieve myself of it all and simply put it on a shelf amongst other stories. There on a bookshelf outside the mind that troubles me, in between the stories of Jerry Stahl and Ervine Welsh, my pain and mistakes would just be one of any other troubled writer; just not so famous. If only I could change the ending, maybe, I could live with myself I thought.

While reading the first draft of this story, I found that some of these lines, and specifically the act of writing them, is what I'd call… literary morphine. A fix that medicated the ill head I slept with on my own deathbed. Lines that fell from angry fingers to a broken keyboard on top of an old thrift store write-away chest. The act of writing was therapy that relieved me of tons of miserable emotions and visceral passions! Horrid gut feelings that melted from the dark side of my soul like warmed ice from a dying glacier, by typing it out of me! It was then that I realized when I stopped writing, and began obsessing over the bad dreams I was having. That anger bottled up in me and thoughts of attempting suicide surfaced again.

I knew how much that dream I was having of Richy was hurting me. But I could never turn away from seeing my brother again. No matter what it did to me! Just as my young gutter punk friend Green didn't want to let go of her boyfriend in her head. Our attempt at holding on to the ones we lost, prevented us from living well. What we did was repeat behavior that hurt us, simply because we refused to say no to it; thus addicts. I felt a bottom during that time that brought me to a low and insanity I didn't know one could come back from. Lower than one I ever experienced on drugs.

I had to make a change! Do a rewrite! I had to change the ending to this story in my head that haunted me! On the page it's easy. But in an obsessive mind… quite another story indeed.

The drinks and drugs were not numbing me any longer and ignoring everyone in my life wasn't working either. It all still bothered me no matter what. And after hopping trains across the country to make a movie to cure my crash… I knew this book couldn't save my ass if that didn't. I had to make changes inside me and stop trying to create things outside me, to please me. So I breathed on it. In fact that's all I did. Every time I thought of anger, I counted my breaths.

It slowed my racing one-track mind. Then I made some changes to create a clean slate to work with…

First I changed my environment. We moved out of our place in Old Algiers, and into a new place in The French Quarter; a garret by the French Market where I could begin writing again. But the bad dreams followed me! So then I decided to reach out to a hypnotherapist for help. And had him plant seeds in my subconscious to make things more bearable during the day. After those sessions, when I had to stop to count my breaths, I began to see my anger rise to the sun, from my forehead, in little clear bubbles. Evidently directed to do so when I was hypnotized. And then I had an AA sponsor come to my home and work the 12 steps with me. Once things slowed down in my mind and life got manageable once again, it was time to rewrite the dream that plagued me!

"Take it slow.
Think less."
I'd remind myself.

I decided that would be my focus every time I closed my eyes to go to sleep… to just slow down, and think less, in a passive aggressive attempt to become the supreme director of my thoughts during REM sleep.

When I got there in dreamland with Richy, I engaged our conversations with every ray of energy I could gather in that state of mind. I made sure to tell him about the progress I was making with my grief; he indeed knew he was already dead. But that didn't stop him from jumping again and again. Death it appears is not the best cure for insanity. I asked him once why he jumped off the bridge. He said…

"I don't remember Bee,
but I regret it.
Tell Mommy please."

Just the mention of it, crushed him! And I was not there to channel my brother to upset him. So I never brought it up again.

Knowing how this dream had been ending thus far and not wanting to actually talk him down and disturb our conversations about everything but… I made suggestions via body language for him to follow me away from the edge. He'd take a few steps in my direction, but without warning he'd pivot back quickly and…

"I'll see ya Braze."
He'd say.

Then he'd jump from the top of the world and off the peaceful, imaginary Tower in New York I created in my dreams. Devastating me once again! Yet I began to notice something new at the end of the dream, it appeared that he smiled at me, just before he jumped! Maybe because he knew it was already all over for him, or he knew he'd see me again the next night. But he in fact started to smile at me as he jumped. It was… fantastic! To me, that was fearless! But of course, not how I wanted his story to ever end.

Completely frustrated with the final act in the dreams, I started anticipating his departure and began reaching out for him at the last moment. But I couldn't grab him! He was just out of reach! I woke up each time completely spent, but not screaming anymore. It was progress.

And so it continued, each night I'd fall asleep and find him up there on the edge. And each night I'd drag out our conversation and slow things down a little more to spend as much time with him as I could. Then, I slowed things down to a slither. And at that pace, I noticed not only his smile at me, but relief in his eyes the moment he stepped from the edge. And at that point it appeared to me his last act ultimately brought him the peace that evaded him near the end of his life on Earth. That was something I could live with. I had too.

During my waking moments, I started to prepare for the dreams that night, by not thinking about them all day. Instead, I practiced mindfulness at all times. I'd actually stay focused on nothing as much as possible, which kept obsessions about getting well and random feelings from my head. When something entered my mind I'd identify it as a thought, or an emotion, and then let it pass. Personal benefits of this higher state of consciousness had profound effects on my quality of living. I was just feeling better, and exuded it in most every waking moment. And, I began to get to sleep easier. Despite what was in store for me each night in the dream. Because once in REM I'd still see Rich there, jumping. But I began to be more at peace with myself, and with his final step. By now, I had no doubts it was his last step to take in life, and not my doing what so ever. I couldn't stop it, but I had to live with it. Though I couldn't go on much longer with the way it was ending in my head. It was time to start slowing things down, to an epic pace!

The following night, after praying under the bridge he actually jumped off in New Orleans, I went home to bed and closed my eyes to visit with Richy again. And, just as always, I found Richy in my head, on the edge, nearing his final act. And once again, I spoke to him through some tears before he said his good-bye. But that night, when he took the step from the edge, and it filled his face with peace and relief… I took lucid control of the dream in epic proportions as he jumped! Just before he could finish saying his good-bye…

"I'll see ya…

I projected him from the Tower we stood on and over lower Manhattan to the vibrancy of the 5 Pointz graffiti mecca at light speed! Over the silent art of graffiti, I could say my final goodbye to him…

…Braze?"

"Good-bye Richy.
You're forever… my guy."

Over the 5 Pointz Building in my dream, he doesn't fall, but glides in mind! I couldn't stop him, but up there, I could let him go. When I woke the next morning, I felt I gave an end to his story, and put his final act, in a place I could live with.

"In my story you leave your life
in style my brother."

Now, my brother floats forever in that undying moment in the 5 Pointz of my mind. And though my brother is gone, in this Book Safe he lives on. And now, my parting memory of Richy is not walking out of my front door before he jumped off the bridge in New Orleans, but rather frozen in the air over a sea of graffiti. Up there with him, I placed the angels in war paint on the edge of the roof, playing guitars and singing My Guy. I of course can't bring him back, yet. But I can live with him in the meantime in a dream suspended in the ocean of time and stored in this Book Safe where his life won't go unsung. Until I reunite us in the heavens after I introduce "spiritual tourism architecture" to the world.

Now… I'm not angry any longer. And I enjoy more than ever gently kissing Bella in the morning before she opens her eyes. And… I can boil water for tea, and not scream at the pot like a mad man. I'm no longer troubled by those dreams, but miss him in them. Our story together didn't have to end this way. It shouldn't have. He deserved more! And though I'm still bothered by the wrong road I led him down when we were kids, I'm not going to let it kill me. But, I can still hear my Mom in the upper chapel of my mind, crying…

"Why Braze? Why Braze?
Why BRAZE!"

"I… duh-know Mom."
I murmur.

I take a deep breath at moments like these, very deep breath. And just acknowledge it as a thought, and let the feelings pass, and her echo fades…

Why Braze?
Why
Why

I'm heartbroken we lost him the way we did Mom. I just tell myself that in time, we all lose each other on the skin of this planet; its kismet. But his story's not over as long as mine continues to evolve. In future books I'm inspired by his history in *Selling The Maybe*. Introduce him to a spiritual soul-train in *Two Headed Braze*. And once again we'll be together in *The Acme Kid!* In my head… you're not dead my brother.

Scenarios

BRIGHTDAWN

Photography

Matthew Newman-Saul

In memory of my Friend

Daoina-Sidhe

Always dedicated to my Brother

Daniel John Higgins

BOOK SAFE

The Players

Danny Higgins.. RICHY

Jerri Scanlan .... MOM

Paul Higgins..DAD

Ben McGregor .... NEB

Stumps Duh Clown .... HIMSELF

Matthew Newman-Saul .... SEPHER

Sara Snell...RUIN

Daoine-Sidhe ....GREEN

Lorraine Beatrice...BELLA

Todd Taylor... Skater

and

Brian Paul Higgins

as

BRIGHTDAWN, BRAZE SCANLAN & MES

This has been a work of true fiction.

The book is based on the
Best Screenplay, Best Documentary, Best Picture

CURE for the CRASH
The Art of Train Hopping

www.CUREfortheCRASH.com

"The secret freedoms of train hopping."

Award Winning Film...
CURE FOR THE CRASH
...The Art of Train Hoppin'.

"A fascinating look inside the minds of train hoppers."

National Geographic
"The secret freedoms of train hopping…
A fascinating look into the minds of train hoppers."
-Aric S. Queen

MOVIEMAKER Magazine
"Cure for the Crash created by Brian Paul and
Mathew Newman-Saul… named Top Grit at Indie Grits."
-Rebecca Pahle

The Philadelphia Inquire
"What would you give up in the name of art?
Filmmaker Brian Paul goes all the way."
-Tirdad Derakhshani

Louisiana Film & Video Magazine
"A fascinating story unlike any other
recognizable genre!"
-Michael Dardent

FILMMAKER Magazine
"Filmmaker Brian Paul is a man who lives his films."
-Paul Devlin

The Garret Scenarios

Include…

Book Safe Glacier
How The Rails Became My Rehab

AND COMING SOON…

Selling The Maybe
A Redlight District Love Story

Two Headed Braze
Dreams Like This Are Dangerous

The Acme Kid
A Relationship With Shopping Karts

Garret Scenario 002 of 004 will be…

CONTACT

www.SELLINGtheMAYBE.com

bpBrightdawn@Gmail.com

BrianPaulBrightdawn/Amazon.com

BRIGHTDAWN

Many names, characters, places, lyrics, and incidents are either the products of the author's imagination or are used fictitiously. Any resemblance to published lyrics and actual persons mentioned, living or dead, events or locales are entirely unintentional or coincidental.

The writer will not answer questions in emails, interviews, signings, social media, markets or other, regarding the basis or inspiration of characters in the book. Although the story is based on the writer's experiences and research, he's not sharing a completely true story, but within it, true messages about recovery and coming of age. This book in no way speaks for the experiences of anyone else in the world other than some of the writer's and his imagination, as do his books that follow.

Music titles and artists are mention/celebrated in the book, but no published lyrics protected under copyrights are used in this work.
Circa 2015

The California House Garret of The Scenarist

BrightDawn

If another battle is won in the war with Himself,
He'll deliver The Maybe if he still has his Health.

INNER CITY OUTLIER PAPERBACKS
THE ICOP CAMP

;